THE
CUSTOMER
CENTURY

THE CUSTOMER CENTURY

LESSONS FROM WORLD-CLASS COMPANIES IN INTEGRATED MARKETING AND COMMUNICATIONS

Anders Gronstedt, Ph.D.

Routledge
New York ▲ London

Published in 2000 by
Routledge
29 West 35th Street
New York, NY 10001

Published in Great Britain by
Routledge
11 New Fetter Lane
London EC4P 4EE

Printed in the United States of America on acid-free paper.

Library of Congress Cataloging-in-Publication Data

Gronstedt, Anders.
    The customer century : lessons from world-class companies in inte-
grated marketing and communications / by Anders Gronstedt.
        p.   cm.
    Includes bibliographical references.
    ISBN 0-415-92199-6 (cloth)
    1. Business communication—Case studies.   2. Communication in
management—Case studies. 3. Marketing—Case studies.
    4. Consumer satisfaction—Case studies.   I. Title.
    HF5718.G77   2000
    658.4'5—dc21   99-35001
                                                              CIP

CONTENTS

For Anita, Camilla, and Carl Philip

PREFACE

The seeds of this book were planted when I entered the field of communications as a young writer for Scandinavia's largest communications agency, Kreab. The firm owes its success to a radical concept: helping clients integrate communications with customers, employees, investors, and other stakeholders. Realizing the value of this idea, I began a quest to seek out all the information available on the topic. To my surprise, hardly any literature, theory, or case studies could be found on how to effectively integrate communications. This prompted my mission to research the most successful practices of corporations in the United States and Europe.

The journey began almost a decade ago with my doctoral dissertation at the University of Wisconsin-Madison. During those early years of the 1990s, the marketing and communications professions were in the midst of transition. Advertising agencies, PR firms, and other communications specialists were transforming (at least in rhetoric) into "integrated marketing communications" agencies. Marketing was shifting focus from transactions to relationships. Meanwhile, business leaders were rediscovering market orientation, without the help of marketing or communications professionals. Inspired by the success of Japanese industry, engineers and statisticians were reengineering business processes around customers' needs. As I traveled around the United States and conducted in-depth interviews with senior marketing and communications managers of world-renowned, total quality management companies like Hewlett-Packard, Saturn, and Xerox, I made a startling discovery: Power was shifting to the consumer, and the management of communications processes was being elevated to strategic levels to help build customer relationships and drive business results. An integrated communications revolution was brewing.

When I joined the graduate Integrated Marketing Communications faculty at the University of Colorado, my focus became more international. I expanded my research to integrated communications practices among leading European corporations. In interviewing senior managers across the European continent at companies like Ericsson, ISS, and Philips, I learned that integrated communications was as urgent and important in Europe as in the United States. While challenges and issues varied greatly from company to company, some underlying processes of successful integrated communications emerged. I began to present the model that I developed at events ranging from in-house senior management meetings and graduate classes to professional and scholarly conferences. As the model evolved, it has withstood the scrutiny of professionals and academics around the world and sparked a wave of interest. With that interest came more and more consulting work. The pressures of my night job grew to the point where I decided to leave my day job at the university to start my own consulting and training business. As president of my Colorado-based firm, the Gronstedt Group, I have had the good fortune to work with a number of leading U.S.- and European-based companies, including Volvo Car Corporation, Emerson Electric, and Electrolux. Our consulting work and training programs with these and other companies have served as fertile testing grounds for the emerging philosophies of integrated communications expounded in this book.

Nine years into my search, I'm now happy to present a book that offers cutting-edge insights from some of the best managers and companies in the world on how to integrate communications for the new century. Packed with practical cases, examples, and advice, this book will be of great value to professionals in marketing, communications, and quality, as well as to scholars and students in these fields. I also hope it will find its way into the hands of senior-level executives who want to grow their businesses, defy the status quo, and make a genuine difference. This book is written for the business leaders, thought leaders, and marketing and communications practice leaders of the Customer Century. It is a manifesto of the integrated communications revolution!

ACKNOWLEDGMENTS

I have been helped more than I deserve by a large number of people who have made this book possible. First of all I want to acknowledge my vice president and chief sounding board, Lisa Siracuse, who has assisted with much of the research and writing of this book. Without her involvement, it would still be a jumble of disjointed case studies and academic gobbledygook. My debt to Lisa is profound. I also owe a huge gratitude to my colleague and friend Torbjörn Larsson, who has contributed extensive research and administrative support to this book. My former associate, Kristen Detrick, has also made substantial contributions in both research and writing. A person who has been instrumental in the development of this project is my business partner and mentor, Professor Clarke Caywood, director of Northwestern University's Department of Integrated Marketing Communications. He suggested the focus on leading total quality management firms, gave me access to his vast network of contacts, and provided guidance throughout the project.

I also owe special thanks to another Northwestern professor, Don Schultz, who read multiple drafts of the manuscript and helped shape it, and to Professor Tom Duncan, my former faculty colleague at the University of Colorado who helped conceive my 3-D model. The European case studies featured in this book would not have been possible without the generous support of my travel expenses by the European communications firm Kreab. I want to thank its owner and CEO and my longtime boss, Peje Emilsson, for his vision and support. My thanks go out to Mikkel Mørup, manager at Nokia, who connected me with people at ISS, Rank-Xerox, and Danfoss. I remain grateful to my Ph.D. adviser, Professor Esther Thorson, who helped design my dissertation study and kept me under her wing even after she left the University of Wisconsin to become associate dean at the University of Missouri; and to my other dissertation committee members, Professors Mark Finster, Ivan Preston, Clif Conrad, and Lew Friedland. Thanks are also due to Ketchum and the Institute of Public Relations that awarded me a grant for my research. My editor at Routledge, Melissa Rosati, deserves much credit for this book. She was a tremendous support in sharpening both the focus and the language to make it more relevant and compelling for managers and professionals to read.

A number of other friends have read the manuscript during various stages of development and greatly improved it with their suggestions and criticism. They include Göran Thorstensson, president of Vindrosen and a longtime friend who helped restrain my zeal and make the book more balanced; Lars Göran Johansson, corporate communications director of home appliance giant Electrolux, who kept me focused on the issues facing today's global multibrand corporations; Professor Frank Durham, of the University of Texas, whose support meant more to me than he probably realizes; Professor Sandra Moriarty, University of Colorado, who helped develop the framework of the book; Professor Brett Robbs, who helped develop the teamwork section; and Professor Christian Grönroos, who helped me move beyond the integration of marketing and communications departments to the strategic relationship building processes of the corporation.

In addition, I have benefited enormously from conversations with the following people who lent their wisdom to this project: Professor Bob Lauterborn, University of North Carolina; Walt Lindenmann, Ketchum; Mikael Thulin, Ericsson; Anders Högström and Sven Windahl, Nordisk Kommunikation; Anders Hesselbom and Sören Johansson, Volvo Car Corporation; Hans V. A. Johnsson, Sture Palmgren, and Åsa Myrdal-Bratt, Kreab; Larry Weisberg, the University of Colorado; Charles Liedtke, consultant; Thomas Hunter, Ph.D. student; and Professors Jim Hutton and Jim Grunig.

Finally, I wish to thank the over eighty senior managers of the leading companies featured in this book that I have interviewed. They contributed generously of their time and insights and are in a real sense collaborators of this study. I especially want to thank the following people who helped set up my interviews at each company: Tom Martin, formerly public relations director at FedEx, now at ITT Industries; Nils Ingvar Lundin, formerly corporate communications director of Ericsson, now at Investor; Rod Irvin, director of corporate communications at Eastman Chemical Company; Chuck Sengstock, retired corporate communications director at Motorola; Ed Allen, retired vice president of Allen-Bradley; Greg Martin, public relations director at Saturn; Joe Cahalan, director of corporate communications at Xerox Corp; Roger Johansson, corporate communications director at ABB; John Jakobsen, quality manager at Danfoss; Mary Anne Easley, corporate communications director at Hewlett-Packard; Bojana Fazarinc, marketing communications director at Hewlett-Packard; and Dayvon Goodsell, quality manager at Celestica.

Most of all, I want to thank my loving wife and business partner, Anita, for putting up with my obsession with this project. I also want to acknowledge my daughter, Camilla, and son, Carl Philip, who have been immensely patient with me, although they cannot understand why anyone would write a book without pictures. This project has lasted their entire lifetimes and they have been looking forward to the completion of it as much as I have.

Superior, Colorado
Anders Gronstedt

Introduction

FROM BULLS TO GEESE

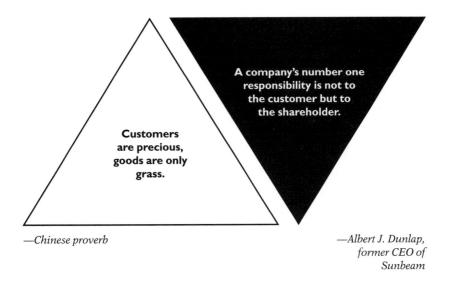

Customers are precious, goods are only grass.

—Chinese proverb

A company's number one responsibility is not to the customer but to the shareholder.

*—Albert J. Dunlap,
former CEO of
Sunbeam*

Few examples illustrate the need for a new integrated approach to marketing and communications better than the sordid tale of Mercedes-Benz's A-Class, a new city car for the European market. The introduction of the new "Baby Benz" was the culmination of a two-year advertising and publicity blitz, pounding home the safety of the car. By cleverly placing the engine under the floor, it would slide underneath the body in the event of a frontal crash and the high seating position would put driver and passengers out of harm's way in a side impact. The carmaker justified the premium price tag for the car with these superior safety features.

The A-Class received standing ovations when it was unveiled with the splendor of a Hollywood premiere at the Frankfurt Motor Show. "A turning point in the industry," gushed the *Financial Times* with unconscious irony. The success ended just a few days later to the tune of bent metal and shattered windshields when a group of Swedish auto journalists flipped over during a test drive of the car. Several of them were hurried to the hospital for minor injuries. The video and photos of the accident became ubiquitous on TV news and magazine covers throughout Europe. This was not the first time auto journalists had raised concerns about this particular safety problem with the car. One month before its world introduction, the A-Class went up on two wheels during a test drive with a team of European auto journalists. Two different cars with different tires were tested, but the problem remained. Mercedes, however, trivialized the problem and rolled forward with the launch.

To add insult to injury, Mercedes decided to throw the blame on the press corps and the injured journalists for staging what it deemed an extreme "moose test." Mercedes argued that the need to make such a sharp, evasive turn to avoid an obstacle in the road was isolated to Sweden, because of its large moose population. The automaker's director of sales for Sweden went a step further and sent a fax to all of its dealers, arguing that the test drive had no relevance to normal traffic conditions; "only Russian lumber trucks" had to be tested under such conditions.

Within days after the rollover accident, two of Germany's leading auto publications repeated the test drive. The test driver from one of the publications rolled over. The other stopped the test drive after the car began to tip on its side. Up to that point, Mercedes had benefited from its loyal German media, which rushed to the carmaker's defense during the first days of the crisis. But as evidence mounted against Mercedes, the German press corps turned adversarial. A barrage of negative publicity in German and international media gave the company a painful lesson in accountability and open communication. Mercedes called a press conference to apologize for its accusations against the journalists and proceeded to blame its tire supplier. Mercedes's managers claimed that replacing those pesky Goodyears with Michelins and adding a gadget called an "electronic stability control" would fix the problem. But most outside experts agreed that such superficial changes wouldn't make much difference. "It's like putting a Band-Aid on an abscess," commented one pundit. Mercedes promptly reprimanded these experts for having the audacity to point out that the emperor didn't have any clothes. A Swedish professor specializing in the auto industry got a call from a Mercedes official who scolded him for claiming that more drastic changes would be required to make the car stable. "I have never experienced anything like that," exclaimed Professor Christer Karlsson.[1]

Treating journalists and experts like bumbling imbeciles did not prove to be a winning strategy for Mercedes. Its arrogant posturing quickly became the ridicule of Europe. The "moose test" was on everyone's lips. A German weatherman reported a low-pressure system heading toward Scandinavia to perform the moose test. A London *Sunday Times* columnist suggested that the new British cabinet should experience a moose test to see how well it would handle pressure. The once premier automotive brand became the butt of jokes in sitcoms and newspaper cartoons. A plethora of anti-Mercedes websites still flourishes on the Internet as a reminder of the incident. My personal favorite features an A-Class car with training wheels, and when you click on it, the whole webpage turns upside down![2] Meanwhile, the news media speculated that either Mercedes knowingly launched a car that would put people's lives at risk, or its product development was too sloppy and unprofessional to catch the mistake. Either way, the whole incident reflected badly on the carmaker. Pundits pointed out that a "moose" in the road could easily be a "child," and that the A-Class was the only car to fail the "child test" in twenty years except for the Czech-made Skoda.

It took several weeks for Daimler-Benz's CEO, Jürgen Schrempp, to wake up and publicly order the design engineers back to the drawing board. Several months later, Mercedes finally relaunched a redesigned, safer version of the A-Class. The original Swedish test driver who rolled over the car, Robert Collin, was the first journalist to test-drive the redesigned car. After driving the car, he agreed to make a statement endorsing it, which Mercedes told him would only be used in a press release. That promise was broken before the ink was dry. The German carmaker made certain they got the full mileage out of the inch provided by the journalist, making his endorsement the centerpiece of an advertising blitz in 180 German newspapers, television commercials, and video news releases sent to newsrooms around Europe. "I feel betrayed by Mercedes," says

Collin, whose repeated protests against using his name in the advertisements were ignored by the carmaker.

Mercedes paid a steep price for its failure to integrate communications. Customers who preordered the A-Class car were canceling by the thousands. The production of the car was delayed by three months, at a cost of $175 million. And that's not including the expense of the 180 full-page ads Mercedes ran after the reintroduction. Yet, these numbers fade in comparison to the seven-and-a-half-billion-dollar tumble of Daimler-Benz's market value, which took place in just three weeks. The relentlessly forward-looking stock market had no patience with a company that was squandering its brand relationships with disintegrated communications.

For almost a century, Mercedes-Benz had been one of the world's premier brands, with attributes of quality, safety, and prestige. Customers willingly paid a hefty price to get the three-pointed Mercedes star on the hood of their car. During the course of just a few months, the star fell. Mercedes cars were no longer perceived as the epitome of safety, and the Daimler-Benz Corporation was perceived as a bully. Customers and the media are unlikely to give Mercedes the benefit of the doubt next time it experiences a crisis. Precious relationship equity was lost and will take years to rebuild.

Just when you might have thought things couldn't get any worse, Mercedes added fuel to the fire by continuing to run the original advertisements about the unique safety features of the A-Class throughout the debacle. "The advertising will not change significantly. Daimler-Benz still has a wealth of information to offer A-Class customers, even without giant beasts from the north," announced Mercedes's marketing director, Jochen Pläcking, in mock despair. I won't even comment on that statement, except to paraphrase Ralph Waldo Emerson's remark: "What you *are* shouts so loud in my ears I cannot hear what you *say*." The "body language" of the brand clearly outshouted the advertising message. While the Mercedes brand was the laughingstock of the world, it was business as usual in the marketing department in Stuttgart. Management assumed that their customers would simply be seduced by the commercials and disregard all the news reports about the car and the company. As it turned out, all the king's ads and all the king's marketing men couldn't put this brand back together again.

Butting Heads in the Production Century

Now, why did a large professional company like Mercedes spend hundreds of millions of dollars marketing this wobbly little car based on its safety? Why didn't Mercedes put its money where its mouth was and actually make the car safe? And why did it risk the reputation of the Mercedes brand name by backing into a corner of sleaze and innuendo, denial and name-calling, smoke and mirrors, instead of immediately taking responsibility and correcting its mistakes? And why would professional marketers decide to dish out millions of deutsche marks, kronor, and pounds for advertising that reminded people of the A-Class fiasco?

The answer to these questions is that Mercedes-Benz, like most companies, is organized like a herd of fighting bulls, with departments and business units fighting against each other for limited budget resources and senior management's attention. Mercedes's Swedish advertising agency blamed its German client for not keeping them informed about what was happening. The corporate PR department blamed its Swedish managers for not being able to contain the story from the news media. The engineers blamed their tire supplier. And the marketing director blamed the moose. This type of rampant internal bickering, with disparate departments and opposing goals, has been the norm in the twentieth century, or the the "Production Century."

Production Century companies are organized to efficiently produce and distribute goods. They relegate customer management and brand building to marketing and communications departments and agencies that sequester themselves in separate offices, isolated both from each other and from their customers, churning out advertising and other communications material to an information-overloaded world. These Production Century marketing departments make a virtue of outspending and outshouting the competition. Run more ads. Maximize the number of impressions. Get more editorial "ink." Dump more coupons. They are frittering away billions of dollars a year in a marketing communications arms race, which has bestowed upon mankind the wonders of fifty packaging variations of Coke, fifty-five different permutations of Crest toothpaste, and four thousand advertising messages inundating the average consumer every day.[3]

Lacking a process of integration, most Production Century

companies are really collections of free-willed divisions and departments. Incidentally, the word "department" originates from the French word *departir*, which means "to separate." At best, the various departments that touch customers fail to take advantage of opportunities for synergy. At worst, they are hurting each other. Customers watch a commercial designed by an ad agency aspiring to win creative awards; they get calls from two different salespeople representing competing business units of the same company; they log onto a website designed by a techno-weaned nineteen-year-old at a Silicon Valley start-up company; they make purchases from a minimum-wage worker at an independently owned franchise; they call companies' 800 numbers and get a nasty response from a call center outsourced to a supplier in Omaha; they get a rude reminder of an overdue bill from a financial department in Dallas. Each department is congregating within its own functional silo, divided by vocabulary, culture, training, and mutual disrespect for one another.

Yet all these departments make an impact on customers. Every interaction and transaction sends a powerful message that enables customers to give meaning to the brand and the company. Something as seemingly benign as the tone of voice with which a person answers the phone helps build a negative or positive impression in the customer's mind. Every time customers receive new information, it is integrated with their prior perceptions. When different points of contact send contradicting messages, companies have ceased to control the way customers understand and make sense of them.

Flying High in the Customer Century

In contrast, the companies highlighted in this book reap the benefits of synergy by strategically managing and integrating customer contact points to reinforce a desired reputation. These world-class companies earn a return on their cooperative efforts that adds up to more than the sum of the parts. And they will take their continued successes into the twenty-first century, the "Customer Century." Rather than organizing communications like a herd of fighting bulls, the winners of the new century will organize themselves like geese flying in a V formation. Flying in formation allows geese to fly 71 percent farther than they could fly alone. They optimize the performance of the group as a whole instead of suboptimizing the performance of individuals. Geese actually take turns leading the group. When the lead goose gets tired, he or she flies back to the end and the next goose takes the lead, because they all know where they are going. How do the geese know where they are going? One theory is that they have a built-in compass. Scientists have measured iron-rich tissue in the brains of birds that they believe responds to the earth's magnetic field, guiding the geese on their migrations. What a model for organizations!

Much as magnetic north provides direction for geese, the magnetic force for today's world-class companies is the *customer*. Obvious though this may seem, it's a surprisingly counterintuitive idea for most managers and organizations. Caught in the revolving door of management philosophies, many managers have lost sight of the fact that customer relationships are the only thing that really generate business value. Even a large number of marketing managers have forgotten that lesson in their preoccupation with the "four Ps" that have defined the field of marketing since 1957. Instead of manipulating customers with price, product, promotion, and place, customers themselves are seizing control of these levers. *Price* is no longer determined by the selling party based on cost-plus, but by customers who can name their own prices based on value-minus.[4] *Products* are no longer made in batches and pushed on customers, but made to order by customers who can design everything from jeans to computers to fit their idiosyncratic butts or work habits. The *promotional* monologue of advertising at the seller's convenience is being replaced by dialogue at the customer's convenience. The market *place* is currently moving into the market *space* of the Internet, where the customer determines the place of order and delivery.

Customers around the globe are becoming increasingly more savvy, informed, demanding, cynical, price conscious, and empowered, with a relentless appetite for quality, service, customization, convenience, and speed. There's only one way to reach their hearts, minds, and wallets: through *communication*, which is the process that people engage in to share understanding and meaning. Communicating with individual customers across all contact points requires painstaking *integration*, which is commonly defined as the process of achieving a unity of effort in various organizational subsystems. Ergo, *integrated communications* is the stuff that profitable relationships are built on in the Customer Century. As the card-carrying academic I once was, I'm behooved to provide my own definition of this term:

> Integrated communications is the strategic management process of facilitating a desired meaning of the company and its brands by creating unity of effort at every point of contact with key customers and stakeholders for the purpose of building profitable relationships with them.

Note that it's a "strategic management process" that must permeate through entire organizations, rather than a quick-fix crash program or campaign from the marketing or communications departments. It goes beyond customers, to involve other "stakeholders" as well, which includes every group or individual with a stake in the company's success. They include the opinion leaders who legitimize the company and its products; the government that might legislate against them; the media that critique them; the activist groups that might condemn them; the financial community that invests in the production of them; and the employees who spend a large portion of their lives at the company's desks. Every point of contact with important customers and stakeholders has to be strategically integrated to build profitable relationships. Customer and stakeholder relationships are the only source of truly sustainable competitive advantage in the Customer Century. Yet most companies don't have a process to manage and grow this asset. Integrated communications offers this process.

Don't mistake this definition of integrated communications for a warmed-up version of the cries in the early 1990s for "integrated marketing communications" (IMC), the catalyst for a myriad of conferences, articles, books, and classes. IMC has been an important step in the direction of integrated communications, but an insufficient one, motivated in large part by communications agencies' appetite for more business. The supply-driven fad of IMC represented a Production Century view of packaging and transmitting marketing communications messages that speak with one voice. The difference between the conventional version of IMC and the strategic approach to integrated communications described in this book is the difference between chicken manure and chicken salad. Instead of a skin-deep integration of messages and creative execution, this book defines integrated communications as a process of dialogue, interaction, and learning, with the purpose of adding value and cultivating relationships with key customers and stakeholders.

Introducing the World-Class Companies

This book will tell the inspirational stories of how some of the world's leading companies are preparing to meet the challenges of the Customer Century with integrated communications. During the course of my research, I turned to leading total quality management (TQM) firms. The management philosophy of TQM fully integrates the entire business organization from the customer's point of view, providing value through ongoing dialogue between everyone in the company and their customers. The companies in this book use the TQM philosophy, tools, and methods of involving everyone from senior managers to factory workers in listening to the customer's needs, and improving processes to consistently satisfy and exceed customers' expectations. Most of the companies are now embracing these principles without the fanfare of the TQM acronym. While the TQM label has lost its luster, its principles lay a foundation for integrated communications. The trend set in motion by TQM is creating new forms of flexible, fluid, and boundaryless organizations, laying the groundwork for the integrated communications practices required in the postindustrial age.

This book is the fruit of a nine-year study of the role of communications at fourteen of America's and Europe's leading corporations. A panel of marketing, communications, and total quality management experts, professors, and senior managers assisted in selecting the companies that are successfully practicing total quality management and integrated communications. Five of the sampled companies are Baldrige Quality Award–winners, two are European Quality Award–winners, four have won British, Danish, Dutch, or Swedish national quality awards, and one has a unit that won the Deming Award. All of them are multinational, multibillion-dollar companies. None of them have arrived at perfect solutions. But they are addressing important questions, experimenting with new ideas, and forming new insights, which can help other businesses.

I conducted hundreds of hours of personal in-depth interviews in seven countries with over eighty senior marketing, communications, and quality managers, plus a few human resources, research and development, and information systems managers. They were predominantly senior vice presidents or managers reporting to senior VPs. In addition, the book is based on published and unpublished documentation from the companies and news articles about them. This research offered rare insight into the successes of these leading companies: how Eastman Chemical Company has successfully merged small-town southern industrial culture with Japanese-style total quality management; how evident the sense of pride is at Xerox, a company that stared death in the face only a decade and a half ago and is now the only company in the world to have won the most prestigious quality awards in the United States, Europe, and Japan; and how ISS, a company in the business of sweeping floors, has developed into an international high-tech powerhouse.

The companies featured in this book

U.S.-based companies	Industry	1998 Sales in USD
Allen-Bradley (now a division of Rockwell Automation)	Plant floor automation equipment	$4.5 billion*
Eastman Chemical Co.	Chemicals	$4.8 billion
Federal Express	Delivery service	$15.8 billion
Hewlett-Packard	Computer and measurement equipment	$46.5 billion
Motorola	Wireless communications and electronics	$29.4 billion
Saturn	Automobile	$4 billion*
Xerox	Document equipment	$19.4 billion
European-based companies		
ABB	Diversified industrial equipment	$30.8 billion
Danfoss	Heating and cooling equipment	$2.2 billion
Design to Distribution, D2D (now Celestica)	Contract electronics manufacturing	$3.2 billion

Ericsson	Phone systems	$22.8 billion
ISS	Cleaning service	$1.9 billion
Philips	Electronic equipment	$33.9 billion
Rank-Xerox	Document equipment	$6 billion*

*1997 sales.

These fourteen companies represent all walks of business life. They make pagers and printers, scanners and stereos, copy machines and camera film, train cars and family cars, software applications and soft-drink bottles, cell phones and sunscreen lotion. Some are over a century old; others are still start-ups. Some are public, others are private. Some are based in the United States and others in Europe. Despite their differences, the companies share a number of traits. The most salient common denominator is their obsessive customer focus. That's not a cliché, but a clinical observation. They identify their key customers and make it everyone's responsibility— from the receptionist and plant-floor workers, to senior management and the board—to establish long-term relationships with them. The same rigor is applied to communication with other key stakeholders, including investors, news media, and local communities. This integration of *external* communications with customers and stakeholders starts at home, by integrating internal communications in the two management directions: *vertically*, between the employees who are close to the customers and the operations, and the senior management with the power to change systemwide processes; and *horizontally*, across departments, business units, and country borders. Their not-so-secret key to success is in keeping communication lines open in these three directions: *externally*, *vertically*, and *horizontally*. This "3-D Integrated Communications Model" is the organizing framework for this book. The expression "3-D" is used because companies must learn how to communicate in all three dimensions simultaneously for effective integrated communications. Excelling in one dimension but neglecting the others doesn't cut it. What gives these companies the "world-class" epithet is their ability to successfully integrate all three dimensions.

With that said, I would be remiss in not acknowledging that the companies featured in this book have not been unscathed. They have all had their share of problems during the course of my nine-year research. Particularly, Motorola, Ericsson, ISS, and Saturn have suffered from sluggish markets and some strategic decision gaffes. It only goes to show that no company can arrive at a perfect state of excellence. Integrated communications is an ever-evolving endeavor. Regardless of any snags that have and will effect the world-class companies in this book from time to time, their unconventional approaches and indisputable successes are a source of inspiration for every company. This journey through some of America and Europe's top-performing companies will inspire business leaders to ask strategic questions about how they can more effectively add value to their organizations, help strengthen relationships with key stakeholders, build brands, and improve corporate reputation—by integrating communications in 3-D. It's a timely message. In this day and age of cost-cutting and downsizing, managers are beginning to ask themselves how much corporate muscle they cut out with the fat, how much of the future they've been mortgaging by squeezing out short-term profit, and how they will get their anorexic business to grow. As the last drops of waste are being wrung out of the cost side of the business equation, managers need to turn to the demand side of the equation. The inspirational examples in this book will show them how to grow business in the Customer Century.

If They Had Only Read This Book . . .

Reading this book before the A-Class disaster could have saved the managers of Mercedes-Benz from the painful experience of that debacle. I'm not making such a bold assertion to tout the brilliance of my own work, but to extol the lessons from the extraordinary companies I studied. Taking a page from leading integrated communications companies would require a new mind-set of Mercedes's senior managers. They would have had to focus less on the operational, financial, and legal implications of their decisions—and more on communications implications to customers and stakeholders.

By integrating its *vertical* communications among senior management, middle management, and front-line workers, Mercedes would have been able to fix the flipover problem years before the launch of the car. During the course of ongoing and open dialogue between senior management and the engineers in the A-Class development team, the problem would surely have surfaced. The top brass in Stuttgart would have been in tune with the problems and ordered remedial actions early on in the process. Even if the problem still prevailed by the time journalists first discovered it, Mercedes could have averted the crisis with integrated *horizontal* communications, across departments and countries. If Mercedes's managers of R&D, marketing, public relations, and Swedish sales were on speaking terms with each other, they could have immediately decided to redesign the car and postpone the introduction by a few months. Such a decision would have gone a long way toward restoring consumer confidence, given that Mercedes's *external* communications were up to par with world-class companies. Mercedes could have acted right away on the concerns of the journalists who discovered the problem, instead of publicly raising its middle finger at them. Treating the media with civility and respect would have turned the journalists into staunch supporters of Mercedes's actions, effectively ending the crisis before it started.

Applying this three-dimensional model of integrated communications to a company like Mercedes is not an easy "just add water" fix, but a framework for thinking about change for an organization. It's not an isolated program, but a continuous effort. As such, it can provide a competitive advantage that cannot be easily duplicated. It determines whether a company can attract and keep talented people, reliable investors, and, most importantly, profitable customers. This book offers a unique backstage look at how some of the world's leading companies pull that off.

What to Do Monday through Friday Mornings:

Each chapter is concluded with a box that provides practical action steps on how to begin the journey to the Customer Century. The boxes are metaphorically entitled "What to Do Monday through Friday Morning," suggesting these action steps be done in the sequence of the chapters.

Before you can even begin the "What to do's," it's essential that CEOs wholeheartedly endorse the integrated communications process. Here are some talking points to help you make the case to the Big Cheese.... Now if that happens to be you, the following points are just as useful to get your managers rallying behind the idea.

- Integrated communications builds customer relationships, which are the only sustainable source of competitive advantage in today's commoditized marketplace. Loyal customers are less costly to maintain, less price-focused, and more inclined to give references to others.
- Integrated communications forges relationships with other stakeholders as well, which reduces the cost of litigation, regulation, and boycotts, and makes money by attracting investment capital, skilled employees, and positive media coverage.
- Integrated communications is more *effective* because it gives companies greater control of the messages and contact points that will ultimately be integrated in the customers' and stakeholders' minds, enabling companies to better manage and cultivate relationships with them.
- Integrated communications is more *efficient,* saving time and money by leveraging efforts and reducing duplication and waste.
- Integrated communications strengthens employee relationships, by valuing and acting on their ideas, sharing their resources, and providing the information they need to do their jobs.
- Integrated communications is the entry ticket to the Customer Century: competitors are doing it, customers are expecting it, and stakeholders are requiring it.

Notes

1. TT Nyhetsbanken, Mercedes kan stoppa leveranser av nya A-Modellen, Nov. 8, 1997.
2. http://scharl.wu-wien.ac.at/ElchTest
3. Day, Adrian C. (1997). "Following the Trend Toward Corporate Branding, Shaping a Superior Corporate Image." Conference Board Report # 1156-96-CH, pp. 22–24.
4. Suggested by Professor Jagdish Sheth in a speech to the annual conference of the Academy of Marketing Science in 1999.

I

INTEGRATING COMMUNICATIONS IN 3-D

A Bird's-Eye View

Loyalty today is no longer a function of rote or duty, but rather passion. You must do things so astonishingly well that customers become not merely loyalists, but rather outright apostles.

As for the car, I thought Saturn a doomed quest. It would probably be just another poorly made American steel box that advertising would lie about.

—*Skip LeFauve, former chairman, Saturn*

—*Joe Sherman, author of*
In the Rings of Saturn

They came from Alaska and Florida, some from as far away as Taiwan, to an assembly plant in the middle of the American South, on their own nickel. Some 44,000 proud owners of General Motors's Saturn automobiles made their way to Spring Hill, Tennessee, on a rainy Saturday in June of 1994. They came to see the plant where their cars were born, meet the men and women who built them, and get to know their fellow "Saturnites." Participants were treated to music and theatrical performances on six stages simultaneously. Celebrities taking part in the event ranged from country music star Wynonna Judd to Olympic skating champ Dan Jansen. The kids got to jump on the flexible polymer material that Saturn doors are constructed from. They could even have a Saturn logo tattooed on their arms (okay, the tattoos were temporary). The main attraction was the guided tour through the car plant. In fact, it was the large number of requests from Saturn owners to see the plant that sparked the idea for the homecoming event. Hosts of the plant tour were 2,300 Saturn workers—whoops, I mean "team members," who volunteered for the event. The same day, over 130,000 additional Saturnites took part in picnics and barbecues at Saturn retailers around the nation. In fact, one out of every six Saturn owners participated in a Saturn event that day. A second homecoming event took place in July of 1999. This time it involved parades, fireworks, an air show, and, of course, the plant tour. Visitors could bring home plenty of Saturn souvenirs, including a $17,000 commemorative green car with homecoming graphics flashing on the instrument panel and stitched in the floor mat. Proceeds from the event went to the Special Olympics. An additional 50,000 Saturnites make pilgrimages to their mecca of Spring Hill every year to tour the plant. To better serve the onslaught of visitors, the company renovated a horse barn and turned it into a Saturn Welcome Center with interactive exhibits showcasing Saturn's history.

Saturn devotees lusting for more regular doses of worship will find sanctuary at local Saturn Clubs. The eighty-chapter, 10,000-plus-member Saturn Car Clubs raise money and do work for charitable causes. For example, Saturn clubs in New Jersey and New York built twelve new playgrounds for underprivileged children during a single day in 1995. The material used to build the playgrounds was donated by Saturn retailers, and the labor was performed by Saturn customers and employees—including Saturn's president and assembly-line workers who flew up to take part in the events.

These are just a few of the unconventional ways in which the General Motors Corporation subsidiary gets all its employees and resellers involved in customer communications. And they prompt a question. Is this marketing or public relations? Is it employee relations or community outreach? Is it customer service or event marketing? It's all of that and more. In two words, it is integrated communications.

Customers, members of the local community, and employees

working side by side building playgrounds together, and employees giving plant tours to eager fans are vivid illustrations of the three dimensions of integrated communications, illustrated and defined in figure 1.1. The model depicts your own company as the triangle in front, with senior management at the top, middle management in the middle, and front-line employees at the bottom. I'm defining "front-line" broadly, as anyone below middle management who is adding value directly or indirectly to the customer. The triangle behind represents stakeholders, such as the local community, the media, investors, and government regulators. The last triangle is customers. The point of illustrating these groups as overlaying triangles is to show that Customer Century companies need to involve people of all ranks and from every department in ongoing dialogues with customers and other stakeholders.

The first dimension of *integrated external communications* is the process of involving everyone in the organization in both inbound and outbound communications with customers and stakeholders. To make that happen, senior management has to train, empower, and support frontline employees through a process of *integrated vertical communications*. This second dimension is about opening up forthright, frequent, and two-way communications among senior management, middle management, and employees. It keeps the top brass in touch with the front-line workers and through them the customers, and employees in tune with the strategic context of their work. But as long as communication is confined to the vertical silos of functions, business units, and countries it is not going to appear integrated to the customer. The real breakthroughs come from the cross-function, cross-business, and cross-region alignment of *integrated horizontal communications*. This third dimension integrates communication among people working at different business units, departments, and countries. The three dimensions illustrate that integrated communications needs to take place throughout organizations (external integration), ranks (vertical integration), and functions, business units, and regions (horizontal integration). Integrated communications is not any one of these dimensions alone. Companies that try to have a bite here and a bite there without sitting down for the whole meal are poised to fail. All three dimensions need to be in place to reap the full benefits of integrated communications in the Customer Century.

Figure 1.1. The Three Dimensions of
Integrated Communications.

1st Dimension:
External Integration

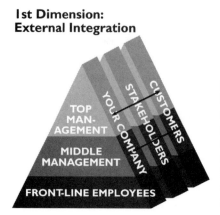

External Communications—Building profitable relationships by integrating communications at every point of customer and
stakeholder contact. Everyone in the organization, no matter what rank or what
department, is involved in dialogue and
learning with key customers and stakeholders to better anticipate and exceed their
ever-changing needs.

2nd Dimension:
Vertical Integration

Vertical Communications—Linking frontline
workers who are closest to the customer
and the action, with top management that
has the power to act on the information
and make systemwide improvements.
Senior managers are in constant touch
with their employees and through them,
their customers; and employees are proud
and well-informed ambassadors of the
organization.

3rd Dimension:
Horizontal Integration

Horizontal Communications—Implementing
effective processes of cross-functional,
cross-business, and cross-border communications. Reinforcing a consistent brand,
leveraging knowledge, skills, and assets, creating synergies, and reaping the advantages
of scale and scope, by facilitating a free flow
of communication across the organization.

An Old Dog's New Tricks

Ironically, the idea behind one of the most powerful examples of integrated communications was born in the bastion of the Production Century, during its heyday. In the early 1980s, on the fourteenth floor of General Motors's Detroit headquarters tower, senior GM managers looked up from their navels one day to realize that American consumers were scarfing up Japanese vehicles. In response to skyrocketing sales of imported small Japanese cars, they reacted hastily by launching smaller versions of their existing cars. The new "economy" Chevrolets, Buicks, and Cadillacs were shrunken in size, but not in price. CEO Roger Smith finally decided to kill the small car projects entirely and start from scratch. He appointed a "Group of 99," comprised of United Auto Workers members and General Motors managers and staff from fifty-five plants in seventeen GM divisions. This team adopted a clean-slate approach to free themselves from traditional industry practices. They visited forty-nine different General Motors plants and sixty other companies around the world for inspiration. The project resulted in the establishment of the first new American car brand since the Edsel and the first fully integrated automobile factory in America since 1927. Named after the Saturn rocket that carried Americans to the Moon during the space race with the USSR, General Motors created the Saturn subsidiary to beat the Japanese in the small-car race. Saturn was an experimental laboratory on a mission to not only beat the Japanese in the small-car market, but also to induce radical rethinking in every aspect of the car business.

Managing and Integrating "Moments of Truth"

Exhaustive customer research guided Saturn's strategies and inspired the team to look at car buying not as a single transaction, but as a whole experience. Before the car was even launched, Saturn management compiled a list of forty points of contact between the company and the customer, or "moments of truth," in Saturn vernacular. They ranged from the moment a customer is exposed to a Saturn ad for the first time, to the moment the customer walks into a showroom, to the moment when a customer picks up a car. The list of truths also includes the service a customer receives while owning the car and, finally, the moment a customer trades in the car for a new one. Says Public Relations Director Greg Martin, "Those are the forty times during 'the Saturn Experience' that we have identified as key moments that really are going to define the relationship we have with the customer."

The purpose of the list is to help Saturn better manage these moments and communicate a more consistent image of the Saturn brand. The list's true significance, though, is that it helped Saturn grasp another truth, one that's both subtle and profound. The communication that really matters to consumers is not the work of marketing or communications professionals. It is the work of the "part-time communicators" in other departments and independent retailers. Saturn's success demonstrates the importance of making all front-line employees and the people supporting them, including distributors, suppliers, and other business partners, understand their role in meeting and exceeding customer expectations. They need to be provided the power, training, and opportunity to deliver consistent brand messages—in words and deeds—to the customers, and to bring back customer feedback to the organization.

In the mind of the customer, every moment of truth is a microcosm of the company. Think of it as a hologram. No matter how many small parts the hologram is divided into, each piece still contains the whole picture. Every contact with a company represents the entire company to the customer. The interactions with the customer form the whole basis of customer communications, regardless if an interaction is based on talking to a person, using the product, reading the owner's manual, or watching a commercial by the company. The idea of managing the moments of truth, sometimes called "moments of opportunity" or "brand contact points," was popularized by one of my fellow Swedes, the former CEO of the Scandinavian Airline Systems, Jan Carlzon.[1] He calculated that each one of the ten million passengers who flew every year came into contact with five SAS employees on an average flight, and that each such encounter lasted an average of fifteen seconds. Carlzon argued that what really makes the difference to consumers is the fifty million moments of truth they experience every year. A passenger's impression of the airline company is the sum total of these moments. Passengers who have pleasant experiences when interacting with SAS employees will view the company favorably. In order to integrate external communications by managing these moments, Carlzon focused on vertical communication by sending all of his front-line personnel to seminars, giving them more decision-making power, and designing new uniforms. He inspired, taught, and empowered employees to send customers a consistently positive message about the company.

Saturn's first moment of truth was a twenty-six-minute "documercial," a documentary about the start-up of a project dedicated to "building cars in a brand new way." Building on interviews of workers and people living in the local community of Spring Hill, the film played an extraordinary role in helping to explain the Saturn idea to new employees, suppliers, and the press. Dealers used it in presentations for bank loans and zoning variances. The film finally introduced Saturn to the consumer market by being aired as an infomercial on cable networks.

The theme of the documercial and all subsequent Saturn advertisements put the company before the product: "A Different Kind of Company, a Different Kind of Car." The ads started running two years before the car was on the market. Its folksy advertising featured Saturn workers talking about the participative management style of the company. A few years later, the emphasis shifted from Saturn employees to Saturn owners. In a refreshing break from the industry tradition of auto-fetishism commercials featuring cars racing in deserts and mountains, the Saturn ads showcased real customers talking about their experiences with Saturn. The owners were selected through their letters and anecdotes passed on by retailers. The first prize of a recent Saturn sweepstakes featured in an ad was to go to Spring Hill and build your own car!

Dealers Dealing with Moments of Truth

Another key moment of truth for Saturn is the purchasing experience. Saturn found that women in particular dreaded the haggling process. They would rather hand-feed crocodiles than go through the trauma of buying a car. This provided a tremendous opportunity for GM to seize on an important need—to make car buying a nonthreatening and enjoyable experience devoid of haggling and manipulation. Ten years after its launch, Saturn is still the only auto company that has managed to make the sticker price nonnegotiable. The price of a Saturn car remains constant for all customers and retailers regardless of the time of year. When Saturn cut its sticker price $700 two months into its model year, it reimbursed owners who had already bought the car at the higher price. The sales process is further improved by renaming sales personnel sales *consultants,* who are trained to avoid hard-sell methods. The word "dealership" was replaced with the more customer-friendly term "retailer" to emphasize that Saturn is not in the business of making deals. To make the buying experience as pleasant for the customers as possible, Saturn is currently spending some $40 million renovating the stores. "We want to make the dealerships warmer, more homey," explains Greg Martin. The stores are becoming cozy, studylike areas with working fireplaces, large aquariums, upholstered leather chairs, wooden desks, a children's play area, and refreshment centers that dispense complimentary coffee and soft drinks. The renovation was put into place after prospective and current customers expressed that the dealerships were a bit impersonal and too sterile. "The new stores will better reflect the Saturn brand," explains Martin.

The Saturn sales consultants have all undergone a rigorous one-week training program at the Spring Hill manufacturing plant. "There aren't a lot of manufacturers who send their dealers to a training center at a factory," rejoices Thor Gilbertson, the sales manager for a Saturn dealership in Madison, Wisconsin. "It gives them a chance to see the factory, and allows them to talk to the plant floor workers. They come back really charged up, ready to go." The retailers are brought back regularly to Spring Hill to support their jobs as ambassadors of the Saturn brand. They don't just tour the plant and listen to presentations, they work together building cars or helping the community. "This last year, all the retailers got together and with Saturn's help, we built this huge playground for the community," remarks Tom Zimbrick, owner of Saturn of Madison. "It was the first time I've gone to a manufacturer's meeting where we got anything done," chuckles Zimbrick, proudly pointing to a framed picture of them building the playground. This veteran dealer assures that he has never experienced this kind of support from any other auto manufacturer. "That is extraordinary—to have this kind of training in the automobile industry. Usually training is just the manufacturer sending out a videotape."

Saturn has a field staff dedicated to supporting its retailers and keeping them connected to the company. Says Zimbrick, "Saturn field executives will come in annually and help us put together a business plan for the year." He particularly appreciates the wealth of customer data that the Saturn field representatives share. "Demographics, buying patterns, market share are all provided to us . . . current owners, prospective owners, why they buy, why they don't buy, what else they are looking for, how often they trade, what they like and dislike . . . this kind of research is something most dealers couldn't afford to do." The retailers are not merely integrated vertically with the manufacturer, but also horizontally with each other. "If you buy a car in Missouri, I can send that service information to Madison, Wisconsin," notes Zimbrick. This support makes a tremendous difference for the retailers, who have the most direct contact with customers and become proud representatives of the Saturn brand.

Picking up a newly purchased car is considered another critical moment of truth to Saturn. Its retailers stage a "send-off" where all staff members gather around the car and cheer for the new owner. A Polaroid picture is taken of the happy car owner, which is tacked on a bulletin board featured prominently at every Saturn retail store. After the new owner drives off the lot, Saturn stays in touch with them through a twice-annual magazine called *Vision*, service reminders, a card commemorating the car's delivery date, and announcements of upcoming events at the dealership.

Delivering a car to a new buyer is a defining moment for the first-time customer, and helps shape her view of the entire car brand. Consumer behavior experts discovered over forty years ago that the time right after purchase is particularly critical, because many customers experience "cognitive dissonance," or more colloquially, "buyer's remorse," right after the purchase. That's an important time for companies to convince their new customers that they've made the right choice. Yet most auto companies don't take advantage of the delivery of the car to reduce this remorse. They treat it as a trivial logistic issue and leave it to happenstance. To

Saturn, however, the send-off is an important contact point that is carefully managed. The Saturn brand has been meticulously built by integrating this and other critical moments of truth. The message of Saturn being a "Different Kind of Company" is embedded with every moment of truth—every print ad, every interaction with a retailer, and every phone call with a customer service rep. The company even used a recall of several hundred thousand cars that had a technical problem as an opportunity to bolster its brand reputation and cultivate customer relationships. Car owners were asked to come in for a free car wash and barbecue while their cars were being repaired. The hot sauce from Thailand was optional. Brilliantly, a potential crisis was turned into a moment of truth, which strengthened Saturn's customer relationships. Says Saturn president Donald Hudler, "We wanted people to feel even better about us after the recall than they did before." Rather than being a chore, the recall left customers feeling great about their cars and the manufacturer. This and other special events reveal how Saturn brand relationships are strategically managed and reinforced, one customer at a time, one moment of truth at a time.

Virtual Moments of Truth

Integrating moments of truth is as important online as offline to Saturn. The carmaker pioneered with a bulletin board on Prodigy that went up in 1992. Saturn responded to as many as one hundred e-mail messages per day back in those dark pre-Internet-age days and encouraged customers to talk to each other. Today, Saturn's website[2] allows customers to enter their own personal information and search its "Extended Family Database" containing over nine thousand fellow Saturn owners. Visitors can search for Saturn owners by name, state, or model year of their automobiles. Once a name is found, they can learn of the Saturn owner's e-mail address, ambitions, inspirations, age, and any other comments they have entered. Customers can post pictures of themselves with their Saturn, find their closest Saturn club, or reserve a place in line for a tour at the Spring Hill plant.

While most companies are troubled by the negative effects of rogue sites popping up in every corner of cyberspace, Saturn has loyal fans creating special websites for enthusiasts. One of the fan sites is called "Saturnalia." Log on and you can chat with other owners, post pictures, find out the latest news and upcoming events. You can even get the scoop on new Saturn car designs planned for the future. Host of "Saturnalia" by night and engineer by day, Charlie Eickmeyer has put many hours into building and maintaining the site: "It's been a lot of fun, although over the last nights, the lack of sleep has started to creep up on me!"[3] Another Saturn enthusiast developed the site "Online Homecoming," dedicated to the Homecoming event of '94. Avid fans can take a virtual tour of the plant, admire vehicles at a "car show," and chat with others visitors. The site draws an average of nearly two hundred visitors a day.

Going the Extra Mile

Saturn integrates not only outbound communications but also inbound communications. It involves everyone in the organization in listening to customers and stakeholders. Through open vertical communications, the second dimension of the 3-D model, this information is relayed to the senior levels where strategic decisions are being made. The listening goes beyond merely reacting to what customers say, to anticipating their future needs. Saturn managers work closely with front-line workers and retailers to sense new trends and generate new ideas. The story of the blockbuster third door on the Saturn coupe is a great case in point. The idea originated with Saturn retailer Stuart Lasser, or rather his ten-year-old son, Hal. During a product development task force meeting with retailers, plant floor workers, and design engineers, Lasser burst out, "It's always been a pain in the neck to get my son in and out of the backseat of my coup. Why don't we add a rear-access door?"[4] An impressive six weeks later, the group was shown a prototype of the new vehicle. An idea that helped revive its entire coupe line was born. Through such attentive listening, Saturn management is constantly anticipating, embracing, and exploiting changes in customer expectations. A dealer wants a third door on the coupe. He gets it. Customers find the retailer stores too cold and uninviting. No problem, let's turn them into living rooms. Legislators and customers are demanding electric cars. They've got it. All along, genuine bonds grow among employees, customers, and stakeholders, as illustrated in figure 1.2. They all feel they are part of the same extended family and evolve into apostles who preach the gospel to anyone who will listen. It is the intimate relationships between company and customers, between managers and workers, between local community and workplace that define the brand and differentiate it from all competitors.

1st Dimension:
External Integration

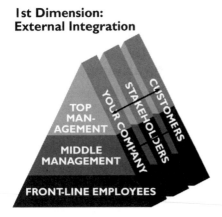

Figure 1.2. The first dimension of integrated communications: Integrating external communications between everyone in the organization and the most critical customers and stakeholders.

Saturn's success is remarkable by any standard. In 1995, it overtook Ford Escort to become the best-selling small car in the United States, capturing an astonishing 10.4 percent share of the small car and sports car market. The following year, Saturn was rated best in overall satisfaction among all car brands, including luxury brands like Lexus and Mercedes-Benz. Saturn is the top-ranking small-size car in Polk's study of automotive brand loyalty. J. D. Power and Associates, the nationally recognized automotive research firm, has ranked Saturn as the best car-buying experience in the industry for three years running. Saturn's own research shows that 97 percent of Saturn owners say they would "enthusiastically recommend the purchase of a Saturn car." And it all stems from a unique communications approach to building relationships and a community of owners. It comes from treating customers as friends, sending them thank-you letters, offering value, and building playgrounds together. "If we have any legacy at Saturn," proclaims Don Hudler, "it will be that we built an outstanding brand."

The challenge is to continue to be "A Different Kind of Company, a Different Kind of Car," in a time when the global auto industry is consolidating and Saturn is becoming more General Motorized. GM made the decision to build its new mid-size "Saturn Innovate," a clone of its German-made Opel Vectra, in a GM plant in Wilmington, Delaware. And after 2002 all Saturn models will be based on a single platform, to be shared with its corporate cousins Chevrolet, Pontiac, Saab, and Opel. But Saturn's management team appears unfazed about the risks of diluting the Saturn brand. "Wilmington is a progressive plant and we're transplanting our entire management concept to it," demurs Greg Martin who seems to think that Saturn will remain as groovy as ever. Its appointment of the first woman ever to head a U.S. car company does little to refute that notion. Cynthia Trudell, a GM executive recognized for her diplomacy and hands-on approach, is excited at the prospect of heading up Saturn. Given that Saturn sells more than two-thirds of its cars to women, it seems only logical to have a woman at the helm. Says the confident Trudell, "It will certainly help to make sure the vehicles are designed with women in mind, and as a woman, I understand the family and what its needs are for vehicles."[5]

Saturn's management is determined to maintain its distinctive role in the lives of its customers even though the missionary fervor that put Saturn on the map seems to be ebbing. But it's not taking it for granted: "We need to be vigilant about building our customer relationships, the day we get content will be the end of it," retorts Martin. Its success at managing these relationships with integrated communications will determine the future of the company.

A Case Worth Copying

Unlike Saturn, some world-class integrated communications companies are made, not born. Few examples of companies that are made through the initiative of visionary leaders are more poignant than the fall and rise of Xerox. It enjoyed enormous growth during the height of the Production Century. In just ten years' time, from 1970 to 1980, revenues grew from $1.6 billion to $8 billion and profit from $190 million to $565 million. But even as Xerox was flourishing, the seeds of failure were sprouting. Protected by patents, Xerox sold copy machines that were embarrassingly riddled with flaws. "Quality in those days was considered nothing more than an expense—and who wanted extra expenses?" reflects David Kearns, CEO at the time.[6] The company sent new products out to market prematurely without proper testing. Instead of improving the equipment, Xerox hired seven hundred more service representatives to go out and fix broken machines. In essence, regular customers became beta-testers for the new machines, constantly having them fixed and corrected. Morale was dwindling and employees and customers alike were leaving the sinking ship in droves. However, management simply decided to deal with customer attrition by seeking out new business and not worrying about all the customers they lost along the roadside.

Xerox's directors watched their train wreck for years. The severity of the situation did not dawn on them because their eyes were directed to the rearview mirror—the financial statements. The Xerox managers neglected to see beyond the numbers to the unhappy faces of their customers. They did not realize that revenues were coming largely from customers who were buying backup machines because of the poor quality of their copiers, and from providing service to copiers that broke down. Along with countless other revered American Production Century companies such as IBM, GM, Sears, and Digital Equipment Corporation, Xerox suffered a rapid decline in customer relationship assets long before the problems showed up on profit-and-loss statements. Xerox was oblivious to its competitors as well. The navel-gazing Xerox culture measured the quality of one Xerox machine with other Xerox machines, and compared the sales results with the company's previous years'.[7] The bottom dropped out for Xerox in the early 1980s when its patents expired and its Japanese competitors began to compete head-on by offering higher-quality copiers at almost half of Xerox's manufacturing costs. The assault took a heavy toll on Xerox, which saw its market share fall from 90 percent to less than 15 percent in just a few years' time.[8] Against daunting odds, Xerox saved itself from annihilation and managed a remarkable turnaround. "In our near-death situation, everyone from the cleaning people to the chairman would have to think differently," reflected Kearns.[9] Xerox got back on a strong track to building its customer relationships.

Xerox survived by dramatically changing focus to strategically integrate customer communications. Today, Xerox's chief executive officer, Paul Allaire, answers phone calls from Xerox customers one day each month. The calls he receives are not just from senior managers at client companies but also from secretaries responsible for a single Xerox machine. He follows through with the complaints until they are completely resolved. This way, Allaire gets to know his company from the customer's point of view. The telephone duty rotates among Xerox's top twenty-five managers. On any given business day, any customer can reach one of the company's top brass. In addition, all senior managers are responsible for maintaining select client relationships. "I'm responsible for sales and service with my alma mater and with a consulting firm that my department does business with," says Dr. Joseph Cahalan, corporate communications director. Not even Corporate Controller Phil Fishbach escapes this responsibility. He has been the "focused executive" for one of Xerox's customers, Philip Morris, for the last ten years. Together with Xerox's global account manager for Philip Morris, Dick Nelson, who is in charge of the daily customer contacts, they meet with senior-level Philip Morris executives every six months. "It can be anything from a discussion of the market and financial plans with the CIO to a discussion of quality control programs with an operations program," says Nelson about the meetings, adding that the involvement of the controller has greatly enhanced their relationships with the customer.[10] Instead of pushing its ink-stained gears, Xerox is becoming a strategic partner and service provider. Instead of assigning salespeople a geographic region, they are members of "industry-solution groups," specializing in serving particular industries like government agencies and graphic arts companies.[11]

Every CEO staff meeting at Xerox begins with Allaire asking the six directors reporting to him two series of questions. The first is: "What customers have you visited in the last month and what have you learned?" The second question is: "What employee communications events have you had, and what did you learn?" Cahalan recalls the first time they were asked: "When that started three years ago there was a lot of silence in the room, but now everybody has a good story to tell." Asking these questions had dramatic effects. "This has really caught on so now all six want to please the CEO of course, so they are almost tripping over each other putting on customer and employee communications events," reflects Cahalan.

Senior management's commitment to customer communication percolates to front-line workers around the world. Employees who don't have direct customer contact are encouraged to better support those who do. The goal is not so much to capture a large share of mind in the public, but to deliver peace of mind to key customers. In other words, every point of customer contact is used as an opportunity to revitalize and reinforce the brand proposition of the digital "Document Company," to improve satisfaction with Xerox, and to identify problems and listen to customers' concerns. Front-line workers are empowered to act as "customer advocates," doing what it takes to please the customer. They are given what Xerox calls "line of sight" training in which they learn how their jobs fit with upstream and downstream activities, to make sure that going out of their way for one customer doesn't disrupt the process flow in a way that would negatively effect another customer.[12] Xerox's European subsidiary, Rank-Xerox, went as far as blowing up its traditional product lines and reorganizing into "customer business units," responsible for particular customer segments. Xerox listens to the voice of the customer by distributing an amazing 55,000 customer satisfaction surveys every month. The results of these surveys, along with information from the customer complaint management system and reports from the field force, are carefully disseminated to everyone in the organization. Customer service representatives make calls to every dissatisfied customer who has been identified in the surveys. All in all, 10,000 complaints are followed up every month. Survey results are also shared with the design and manufacturing departments for root cause analysis and corrective actions. A senior management team meets regularly to review the survey and discuss actions to improve the "top ten dissatisfiers." A global customer satisfaction system is the cornerstone of Xerox's vision of 100 percent customer satisfaction. Before the system was established, customer satisfaction research was optional for local Xerox subsidiaries. To the degree that the local Xerox subsidiaries even surveyed their customers, they asked different questions, using different rating scales. It was not possible to compare scores across regions and determine if particular dissatisfaction problems were endemic to a single country or the entire company.[13] Hardwiring the "voice of the customer" into the entire company this way has provided Xerox an edge in the Production Century, but it will be the entry ticket to any market in the Customer Century.

Xerox has taken the voice of the customer and used it to redefine itself. The Xerox brand has been carefully groomed to transcend its physical products and instead represent a broad range of document "solutions." It's offering professional services such as building digital office networks and even running outsourced printing and copying operations. The onetime maker of photocopiers is now "The Document Company," a one-stop shop for scanning, storing, custom printing, and faxing products and services—a digital powerhouse in the information age. And the efforts have paid off. The year before this book went to print, Xerox scored record profits of $2.7 billion.

Integrating Stakeholder Communications: An Overnight Success Case

Communications of the Xerox and Saturn brands go beyond customers' direct contacts with the companies. Articles from the morning paper, comments from a trusted friend, criticism from an environmental group, and other credible third-party sources are moments of truth with an even stronger impact on customers. External communications needs to encompass all "stakeholders," which are groups and individuals with a stake in the company's success. They are people or organizations who can help or hurt the company. Some are constituents, such as customers, employees, shareholders, or suppliers. Others can be adversaries such as competitors, unions, legislators, or watchdog activist groups. The stakes of stakeholders have never been higher, as evidenced by the rise in business litigation, the decline of employee morale, confrontations with interest groups, scrutiny from the media, and activism by the board. Not only are their stakes mounting, but they are also getting more connected. Around the world, they log on to the same World Wide Web, watch the same satellite television channels, and travel to the same places. Companies cannot afford to be different things to different stakeholders. That's not to say that communication to each stakeholder should be identical. But it needs to be, at a minimum, consistent, and at best, leveraged.

A dramatic case of how employees and the media can be used as levers against government legislators is Federal Express's handling of a trade dispute with the Japanese government. At issue was Japan's denial of FedEx's right to serve its new air cargo hub in Subic Bay, the Philippines, from Japan. "It really was a serious situation because we had invested a lot of money in this inter-Asian hub and it formed the basis for our growth in Japan," explains Tom Martin, FedEx's public relations director at the time. Through intensive Washington lobbying, including two high-profile congressional appearances by FedEx's founder/CEO Fred Smith, the delivery company convinced the U.S. government to retaliate against Japan. The United States threatened to cut Japanese cargo flights to the U.S. if Japan did not allow FedEx to serve Asia from Japan. Simultaneously, Fred Smith and other senior FedEx executives made frequent visits to the press clubs in Tokyo, the central forum for the Japanese press, while also contacting the U.S. correspondents of the Japanese newspapers. "We worked Japanese media both in the U.S. and Japan; it was important to work both sides of the fence," comments Martin, explaining how they got such positive coverage in the powerful Japanese newspapers.

FedEx used its closed-circuit satellite television system both to keep its workforce abreast of the situation and to feed television stations around the world with its side of the story: "We had numerous requests from journalists to do live interviews, and since we weren't able to send Fred Smith all over the world, we were able to provide live and taped feeds with Smith and our senior VP of Asian operations to key media outlets around the world." Not only did FedEx win the trade issue just months after it erupted, the communications effort resulted in 350 million media impressions around the world. Martin is careful in prefacing that this is only one measure of success, "but clearly, gaining that kind of coverage day in and day out enhanced our stature as a predominant Asian carrier." The reputation boost was particularly important to FedEx's own employees in Japan. "Prior to this, our employees were almost embarrassed to work for us because no one had heard of FedEx," notes Martin, who went to Japan to talk with employees with Fred Smith after the issue was settled. "Our employees told us in meetings that their friends read about FedEx as a powerful U.S. employer." The notoriety of FedEx turned employees into proud ambassadors of the company.

The cases of Saturn, Xerox, and FedEx clearly illustrate that integrated communications goes beyond the single transaction to focus on relationships, beyond a single-minded focus on the customer to include a wider range of key stakeholders, and beyond the communications and marketing departments to involve everyone in the whole organization. The problem with Production Century companies is that people outside of marketing and communications don't perceive customer and stakeholder communications as one of their tasks. Yet these "part-time communicators" throughout the company, be it in finance, operations, or customer service,[14] are the people who handle the communication that really matters to consumers. They represent the "body language" of the company if you will, while the full-time communicators in the marketing and communications departments and agencies represent the "spoken word." The part-time communicators not only outnumber the full-time ones, they frequently have a greater impact on customers. The bills they send and the services they provide can communicate much stronger messages than any ads or brochures. The challenge for the full-time communicators is to leverage the effectiveness of their part-time communicators, making communications second nature to everyone in the organization.

Integrating Vertical Communications: Top 2 Bottom with D2D

Integrated external communications starts with integrated internal communications in both vertical and horizontal directions among all part-time communicators. In fact, Saturn allocates almost 70 percent of its communications budget to internal communications, and FedEx's employee communications staff of sixty people is twice the size of its thirty-member public relations department. While the allocation of communications budgets and staffs doesn't give the full story, it sure suggests where the priorities are at these companies.

The second dimension of vertical communications is the process of linking front-line workers who are closest to the customer and the action with top management that has the power to act on the information and make systemwide improvements (figure 1.3). The starting point of vertical communications is to rally employees around a clear vision. The vision of a world-class company is not dreamed up by the CEO while taking a hot shower, brainstormed during a retreat by senior managers with bloated bladders, or evoked during a rain dance by a management consultant. Instead, it evolves from a process of "bottom-up communications," an ongoing dialogue among employees of all ranks. Once consensus is reached around a clear vision of the company, it is relentlessly communicated by top management to both front-line employees and customers.

**2nd Dimension:
Vertical Integration**

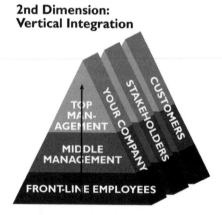

Figure 1.3. The second dimension of integrated communications: Integrating vertical communications between senior management and front-line workers.

The planning process at the British contract electronics manufacturer Design to Distribution, or D2D (now called Celestica Ltd. after being absorbed by the new parent company),[15] is a testament to the power of integrated vertical communications. All of its two thousand-plus employees take a survey every October to identify improvement issues. A four-day kickoff event is held in January when the managing director (the British equivalent of president) presents the results of the employee survey and the proposed plan of action during a series of meetings with twenty to fifty employees at a time. He spends four days from seven in the morning to ten in the evening discussing core messages about the company and actively soliciting feedback and making sure every question gets answered. The annual plan that emerges from these meetings is later "cascaded" down the organization. All senior managers meet with the people reporting to them to plan how their units will contribute to corporate goals. The next-level managers meet with their subordinates to develop more specific plans. The process is cascaded down five management levels to every employee, from January to May. At each level, the plan is translated to more specific actions, which managers commit to implement. The process creates understanding and buy-in of key messages throughout the organization because every manager will first hear the message from their boss, then communicate it to the people reporting to them. To ensure that the message is consistent through this process, the corporate strategy and policy document is put together as a little booklet and summarized on a laminated card for employees to carry with them. The mission and strategies are reviewed every three months in the interest of staying adaptive in the fast-changing world of the computer industry.

Compare D2D's approach with most other companies, where the only corporate-wide planning process is the budget process, and where directives are dictated, creating compliance instead of commitment. D2D puts the horse in front of the cart and starts by building consensus around objectives and action plans before it allocates money. People at all levels plan how they can contribute to a small number of company-wide breakthrough objectives, which are aligned with the company vision.

Once the vision is decided, world-class CEOs communicate it tirelessly to everyone in the organization. FedEx's chairman Frederick W. Smith, for instance, is consumed—no, make that obsessed—with communicating the vision and strategies of his company. His obsession spreads like wildfire to every corner of the organization. He is truly the corporate communications officer. Fred Smith got his first lesson in communications as a marine lieutenant in Vietnam, from a sergeant who told him, "There are only three things you ought to remember: shoot, move and communicate."[16] Smith's unwavering commitment to communications, which grew out of this experience, has made him a cult celebrity among his employees. "Smith can turn up anywhere in the system. He might be at the hub giving a tour to one of his counterparts in the evening. He might show up in a plane, jump seating somewhere. He can turn up having a discussion on some amazing little detail with a courier in some offbeat city," explains Robert Hamilton, marketing manager at Federal Express. "You don't think of people relating to Smith as someone who resides in his own world. Smith is much more the Sam Walton type." His personal example has created esprit de corps and cohesiveness among all his employees.

Through the use of symbols, images, metaphors, and storytelling, top management creates corporate legends that explain and dramatize the companies' visions. At Hewlett-Packard, the legends of the founding fathers still live on. The managers I interviewed spoke reverently of how cofounders David Packard and Bill Hewlett burned the midnight oil in their garage. Quotes by "Dave and Bill" fell like crumbs from their lips. In the same manner, managers of Ericsson have relayed the story of how the company spent thirteen years courting British Telecom as a client so many times that it has become folklore at the phone systems giant. The story has been deliberately cultivated to illustrate one of Ericsson's three corporate values, "perseverance." Bringing the vision alive through such constant communication gives these organizations focus and direction, not unlike geese flying in V formation.

Managers like to complain that it is lonely at the top, and it probably is because they have lost touch with the company and its customers. Integrated vertical communications puts them back in touch. Instead of having the traditional role of the final reviewer who approves plans and proposals, world-class managers interact and shape the skills of their mid-level managers and front-line workers. Vertical integration empowers the people who are closest to the customers and company operations to communicate more openly, more frequently, and more effectively with the managers who have the authority to change the business process.

Integrating Horizontal Communications: Getting Motorolans on the Same Wavelength

The third common element of world-class companies is their practice of horizontal integration across functions, business units, and geographic regions (figure 1.4). Competitive advantage depends increasingly on the processes of leveraging local expertise, linking knowledge, and developing creative innovations. A proliferation of functional councils facilitates horizontal communications at companies like Motorola. "Our key to coordinating our image, key messages and everyday operations in this decentralized environment has been the public relations councils," says Motorola's now retired public relations director, Charles Sengstock. He is the father of the "Communicators Forum," a joint meeting that was held for all public relations, marketing communications, employee communications, community relations, investor relations, and government communications staffs around the world. "You would be exposed to new and different things," explains Steve Biedermann, Motorola's director of employee communications. "If you are a PR person, you would be hearing things about community relations and employee communications that you normally wouldn't. So you would be getting cross-exposure." In the high-tech world of Motorola, the high-touch approach of the personal meeting is a formidable way to facilitate horizontal communications. The cross-functional, cross-business, and cross-geographic nature of these meetings is critical to developing organizational learning, to duplicate success and avoid replicating mistakes, to drive rapid learning and rapid improvements, and to integrate communication to customers.

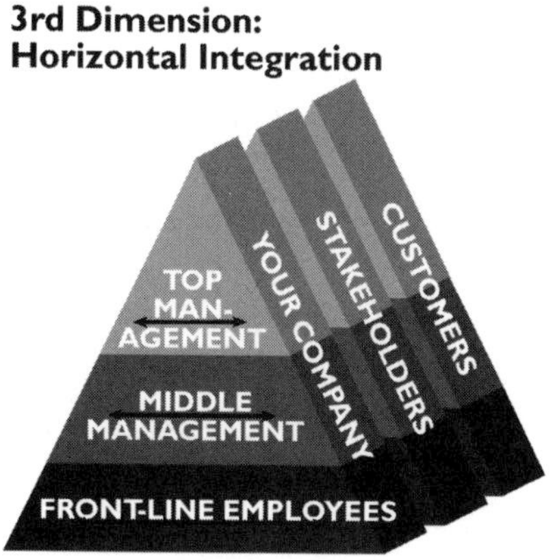

**3rd Dimension:
Horizontal Integration**

Figure 1.4. The third dimension of integrated communications: Integrating horizontal communications at all levels of the organization across departments, business units, and regions.

Effective teamwork is the nucleus of integration, facilitating information sharing and collaboration across areas of expertise, regions, and ranks. Companies like Saturn, Xerox, and ISS put all their employees through training in how to work effectively in teams. For instance, Saturn provides teamwork training based on the "forming, storming, norming, and performing" stages of team development. Xerox has its own step-by-step teamwork processes hanging in all of its conference rooms around the world. "The thing that really hits you is that you can travel to London early in the morning, get into the conference room, sit down, start working immediately, and have a full day of work," says Tom Kenneth, quality director of Rank-Xerox's Nordic region. "We all use the same team processes because you don't have to use time to find out, 'what tools do you normally use?' and 'in what way do I normally work?'" Unlike Xerox, Production Century companies don't provide the time, resources, tools, and training to make the magic of teamwork work.

Yet all these formal processes of vertical and horizontal communications are only half the success story. Most of the communication in any organization takes place outside of the meeting rooms and the pages of the employee newsletter. World-class companies go to great lengths to encourage informal communication across management ranks and departments. They create an atmosphere of open communication by eliminating the caste system of corner offices, special parking spaces, titles, and dress codes. The only dress code at Saturn, for instance, is that employees must dress. Managers dress casually in jeans and sweatshirts, and no one has a title: everyone—worker or manager—is a "team member." Like Saturn, Hewlett-Packard's management facilitates open communication by eliminating doors and walls in its offices. "I was very happy to come to HP where everybody has essentially the same ugly office. It is a little ten-by-ten cubicle. There is no time wasted on who has the better desk, if you have a door to your office, or if you have a company car. There are no trappings like that," says Mary Anne Easley, Hewlett-Packard's public relations director, adding that everyone at HP is on a first-name basis. She recalls a story of when HP cofounder and then-CEO David Packard was called "Mr. Packard" by an employee. He replied, "Mr. Packard is my father. My name is Dave."[17] Current CEO Lew Platt is a buttoned-down former mechanical engineer who has carried on the tradition. His egalitarian philosophy puts everyone on an equal level and facilitates a free flow of communication. Lately, he has taken this communication to the web. "HP's corporate culture has always encouraged open communication among employees. But with the advent of our Intranet, information sharing has taken off like never before," says Platt.[18] Intranets and other internal computer networks play an increasingly important role in opening up the internal floodgates of information.

The most prevailing barrier to open communication is the "kill the messenger syndrome." In the process of committing this sin, managers are effectively killing all useful internal dialogue. Instead, they need to declare freedom of speech—a corporate glasnost if you will—and offer employees the time, training, and means to exercise this freedom. Federal Express and Hewlett-Packard are actually offering lifelong job opportunities to their employees— helping to drive out fear of punishment for speaking up. These companies are providing front-line workers regular opportunities for discussion with immediate managers and top managers, through face-to-face meetings, televised call-in shows on closed-circuit TV networks, and online chat groups. They are tapping into the brainpower of all their workers and creating an army of devoted part-time communicators.

Reinventing the Marketing and Communications Professions

The dawning Customer Century spells both good news and bad news for marketing and communications professionals. The bad news is that their traditional role of crafting a façade of smoke and mirrors through advertising imagery and promotional bribes is history. Traditional marketing communications is no longer a powerful lever on consumer behavior. The good news is that the men and women of the profession can elevate their roles to become strategic managers who use the entire operations and value chains as communications media. In the process, they need to redefine the role of communications from *communicating* the value of the product and company to actually *creating* value for the customer. Rather than passing along information about product benefits and brand propositions, they need to use communication to help identify customers' needs and provide solutions.

Arto Hamberg is an example of a new breed of communications

professional who has moved beyond merely being a service provider to becoming a business driver. He participated in a small team of six people driving the quality management transformation program, labeled "T50," at ABB Sweden's eighty diverse industrial companies. The team was charged with teaching managers to cut cycle time and improve customer focus, identifying success stories at the different ABB companies, and disseminating those success stories to the other companies in the group. Hamberg explains, "The receipt of our success was when an idea we had sent out came back as their own." He cracks a wry smile while the remark is sinking in, adding, "In that respect, it is not a very thankful job. Our job is done when the new ideas are so deeply embedded in our group that people are entirely convinced that they came up with them themselves." He describes his role as that of a coach, facilitator, and adviser, which is the direction in which the marketing and communications profession is moving.

Another renaissance communications professional is Guum Hayen, corporate communications director of home electronics behemoth Philips. This impassioned Dutchman wrote the action plan that served as the catalyst for the 1992 plan of the integration of the European Union. Later he took the initiative to form the European Round Table of business leaders, and the European Quality Foundation—two of the most powerful business associations in Europe. When Philips faced a severe financial crisis in the early 1990s, Hayen led a major restructuring program called Centurion, designed to cut costs and serve customers better. It was Hayen's brainchild to close down every Philips factory around the world for a "Customer Day." Philips's more than 200,000 workers took part in a question-and-answer session with their CEO live via satellite, transmitted on big screens, and solved real problems in teams. Getting the board of directors to commit to such an investment at a time of crisis required a lot of persuasive skills from Hayen. "I reminded them that it was a leap year, and this was an additional day that would not cost the company any lost production," recalls Hayen between drags on his cigarette. The laughing senior managers approved the idea and Customer Day is now a regularly occurring event at Philips.

The corporate communications and marketing functions have

come to a crossroad. The road traveled by Hamberg and Hayen leads straight to the CEO's office. As counselors to the head honcho on the strategy of managing and integrating communications processes in 3-D, they are communications "process owners" rather than functional heads. Their small and agile managerial staffs are responsible for consulting, coaching, teaching, mediating, supporting, networking, and acting as change agents. Rather than doing marketing for the organization, they are market-orienting the entire company. The other road becomes a superhighway of marketing and communications support systems of websites, databases, lead management systems, and consumer research. These increasingly cost-effective, accountable, individualized, interactive, and automated tools and systems require highly skilled specialists and cutting-edge capabilities in emerging technologies. There is no reason to even keep the two functions in the same organization. As the strategic function moves up the organization, the tactical support functions are moving out. Outside agencies frequently bring a scope of resources and skills to do the job better at a lower cost than an in-house staff, provided that they are treated as partners. While advertising has traditionally been outsourced, areas like sales, sales promotion, logistics, marketing information systems, and customer service are increasingly handled by outsiders. That's why some world-class companies are forming close-knit partnerships with global communications agencies, which are uncannily like the Japanese *keiretsus*, the intimate partnerships among Japanese manufacturers and suppliers. Companies like FedEx and HP have found that an "agency *keiretsu*" of a few global agencies offers superior strategic consistency, speed of learning transfer among national markets, and economies of scale and scope.

With support functions outsourced, the in-house marketing and communications staffs assume a more strategic role of driving rather than just supporting the business. Along with the added responsibility comes added accountability for business results. Marketing and communications staffs need to take responsibility for the bottom line by demonstrating return on investments in customer and stakeholder relationships. Not only do they need to measure how *customers* add value to the *company*, but also how well the *company* adds value to the *customers*. Marketing and communications staffs need to be vigorous and persistent in tracking customer and stakeholder perceptions of the company. The purpose of this research goes far beyond justifying their true worth to the organization and cooking up a response to the relentless question from the CEO of "What have you done for me lately?" Instead, it should be presented to management as decision-support information for strategic planning, new product development, and investments.

The future holds tremendous opportunities for the marketing and communications professions. But the first people who need to believe that are the professionals themselves. They need to help their organizations integrate communications both online *and* offline. The Internet is making online integration possible, all the way from product design and material supply, through manufacturing and distribution. Coupled with database technology and mass customized manufacturing, it is poised to bring customers better selection and comfort, lower price, and a community of customers. Meanwhile, the uniquely human ability of *offline* communication is coming to the forefront. Customers are afforded the opportunity to touch, feel, and smell products and to interact, bond, and solve problems with real people, as stores are becoming showrooms, salespeople are becoming consultants, and service reps are becoming customer ombudsmen. The winners of the Customer Century will be companies that successfully integrate and leverage both high-tech and high-touch communication.

Surviving and thriving in the Customer Century requires the strategic combination of high-tech and high-touch channels along the three dimensions of external, vertical, and horizontal communications. No single dimension is powerful enough to transform the organization on its own. Each of them are indispensable, supporting the company like a three-legged stool. What sets the world-class companies apart is their practice of all three dimensions in concert.

Redefining Branding in the Customer Century

Entering the Customer Century, products themselves have become secondary to the powerful brand names attached to them. Consider that most of Hewlett-Packard's products have a life span of less than a year, but the HP brand has served for over sixty years.

Hewlett-Packard estimates that it can add 25 to 50 percent on its products just because of its revered brand name,[19] which goes to show that branding is far from just a concern for consumer goods industries. Mats Rönne, Ericsson's marketing communications manager, goes as far as arguing that a strong brand name is even more important when Ericsson sells large phone systems to the AT&Ts of the world. "Given the complexity of a large business-to-business contract, no one can truly make a neutral and unbiased analysis of which potential supplier has the best offer. Instead, it boils down to the strength of the corporate brand." Or as the old saying went back in the 1980s, "No one has ever been fired for choosing IBM." As the largest supplier of telecommunications equipment in the galaxy, Ericsson is on route to receiving the kind of trust that the IBM brand once enjoyed. That's probably a more valuable asset than all its patents, buildings, and machines combined. "When the product isn't tangible, the people behind it become more important and the brand is built on relationships," asserts Rönne, who makes the case that the Ericsson brand is created by the men and women who service the customer every day. "A prospective client thinks, 'Are they pleasant to deal with? Do they show up on time? Do they keep their promises? Can I see myself dealing with these people for the next five, ten or twenty years?'"

Ericsson's service and relationship-building orientation is illustrative of the Customer Century approach to brand building. After all, what company in today's service economy can boast tangible product benefits anyway? (Answer: a fraction of the 20 percent of U.S. companies that still manufacture products). The United States has become a nation of telephone operators, cosmetologists, lawyers, programmers, shrinks, and masseurs who are serving each other. The rest of the world is heading down the same path, but trailing the United States. The actual "stuff" needed to perform these services is farmed out to offshore suppliers. The only stuff-making industries that haven't yet moved overseas are those requiring highly skilled labor, such as automobile, computer, and airplane manufacturing. And even these products are sold almost exclusively on service, as Saturn has shown the world. The proof of the pudding is in such statistics as the one showing that 50 percent of car owners who experience poor after-sales service switch car brands the next time they buy a new car, and only 25 percent of consumers who receive good service switch brands.[20] As service assumes greater importance than products, branding moves beyond offering "unique selling propositions" to creating "total value solutions" for customers. Gone are the days (if they ever existed) when brands were created through the traditional "branding" activities of colorful logos and witty tag lines, creative commercials and unique packaging. The brand is no longer defined by this coat of cosmetics that is added as an afterthought to the products. Instead, customers' perceptions of the brand are based on the *character* of the brand, as expressed through the entire customer experience. The true brand builders of today are the engineers, receptionists, truck drivers, accountants, and the other part-time communicators. Their performance and relationships with the customer determine the strength of the brand. In fact, world-class brands exist solely in the minds of customers and stakeholders and are defined and reinforced by the quality of the experience with everyone and everything representing the brand. And three-dimensional integrated communications is the only way to build successful brands in the Customer Century.

This change has dramatic implication for brand management because marketing communications is no longer the key link to consumers; instead it's a broad interface of the database, the operations, and the front-line workers that connect the brand with the consumer. This change redefines brand management as a cross-functional responsibility that involves the orchestration of all part-time communicators in the entire service experience. Hewlett-Packard, for instance, has designed a new communications program to raise external brand awareness among HP's workforce. The program's goal is to provide brand training that enables management, employees, and third-party representatives to be able to answer the following questions: What is our brand? What are our core brand values? What is brand management? Why is it important? What is my role?[21] The program will combine *awareness building* through websites and forums with *skill-building* exercises focusing on implementing what the participants have learned. Ian Ryder, HP's director of brand management, believes this is a necessary step in managing the revered brand: "People are a critical component of a brand management system and that old-style management itself is failing to deliver customer value."[22] HP's goal is to have all its 125,000 employees trained during the course of a year.

HP and Saturn have, like few other companies, learned to integrate and leverage communications in 3-D. As we turn our attention to the first dimension of the 3-D model in the next chapter, it will become clear how integrating the voice of outbound communications and sharing the learning experience of inbound communications can lay a foundation for success in the Customer Century.

What to do *before* Monday Morning:

Assess how well your company practices 3-D integrated communications, by asking a sample of managers and employees the following questions. Present the survey results to senior management. Involve them in identifying key improvement areas and assign cross-functional task force teams to address them.

About External Communications:

- Who are the most important customers to the company? How do you know that?
- Who are the most important stakeholders?
- How does your (and your employees') work impact customers?
- How do you get feedback from customers on how your (and your employees') work can be improved?

About Vertical Communications:

- What are the vision and key messages of the company?
- How relevant is the information you're receiving to do your job well?
- How freely can you express your views without fear of reprimands?
- How well does senior management listen and implement your ideas and suggestions?

About Horizontal Communications:

- How well are you kept informed about what's going on in other units of the organization?

- Which cross-functional teams are you currently a member of?
- How frequently do you interact with colleagues in other functions of your business, in other business units, and in other countries of your organization?

Another option is to ask a cross section of managers to take our interactive audit at www.gronstedtgroup.com that calculates a quantitative score and provides an automatic "Gap Analysis" showing how integrated your company is compared to other companies.

Notes

1. Carlzon, J. (1989). *Moments of Truth*. New York: Harper & Row.
2. www.saturncars.com
3. Fann, Gina (1998). "Virtual Homecoming Draws Saturn Lovers: Web Site Reminiscent of '94 Event." *The Tennessean*, August 2.
4. Henry, Jim (1998). "Behind Saturn's Door No. 3: Hal." *Automotive News*, November 30.
5. Steinhart, David (1998) "Saturn's New Boss Brings Female Virtues," *Financial Post*, December 16.
6. Kearns, David T.; Nadler, David A. (1992). *Prophets in the Dark*. New York: HarperCollins Publishers, Inc.
7. "Xerox Corporation: Leadership through Quality" (A). *Harvard Business School Case Study*, # 9-490-008.
8. Kearns, David T.; Nadler, David A. (1992). *Prophets in the Dark*.
9. Ibid.
10. Brewer, Geoffrey (1998). "Getting Top Executives to Sell." *Sales & Marketing Management*, October, p. 39.
11. Diane Brady (1999) "Can new CEO Rick Thomas turn its digital dreams into reality," *Business Week*, April 12, pp. 93–100.
12. Bowen E. David, and Lawler, Edward E. III (1995). "Empowering Service Employees." *Sloan Management Review*, Summer, pp. 73–84.
13. "Xerox Corporation: The Customer Satisfaction Program." *Harvard Business School Case Study*, # 9-591-055.
14. Gummesson coined the term "part-time marketer," which inspired my term "part-time communicator." Gummesson, Evert (1990). "The Part-Time Marketer." Center for Service Research. Karlstad.
15. The book will use the company name D2D throughout the book.
16. Grant, Linda (1997). "Why FedEx Is Flying High." *Fortune*, November 10, pp. 156–160.

17. Easley, Mary Anne (1997). "Everything I Know about Communication I Learned from Two Engineers." *Journal of Employee Communication Management*, July/August, p. 40

18. Martin, Chuck (1997). *The Digital Estate*. New York: McGraw-Hill, p. 138.

19. "Brand Strategy" (1998). *Corporate Branding*, January 23, pp. 4–7

20. Horovitz, Jacques (1996). "Mastering Management." *Financial Times*, March 1.

21. Mellor, Victoria (1999). "Delivering Brand Values Through People." *Strategic Communication Management,* February/March.

22. Ibid.

2

FIRST DIMENSION

Integrating External Communications

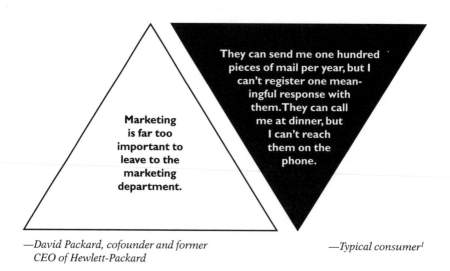

Marketing is far too important to leave to the marketing department.

They can send me one hundred pieces of mail per year, but I can't register one meaningful response with them. They can call me at dinner, but I can't reach them on the phone.

—David Packard, cofounder and former CEO of Hewlett-Packard

—Typical consumer[1]

Quick now: Name a company that considers advanced technology, a high level of professional skills, and a premier global brand image among its key sources of competitive advantage.

Hewlett-Packard? Xerox? Sony?

No, no, and no. Try ABB, the global electrical engineering mammoth formed in the 1987 merger of century-old archrivals Swedish-based ASEA and Swiss-based Brown Boveri & Co. It was, at the time, the largest cross-border merger the world had seen in eighty years. By acquiring an additional seventy companies, ABB became a $30 billion powerhouse in a few years' time. Today, ABB is the principal supplier of the world's electric power generation equipment, high-speed trains, and air pollution control equipment. A few years after the merger, the Swedish subsidiary of ABB was facing an increasingly competitive environment. The diverse group of eighty companies manufacturing everything from nuclear reactors to electrical light switches was under pressure to improve customer service and employee motivation. The biggest customer complaint wasn't the fact that one in seven of ABB's deliveries was late or had defects, but that the engineering-minded company wasn't sensitive enough to the customers' needs. Meanwhile, some of ABB's work units had over 50 percent employee turnover rates. Sick leaves were so rampant that the companies couldn't even plan the production for the next day because they didn't know how many workers would show up. The consensus of its 27,000 workers was that their work was tedious and mindless. Poor morale reigned supreme. Senior management had to find a way of rallying employees, suppliers, and customers around a major change effort.

In what was likely the biggest policy shift of the 1990s aside from Michael Jackson getting married, the shy and stodgy ABB Group decided to embark on a high-profile change program. "The new industrial revolution" was the modest theme of an advertising campaign that kicked off the transformation. Thousands of customers and suppliers were invited to in-depth seminars describing the change process. CEO Percy Barnevik and other senior executives gave interviews and speeches relentlessly. "We decided early on to use mass media," explains Arto Hamberg, communications manager of the program. "That is the best way to show everyone in the organization our commitment and trust to the change process." Senior management used external news media not only to apply pressure on managers, employees, suppliers, and customers to change, but also to generate enthusiasm for the change project. The anonymity that once enveloped the company gave way to a barrage of positive publicity. Success stories of the change effort flourished in the news. Two years later, ABB ran advertisements featuring its success stories. The ads invited the public to order a magazine with cases on the transformation or buy a book describing the process. "The book was entitled *The Transformation*, and described a number of success stories from different ABB companies," comments Lillemor Rolf, ABB marketing communications director. A whopping 51,000 people ordered the book and it sold out—all that in a country with a population about the size of Michigan. "The curiosity about our change program has opened doors for us to new and existing clients that we were unable to access earlier," exclaims Roger Johansson, director of corporate communications in Sweden.

In taking the case to the public, ABB integrated *external* communications to customers and stakeholders, which is the first dimension of the three-dimensional strategy of integrated communications. When ABB managers and employees were reminded about the change process not only at work but also from the evening television news and neighbors, they knew it was for real. "We started with internal communications, then we did external communication, then internal again," explains Johansson. "We started a positive spiral and we are systematically trying to build it. It is all about credibility. You start getting newspaper articles and opinion leaders to endorse what you are doing." Is anybody at Mercedes listening? Contrast ABB's virtuous spiral of reinforcing positive communication internally and externally with Mercedes's vicious downward spiral of lies and deceit. ABB used communication offensively to drive positive change, while Mercedes used it reactively to cover up previous communication failures.

The success of ABB's integrated *external* communications rests on carefully integrated *internal* communications, both vertically up and down the chain of command, and horizontally across departments. *Vertical* communication was set in place when the senior managers of ABB's eighty companies were invited to a three-day conference. "Seven hundred managers were educated about the change program and its potential long-term benefits. Similar seminars were given separately to thousands of customers and suppliers," explains Arto Hamberg. The managers that attended the conferences went back to their companies and conducted seminars with the people reporting to them, who then cascaded the information down to the foremen. This system of communication has been repeated every year. Hamberg emphasizes the importance of such persistence: "If you throw one stone, the ripples disappear soon. You have to throw them all the time. Regular seminars and meetings with senior managers and employees are the only way to keep a change process alive." To reach all the employees directly, management sent out newsletters, and audio- and videotapes about the program. Online communication was used later. "It can be used, once the interest has been created, to make information available," Hamberg points out. "Personal contact, though, is the most important communication channel." ABB also took the message straight to the front-line employees, primarily with electronic communications. This combination of high-tech and high-touch communication methods has proven to be the most effective way to integrate vertical communications at world-class companies.

ABB decided to make "time" the common denominator of the change process, labeling the program "T50." The "T" stood for "time" and the 50 represented the goal of cutting the cycle time of every process by 50 percent in three years. A thousand quality-improvement teams were formed and charged with the task of slashing every manufacturing and administrative cycle time in half. The T50 project was intended on improving *horizontal* integration by flattening hierarchies, orienting work around processes, and opening up lines of communication across the organizational boxes of the company. Manufacturing processes would be reorganized into self-directed teams where workers rotate among different tasks and plan their own work schedules. This would create a more stimulating environment and greater flexibility where people could fill in for each other. The entire value chain from suppliers to customers had to be better integrated. The 200,000 suppliers were going to be cut by 70 to 80 percent, with the surviving suppliers being required to work in closer partnership with ABB. Upstream in the value chain, ABB had to integrate its processes better with its customers' processes. ABB Sweden was going to blow up the walls that separated its eighty subsidiaries and the departments and product groups within each company.

ABB's 3-D integrated communications approach has paid off handsomely. "We met our goal of cutting cycle times of every process in three years and have made productivity gains of 10 percent every year since the inception of T50," Hamberg points out with understated pride five years into the program. Profit increased fivefold during the first five years. The goal of T50 later evolved into developing world-class quality. New stretch-goals were set outside-in, based on benchmarks with other world-class organizations. While the content of T50 was evolving, it has been tied to the common theme of T50 and reducing cycle time—50 percent at a time. It's an example of how integrated communications can be practiced as a strategic management process to revive an entire organization. Like any effective change process, it started with external communication.

As seen in figure 2.1, *integrated external communications* is about building close customer and stakeholder relationships at all levels of the organization. This first dimension starts with identifying the most important customers based on their current profit contributions, and potential lifetime customer value. Next, the discordant voices of these customers are integrated into the organization. Satisfaction surveys, retention rates, complaints, inquiries, field operations, market research, and other sources of customer information are judiciously tracked and the information gets widely shared within the organization. Employees of all ranks and job functions get out and experience the products or services from the customer's perspective, talk to the customers in their own environment, learn about their needs, ask about their ideas, and listen to their gripes. Only by listening in a collective sense can world-class organizations build relationships and anticipate the future needs of their customers. The same process is applied to nurture relationships with key stakeholders.

**1st Dimension:
External Integration**

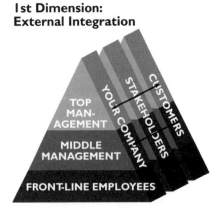

Figure 2.1. The first dimension of integrated communications: Integrating external communications between everyone in the organization and the most critical customers and stakeholders.

A Customer in the Hand Is Worth . . .

If staging seminars and homecoming events for your own customers seems like preaching to the converted, well, that is precisely
the point. Just consider that it costs anywhere between five to
twenty times more to recruit a new customer than to keep an existing one.[2] But that's not all. Research clearly shows that customers
become more profitable over time. Existing customers cost less and
provide more revenues the longer they stay, because the cost of
acquiring the customer goes away, customers become less price
sensitive, they require less attention from sales and customer service personnel, they buy more, and they refer other customers.[3]
From the customer's point of view, a long-term relationship offers
advantages as well. Most consumers enjoy the convenience and
peace of mind of buying the same brands from the same store.
Likewise, business buyers are increasingly turning to small numbers of "preferred suppliers." The appeal of minimal search cost,
the security of knowing what you get, and the promise of volume
discounts are some of the benefits of a relationship experienced by
consumers and business buyers alike.

Indisputably, the path to business success leads through long-
term customer relationships. Sound data now supports the intuitive appeal of a relationship focus. For instance, Ford estimates
that each percentage point gained in car-owner loyalty is worth
$100 million in profit every year.[4] That's not to say that the focus on
existing relationships should be done at the exclusion of recruiting
new customers, just that there needs to be a better balance between
relationships *and* acquisitions. To use the old leaking bucket
metaphor, most companies are too busy pouring new water in the
bucket—recruiting new customers—without paying attention to
how much is leaking out the bottom—customer defection. They
need to shift their attention from adding water to fixing the leaks.
Recruiting new customers still has a role, but prospects should be
carefully selected before they are pursued based on their potential
for long-term relationships. Breakthroughs in data-warehousing
and data-mining technology promise to take such surgical target-
ing to new levels. A data warehouse is an enterprise-wide repository
of databases from different units of the organization and external

sources. Data mining can discover less obvious patterns and connections among thousands of variables in a database, and identify common characteristics of the customers with the best potential based on a myriad of factors, including buying behavior and demographics. The combination of data mining and data warehousing can really turbocharge the ability to identify the best customers and prospects, to target messages, and to grow relationships.

The problem with marketing managers who are deeply steeped in the Production Century model is that they consider the communication process to be completed when a prospect makes the purchase. At that point, the customer returns to being another anonymous prospective client and the marketing process begins all over again. Instead, managers need to focus on migrating customers along the relationship path, from prospects to "evangelists," as indicated in figure 2.2. Communication needs to be carefully integrated to each of these segments with the purpose of migrating customers up a notch on the path to becoming *loyalists* and *evangelists*. Prospects need to get incentives to make the first purchase, occasional buyers need to be enticed to become loyalists, and loyal buyers need to be provided the T-shirts, buttons, talking points, homecoming festivities, or whatever it takes to make them evangelists. Research in the computer software industry shows that customer evangelists on average recruit five new customers and provide coaching and support for an additional nine existing customers.[5] Any company has potential evangelists just waiting to find salvation in your brand and start recruiting new customers. Your company's own employees, suppliers, sales force, and distributors are a good place to start. Very few companies have communication programs to make even these stakeholders proud ambassadors of the brand. Even fewer companies have communication programs to inspire their most devoted customer advocates of the brand.

Needless to say, relationships should not be forced upon every customer by harassing them with phone calls or stuffing their mailboxes with junk, or by trying to gather and leverage customer information on everything from what color underpants they're wearing to when their pet canary was born. Not surprisingly, many consumers don't want to enter a relationship with their favorite paper clip or bathroom tissue supplier. Trying too hard to develop

Migrating Customers

Figure 2.2. The focus of integrated customer communications is on migrating customers to get them to become loyalists and evangelists.

unwanted relationships with existing customers can turn them off. The existence and depth of relationships depends greatly on the intensity of consumer involvement with the product. Suppliers of low-involvement products like potato starch flour or toilet bowl disinfectants should focus more on their relationship with retailers and professional users.

Profitable Customers Are Always Right

Not even world-class companies have the resources to integrate communications with all of God's creatures. So they settle for their most profitable customers. By harnessing the power of database technology, Internet connectivity, and mass customization capabilities, companies can identify the customers with the greatest profit potential and tailor communication and service to their individual needs. World-class companies are aggressively consolidating customer databases from finance, accounting, marketing communications, sales and customer service, from business units and subsidiaries, and from channel members and syndicated sources around the world to get a complete picture of the cost and income flows from individual, end-user customers. If they are removed from their end-user customers, they analyze intermediaries, such as distributors or original equipment manufacturers (OEMs), in the value chain as well. Although these channel members are important customers, world-class companies never lose sight of the people who matter the most, the end-user customers. After all, they are the ones who are ultimately footing the bill and consuming the product or service.

Saturn has database information on every one of its two million owners. Even a sprawling and diverse company such as Hewlett-Packard has a central customer database with between 6.5 and 8 million names, complete with the recentness and frequency of purchase for an individual customer and his or her contact history with HP. This repository of customer information is available for authorized HP staff members on its Intranet,[6] enabling HP to deliver individual messages and service offerings to customers. The database is used for inbound communication as well. Information about corporate customers who call or e-mail for service is entered into a database, complete with the time of contact and type of concern before routing them to a rep with the right knowledge. By analyzing this data and offering customized solutions, HP is garnering additional sales to the tune of $180 million.[7] A learning relationship starts growing as customers teach their suppliers about their needs and get increasingly customized solutions in return. This capability of collecting, synthesizing, analyzing, and acting on the customer information allows the Customer Century company an advantage that no competitor can readily copy.

The emerging hardware, software, and analytical tools give world-class companies the opportunity to track each interaction with customers, including purchases, preferences, payments, returns, responses to promotions, inquiries, satisfaction survey results, and complaints. Add to that the new accounting methods of "activity-based costing," which can determine the actual costs of individual customers, including customer service, credit expenses, handling charges, and product support. Link the purchasing data with cost data and—*voilà*—the profitability of individual customers and customer segments can be determined. Most companies will find a curve that looks like the one in figure 2.3. It illustrates two important insights. Number one is that not all customers are profitable. Almost every company has a number of customers they're losing money on that need to be either gracefully dumped or turned into profitable customers by hiking prices and/or reducing service levels. Obviously, unprofitable customers should be spared this treatment if they have the potential to become profitable in the future, or if they are influential opinion leaders that might attract other customers. The second finding that will surface from a customer cost-benefit analysis, is that a surprisingly small number of customers account for almost the entire profit. The 80/20 rule, which stipulates that about 80 percent of any company's profit is attributed to 20 percent of its customer base is true for any company. This "Pareto effect," first expounded by the Italian economist Wilfredo Pareto, who concluded that 80 percent of wealth was owned by 20 percent of the people, is indeed a stroke of brilliance. It doesn't matter what industry, company, or country, the Pareto effect is as predictable as the law of gravity. By identifying the most profitable customers or customer segments, the level of investment in each of them can be determined, and the returns can be measured. This is a completely new approach to resource allocation, where companies "invest in customers" rather than spend money on marketing.

Profit

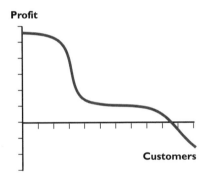

Figure 2.3. Profitability analysis of most companies shows that a small number of customers account for most of the profit and a number of customers are unprofitable.

Customers

But hold on, we're just warming up. Analyzing purchasing history is a good start. After all, the best predictor of future buying behavior (at least in the short term) is past buying behavior. But before jumping to any conclusions about which customers to focus relationship efforts on and how to segment them, their potential lifetime value to the organization has to be estimated. "Lifetime customer value" is the true arbitrator of how much a marketer can afford to spend on a relationship with a particular customer. It's an assessment of how much revenue a marketer can expect from a particular customer from the present until the relationship terminates, i.e., the net present value of future profits of a customer. Statistical modeling can be used to perform this analysis.

Estimated retention rates become an important variable in this equation, because customers who remain loyal for a longer time are more valuable. Another critical variable in any analysis of customers' future profit potential is their "share of wallet"—how much a company has captured of a customer's budget for a category of purchases. Fast food companies need to determine their "share of stomach," automobile companies need to figure out their "share of garage," clothing companies their "share of wardrobe." A family with one Saturn and one Honda in the garage represents a 50 percent share of garage for both companies. Increasing that to 100 percent can be many times more cost-efficient than chasing new customers. FedEx is an example of a company with the savvy to explore additional business opportunities with existing customers and to maximize its "share of mailbox." It identifies customers with a 50 percent share of shipping budget, which might be companies that are using FedEx only for overnight letter service and UPS for boxes. The customer will be approached and persuaded to make FedEx its exclusive freight service provider, thus increasing the "share of mailbox" for that particular customer from 50 percent to 100 percent. The client's lifetime customer value doubles simply by providing enough of an incentive to use FedEx exclusively, and the client benefits from the convenience of a single-source supplier.

But, here's the rub: This customer information is frequently unavailable to the marketing staff to use for custom-tailored communications and one-to-one relationship building. And it's usually at a safe distance from the front-line workers who could use the information to improve communication with customers and enter information from customers into the database. The true breakthroughs come from sharing the customer database broadly within the company, and organizing the company's entire manufacturing, service, delivery, and communications process around individual customer needs.

Integrating the "Voice of the Customer"

Identifying the most important customers sets the stage for listening to them in a collective sense. The "voice of the customer" needs to reach senior executives as well as middle managers and front-line workers. ABB, D2D, and Rank-Xerox capture information on individual consumers and engage their entire organizations in tailoring satisfaction improvements to them. Take ABB subsidiary ABB Atom, for instance. The manufacturer of fuel for nuclear power plants conducts in-depth customer satisfaction interviews with every customer annually. The corporate quality director and the marketing manager for each business unit personally conduct the interviews. Says Kjell Morlin, director of quality, "It is important that the customer is well prepared, so once we have agreed on a meeting, we send a letter and describe the twelve different areas we want to discuss." The project manager of ABB Atom assigned to the day-to-day client contact does not participate in the interview, to encourage open criticism from the customer. "We never respond to critique during the interview, we just listen and take notes," says Morlin. "We don't want clients to refrain from giving us a piece of their minds because we're rebutting and debating." Although a fair number of the questions deal with product quality and technology, most of them are about "soft" relationship issues. "I am convinced that it is the soft issues that make you win the market battles. The customer assumes that we have high product quality. We haven't had a nuclear reactor problem caused by our products in fifteen years, and not one late delivery of a product in the last three years." Morlin believes it's the personal relationships with clients that matter. The surveys are reported back to each customer, along with a detailed action plan outlining how ABB Atom will remedy trouble spots. This process is extremely beneficial for both the client and the company. "We are obsessed with improvements and the survey reports are important to stimulate ideas for improvements," comments Morlin. He is convinced that the return on this investment in time and money is huge. "A lot of people ask: How can you afford to spend so much on quality? The answer is, we can't afford not to. If we became even one-tenth of one percent more efficient, it's all paid for. If we get another order to recharge a nuclear plant as a result of the in-depth interviews with our customers, then all our in-depth interviews are paid for the next ten years."

British computer maker D2D has a more frequent customer satisfaction process. It asks its customers to fill out a scorecard every month to monitor relationships and look for ways to improve. "The principle behind the scorecard," explains Dayvon Goodsell, quality manager, "is you take a number of different facets of the relationship: *Product quality* and *timeliness* are obvious. On top of that, we have *flexibility, willingness to change, responsiveness, communication,* and *technical competence.*" He continues, "We try to get the scorecard every month, at least every quarter. It gives us a target for improving it. The score is communicated internally to the team that produced that client's product."

Danfoss, a Denmark-based heating and cooling equipment supplier, likes to listen to customers speaking in their own words instead of using quantitative scorecards. "What we are interested in is not how satisfied people are, but where they are *dissatisfied.* We do semi-structured interviews over the phone that allow us to probe the attributes they are not satisfied with by asking why, why, why," comments Torben Fich, director of communications and marketing. "The qualitative comments from such a survey are typically very actionable." Danfoss is not the only company where the customer's voice is shared broadly within the organization and promptly acted upon. Rank-Xerox Denmark assigns every single employee to a team responsible for customer satisfaction scores for a specific geographic area. It has divided Denmark into six geographic areas with one team responsible for each. Each of the six teams is composed of about fifty members led by a steering group of ten people. Managers can be used as resources by the team or the steering group as needed. "This is on top of the formal organization. We like to think we gain additional good ideas and quality thinking," says Tom Kenneth, quality director of Rank-Xerox's Nordic region.

Part of every employee's bonus at Rank-Xerox is tied to the customer satisfaction score of the area, making the salespeople (all of a sudden) very interested in customer satisfaction. This forces them to set more realistic customer expectations and consult the service department before making promises to customers. "Before they would promise the customer, 'Of course we can do so and so,'" notes Kenneth, describing the classic situation of disintegrated communications. The salespeople over-promise in the interest of meeting their sales quotas, and the product and service fail to live up to the customer's inflated expectations. Kenneth explains the change: "Today the sales rep is more inclined to say, 'I have to check that with my colleague in service before I promise anything.'" Managing realistic expectations is a pivotal task of external communications. Customers always compare what they are getting from a supplier with their expectations. If expectations are set too high by marketing, sales, or other areas of communications, customers will inevitably be disappointed. In the Production Century model, marketing and sales were responsible for blowing the horn and persuading people to buy at any price. The role of communications was to communicate value in hyperbolic ways. In the Customer Century, the role of communications will be to *create* value, by managing expectations and learning about customer needs.

Managing expectations through integrated external communications is the first step in exceeding them. Merely satisfying customers doesn't cut it any longer. Xerox made that startling discovery a few years ago, when it learned that "completely satisfied" customers are six times more likely to repurchase Xerox products than its "very satisfied" customers, who are only marginally more loyal than the "satisfied" customers. Anything less than complete satisfaction isn't going to sustain customers' loyalty, as illustrated in figure 2.4. Independent research shows this to be true for most industries.[8] Customers need to be delighted. Yet surprisingly few companies have emulated ABB Atom, D2D, Danfoss, and Xerox's systematic processes of discovering what really concerns and excites customers, to ensure that they are completely satisfied. Most companies continue to use the occasional customer satisfaction survey that is little more than an applause meter, averaging out customers' feelings at a particular time. These typically end up in three-ring binders that are relegated to the bookshelves. In contrast, companies like ABB, D2D, and Rank-Xerox make every effort to compile, analyze, and act upon insights about individual customers' needs in order to improve existing services. But more importantly, they also probe for insights about customers' unfulfilled wants and dreams in order to stay abreast of future trends. Foresight about long-term marketplace shifts doesn't come in neatly packaged market research reports, but from firsthand, in-depth dialogue with customers.

Figure 2.4. Xerox has found that "completely satisfied" customers are six times as likely to repurchase and recommend the brand as "very satisfied" customers who are only marginally more loyal than "satisfied" and even "not satisfied" customers.

Source: Christopher W. Hart and Michael D. Johnson, "Growing the Trust Relationship," *Marketing Management*, Spring 199.

The Voice of the Customer Terrorists

World-class companies takes special care to listen to the voice of disgruntled customers. It is particularly important to act swiftly on customer complaints, or else the customer will turn into a "customer terrorist" who will badmouth the company. Eastman Chemical Company, maker of chemicals, fibers, and plastics, has an 800 number that customers can access twenty-four hours a day to voice concerns. The information from these calls is stored in an elaborate database, which is accessible to every Eastman employee who deals with customers. Special "customer advocates" follow up and resolve complaints. Eastman's goal is to respond to 90 percent of the complaints with an acknowledgement to the customer within twenty-four hours and to have 90 percent of complaints resolved within thirty days. The immediate handling of complaints frequently turns potential terrorists into company advocates.

For every complaint, there's typically at least ten other customers out there with the same bad experiences. Customer complaints need to be addressed swiftly and the information shared widely for corrective actions to avoid similar situations in the future. Federal Express's communications managers receive regular reports regarding the concerns and complaints that have been expressed by customers on their hotline. Saturn frequently makes employees who take hotline calls members of problem-solving task-force teams. This systematic use of customer information is the only way to learn from experience and continually improve.

Connecting the Workplace with the Marketplace

The customer dialogues are driven deep into world-class organizations, involving not just marketing and sales staff and management but also factory floor workers. Danfoss, for one, is known for bringing in groups of customers to meet assembly-line workers. It makes sure all employees understand how important each order is to the company and its customers. When Danfoss lands a new customer order, it shares the good news with employees. "Each refrigerator component that comes across the assembly line is labeled with the company name that it is produced for. Workers know that they are not just producing for inventory purposes, but for real live customers," says Uwe Bartram, sales promotion manager of supermarket refrigeration controls. Marketing Manager Bodil Lindhard contrasts this with the past. "In the earlier days, only the marketing department knew about the customers. Today we produce for customer orders, and the factory workers understand how important a particular order is to a customer." As Quality Manager John Jakobsen reminds us, the factory workers of today are knowledge workers who sit in air-conditioned rooms monitoring robots and taking occasional breaks to work in teams on Pareto charts and fishbone diagrams: "When you visit the production areas at Danfoss you will find the walls covered with graphs and charts." Customer orienting plant-floor workers has real impact on both product quality and customer commitment. "I think we gain some big customers because they understand that this particular customer and this particular order is really important to all of us," notes Bodil Lindhard, marketing manager. It shows the personal involvement with customers among the entire company.

Saturn subscribes to the same philosophy of connecting the workplace with the marketplace. The carmaker even aired a commercial featuring the true story of how a worker taped a letter and picture of a third-grade teacher who had ordered a Saturn on the rearview mirror of a car on the assembly line. "To let you know who you are building that blue-green car for, I've enclosed my school picture," she writes, as the commercial shows the worker at the end of the line putting the letter and the picture in the glove compartment. Saturn president Don Hudler believes that disseminating customer insight widely among Saturn "team members" is vital to the success of the company: "Research is invaluable. We do a lot of it. And I find that the more we share that, the better team members are able to respond and meet the needs of the customers." Saturn's director of consumer marketing, Steve Shannon, contends that understanding the customer is the starting point for success. "For Saturn, the target customer is very well defined and very well understood by everybody. That seems to be a prerequisite for integrated marketing."

D2D even gets its assemblers and factory workers vested in the company by sharing confidential information with them regarding profit margins and costs. Trusting them with the information makes the workers feel that they play an important role in the company. Says Dayvon Goodsell, "Ten years ago, we would have never given them this information. We are very careful to keep them informed about what is behind what they are building, what it costs to build, so they become part of the business." Every method of internalizing customer preferences—whether it's Danfoss and Saturn attaching faces to the inanimate products that parade down the assembly line every day, D2D sharing profit-and-loss figures, or Rank-Xerox tying in compensation with customer satisfaction—illustrates the first external dimension of the 3-D communications model. All of these companies have created learning environments where everyone involved directly or indirectly with customer contacts is keenly aware of how their actions affect customer satisfaction.

Buddying up with Ericsson

Integrating the voice of the customer into the organization is the first step in building relationships with them. Ericsson's relationship with one of its clients, British Telecom, is a case in point of how to involve the entire organization in the relationship process. The phone systems supplier tracks every relevant individual at British Telecom—from CEO to receptionist. The names of thousands of BT people are kept in an elaborate database and matched with an "owner" within Ericsson. For instance, each Ericsson secretary is responsible for keeping in touch with an assigned secretary at BT, each engineer is responsible for a particular engineer at

BT. Through this "buddy system," managers and engineers at BT have the convenience of a personal contact at Ericsson. Every now and then, BT employees will even get an invitation to social events such as a symphony or a sponsored seminar from their individual Ericsson counterparts. The informal socializing at multiple points of organizations builds personal relationships and trust with clients. Public Relations Director Paula Wagstaff takes this responsibility very seriously. "My role is to develop relationships with my counterparts on the client side. I take ownership of those people." She continues emphatically, "And I wouldn't let anyone else at my department deal with those customers because I think they need one point of contact. We have heard that from customers. Ericsson is easy to deal with because you have one point of contact." Wagstaff is the "owner" of BT's public relations director and she makes a point of calling her BT counterpart on a regular basis. "I'm not just contacting her when there is a press release to be approved, I ring her up whenever I read something about BT in the paper just to chat about it." These calls are a proactive way of bonding with the client. The enterprise-wide partnership between Ericsson and BT is built not only through the informal communication of the buddy system, but also by formally matching up the functions of both companies with each other. The PR departments of Ericsson and BT collaborate to leverage opportunities for publicity, the R&D groups work in partnerships on new products and services, and the operations groups help each other drive out waste of the system.

It's at the most senior levels where the company has the most pressing needs for customer relationship building. Jackie Karlsson, marketing communications manager, admits that this is Ericsson's weakest link. "We have a lot of contact with BT at the operational level, but not as much as we would like on a senior level." Ericsson's senior managers recognize the need to nurture the relationships with their "buddies," to discuss the strategic direction of the partnership.

The kind of strong and trusting relationships that come from long-term associations benefit both Ericsson and its clients. The business partners go out of their way to help each other. Recently, British Telecom experienced a publicity crisis when its main supplier was forced to lay off people as a result of a reduction in business with BT. To help counteract the negative publicity, Paula Wagstaff contacted her counterpart at BT and provided news stories about how Ericsson was hiring hundreds of graduates as a result of an increase in business from BT. "They used our information at a time when they really needed it, and so our relationship started building." By working seamlessly with customers to serve the needs of the customers' customers and the customers' stakeholders, Ericsson has become the world's largest global supplier of telecommunications equipment, racking up annual earnings growth of 50 percent between 1993 and 1997. As this book was going to print, Ericsson and BT just closed a groundbreaking new five-year contract valued at half a billion dollars, whereby Ericsson will supply BT with an intercity network of voice and data communications traffic.

Ericsson's relationship with BT is, in a sense, the perfect illustration of integrated external communications as the overlapping pyramids (see figure 2.1 earlier in this chapter). That's not to say that this type of relationship is easy, or even that it's the goal for all business-to-business relationships. In fact, the rate of enterprise-wide partnerships that fail during their first twelve months is even higher than the divorce rate of most countries, upwards of 70 percent.[9] The reason is typically a lack of commitment from both parties to integrate communications. Enterprise-wide partnerships with buddy systems and function-to-function matchups require such extraordinary demands on both organizations that they are only feasible with a handful of clients.

Integrating Global Communications

Ericsson's partnership with BT was put to the test a few years ago, when BT expanded into the German market and wanted to continue its supplier partnership with Ericsson. The German subsidiary of Ericsson considered BT a small player in the German market and treated it as such. Needless to say, BT was upset that it didn't get the red-carpet treatment it was accustomed to in the U.K. To remedy the problem, Ericsson reorganized and assigned "global account managers" to its fifty largest global clients. An individual at Ericsson U.K. is now assigned the global responsibility for BT. "BT is very adamant, BT will not deal with Ericsson locally, they will only deal with Ericsson U.K.," says Wagstaff. By the same token, a senior Ericsson manager in the United States has the global responsibility for AT&T, and a global account manger in Stockholm is assigned to Telia, the Swedish telecom. By becoming a global supplier of international clients and offering comprehensive solutions, Ericsson can build more lucrative customer relationships. "Parallel with the traditional line organization with local clients, we're developing an international project organization serving our global clients," says Ericsson's corporate marketing communications Director, Mats Rönne, assuredly.

Integrated *global* communications is the logical extension of integrated communications. To give an idea why most companies are fretting about globalization, try to connect these dots: Consumer preferences are converging as people from all over the world are wearing the same sneakers, drinking the same soft drinks, and working from the same computers. Burgeoning global media companies like Sky, Star, Time Warner, HBO, and Disney are in a race to offer global TV programming. STAR TV reaches 2.7 million people in Asia with a single satellite footprint. Hundreds of millions of people in 144 countries from Bangladesh to Bolivia, from Barbados to Borneo, are watching and drooling over *Baywatch*, the world's most widely viewed television show. Meanwhile, like-minded communities from all over the world are congregating on the Internet to chat, browse, and trade. In the real world, Europeans are throwing away their respective marks, francs, guilders, and lire for a single currency. Trade barriers are being obliterated. As consumer markets are becoming more global, consumer goods companies are consolidating their supplier base to a small number of global vendors. The ripple effects in the entire supply chains are forcing business-to-business companies like Ericsson to restructure to serve global clients effectively. Without a doubt, integrated global communications is imperative in the Customer Century. So much so that the term is rapidly becoming an oxymoron because there will be no other kind of business.

Global Account Managers Are Cleaning Up

Another company facing the challenge of organizing around international clients is ISS. This international cleaning group with

100,000 employees decided a few years ago to stop chasing every new business opportunity head-to-head against small, low-cost competitors. Instead, it opted to grow with existing clients internationally. "Companies are increasingly bundling their purchases of services. They go from cleaning to maintenance, and try to decrease the number of suppliers," explains Fred Nurskij, European marketing manager. He assigns key account managers the responsibility for the service quality and customer satisfaction of particular clients and to build new business with them. These account managers become integral players in their clients' businesses. They develop a keen awareness of their clients' needs and how they might provide added value to the client and, in turn, market more services to that client. Rather than just contracting to do cleaning for clients, key account managers encourage their clients to outsource all internal maintenance of their facilities to ISS. This includes the mailroom and reception operation, coffee and vending machine maintenance, copy machine support, and landscaping. As ISS contends, this allows clients to focus on what they do best. Naturally, it also increases ISS's business.

ISS clients are increasingly consolidating building maintenance to a single global service provider. "Companies will move from local to national, and sometimes, international purchasing. And as such, they become more sophisticated," says Nurskij. Consequently, ISS developed a pan-European key account management system. Major pan-European clients are served by a key account manager, who heads a team of key account managers in all the countries where ISS serves the particular client. The key account team has a phone conference every month to keep everyone up to date on client developments. Each member makes a monthly report available on the company's Intranet to all the other members, and they e-mail each other on a daily basis. Says Fred Nurskij, "If our salespeople in France want to approach Smith Cline & Beecham, they click on it and put in a request to see presentations that other salespeople assigned to SM&B have given to the client company in other countries. They can also request their meeting notes." Through such proactive management of key clients across different countries, ISS can grow with a client internationally. "Right now we provide excellent service for Samsung and Texas Instruments in

Portugal," proclaims Nurskij, and adds, "If we use our service in Portugal as an example of our good service, we can go to Texas Instruments Europe, and suggest we provide these services in other areas. By expanding our business with good customers, we could probably make the revenue five times or more."

The pan-European relationships aren't developing as fast as ISS would like them to, "but companies are restructuring and moving in that direction," says Alain Dehaze, business development director. These client companies, if convinced to use ISS on an international scale, could help ISS clean up all over the world. The benefit to the client company would be to have a vendor that would learn about the particular service requirements of that company and transfer the information across borders. Says Nurskij, "If we are able to get some level of productivity in dishwashing in Germany, the difference shouldn't be too big in Switzerland. In the old environment, we probably would have worked with different products and different machines." Moreover, the clients would have a better overview of their facility-maintenance costs and satisfaction, country by country.

In an additional effort to service key clients, ISS aligns customer and employee surveys. Results of standardized pan-European customer satisfaction surveys are broken down by key clients and compared with employee satisfaction surveys of the employees serving the particular client to develop improvement plans. "Customers are asked if their key account manager is accessible and provides useful information and quality service," explains Nurskij. "Meanwhile, front-line workers are asked if they are getting the right support from management to do their job well and key account managers are surveyed about whether they are provided with the right tools, resources and information to delight the client." The key account manager presents the results to clients on a regular basis. Root causes of problems are identified and remedied in collaboration with clients. Thus, ISS coproduces value with its customers on a global scale. Its global account managers are cleaning up among ISS's different companies and countries, integrating communications and service to every key client.

ISS and Ericsson have come a long way since the days when communication was managed around product lines and local subsidiaries. Unlike Saturn, they didn't have the luxury of starting with a clean slate. Both companies started with amalgamations of wide-ranging businesses scattered around the world. A knife divided business units and subsidiaries, severing ISS people who did landscaping from those who did floor sweeping, and Ericsson public phone system experts in Germany from those in Great Britain. Like most companies, their communications were planned from the *inside out*, focusing on their products and services, instead of *outside in*, from the perspective of their customers. They subscribed to a *supply-side marketing* approach of selling whatever products and services they had in store, instead of *demand-side marketing* of offering customers solutions. Financial reporting and bonus systems, business planning and budget allocations were all structured around separate product lines, rather than customer segments. In only a few years' time, Ericsson and ISS have mounted the complex and ever-evolving task of realigning their entire business operations around their customers. That's how profound the transition is to integrated communications.

When the Stakes Are High

External integration goes beyond customers, to every group or individual with a stake in the company. Success in the Customer Century requires careful attention to all stakeholders, who are any groups or individuals who affect or are affected by the achievement of a corporation's purpose, now and in the future.[10] All stakeholders ask one or both of the following questions: "What can you do *for* me?" and "What can you do *to* me?"

The stakes of the stakeholders are growing in these days of fierce competition, sophisticated consumers, demanding employees, intrusive governments, litigious publics, active shareholders, scrutinizing media, and the 90,000 and growing registered special interest groups in the United States. The successful management of relationships with these groups leads to a cycle of reinforcement where success starts feeding itself. Companies that can attract good employees will attract equally good investors, customers, and partners, and escape some of the harsh criticism from the mass media. The converse is equally true—the mismanagement of stakeholder relationships can put companies in a downward tailspin.

The news media have emerged as particularly critical stakeholders that can make or break a company almost overnight. Business news has gained the same media prominence as royalty, Hollywood, and sporting events. There's no end to the public's appetite for news stories about rising corporate profits, booming financial markets, mergers, acquisitions, spinoffs, breakups, downsizing, and layoffs. Corporate leaders like Andy Grove, Jack Welch, and Percy Barnevik have become perennial cover boys of magazines and book jackets, and prime-time television stars. Other less fortunate and less media-savvy CEOs are ridiculed or vilified and given nicknames like "Chain Saw." In addition to the media, there are a number of other stakeholders of growing importance, including employees, government agencies, legislative bodies, financial markets, interest groups, local communities, suppliers, distributors, trade and professional organizations, opinion leaders, and competitors. Their importance varies greatly with company, industry, and country. But most companies will find some stakeholders to be "mission critical," warranting the same attention as their customers. They will find that the same logic of integrated communications espoused in this chapter applies to noncustomer stakeholders as well.

Research clearly proves that companies with strong stakeholder relationships are more successful by any measure. Harvard Business School research by John P. Kotter and James L. Heskett shows that companies that value employees, customers, and shareholders far outperform companies that put shareholders first. They grew four times faster in revenue, eight times faster in job creation, an amazing 765 times faster in growth of net income, and gave shareholders twelve times as much capital appreciation. This finding is consistent with *Fortune* and Yankelovich Partners' "Corporate Equity" study, based on almost eight thousand completed surveys, which shows a clear correlation between companies' successes and stakeholder perceptions. Its top twenty "high equity companies" have the following in common: customers consistently recommend their products; employees recommend these companies to other prospective employees; industry colleagues recommend them to joint venture partners; the public stands by the companies in times of controversy; and investors find their stocks attractive investments. These findings leave no doubt about the bottom-line effects of integrating stakeholder communications.

The Tangled Web of Stakeholders

Stakeholders are not only becoming more important, they are also becoming more intertwined. The web of stakeholder relationships keeps getting more and more entangled as individuals and organizations have multiple stakes in a company. Motorola is, on any given day, AT&T's supplier, partner, and competitor. Consumers are not just buyers but also environmentalists and investors. Employees are not just workers but shareholders and community members. Collectively, employees have become the largest owners of corporations through pension funds, mutual funds, and profit sharing. The fact that stakeholder roles are so interrelated and overlapping makes it even more important to integrate communications with them. "In this business, you cannot just have one area that you worry about," says now retired Mike O'Neill, former director of communications and public affairs at Eastman Chemical, "because everything spills over. If you communicate to employees, then almost immediately it is in the community. If it is in the community, it is in the media. So there are no sharp lines drawn."

Danfoss keeps all its key stakeholders informed by sending its employee magazine, *Avisen*, free of charge to former employees, every Danish newspaper, leading politicians, union leaders, and anyone else who signs up. "Every two weeks you can be sure there will be articles in Danish newspapers taken from *Avisen*," says Vagn Hesselager, employee communications manager, "so every two weeks, in fact, we have a news release." It is sent to the homes of employees to help keep family members informed. "We like to keep families informed of what their spouse, mother or father is doing, that's part of our company culture," comments Hesselager. Keeping stakeholders informed is like kindergarten, a good place to start. Achieving business objectives through strategic communication, coalition building, and partnership with key decision-makers of major stakeholders, however, is graduate school. A graduate-level case was unveiled when Motorola found itself blocked from entering the Japanese market in the early 1980s.[11] To integrate communications with U.S. and Japanese policymakers and corporate leaders, Motorola consolidated all its Japanese operations into a single unit, headed by a cast of three managers: "Mr. Japan" was based in Motorola's Schaumburg, Illinois, headquarters; "Mr. Here" was based in Washington, D.C., in charge of lobbying the U.S. government on Japanese trade issues; and "Mr. There" was a Japanese national based in Tokyo, in charge of the daily operations in Japan. "Mr. Japan," Stephen L. Levy, explains the problems before this reorganization: "We were not creating the image of a large corporation, but rather the image of several loose pieces of an organization that were not acting together as a coherent unit."[12] Motorola's new organizational unit led a high-profile integrated communications campaign with all key stakeholders to open trade with Japan. It included articles, speeches, testimonies, and an advertising campaign, which ran for four years on the theme of "Meeting Japan's Challenge."

Not only did Motorola integrate its own communications, but also that of the entire industry by getting a number of large companies behind the "Coalition for International Trade Equity." The electronics powerhouse filed three successful suits against the competitive methods used by Japanese companies and publicly supported other companies that filed similar suits. The effort paid off. Motorola succeeded not only in opening the gates to the Japanese market, but also in developing a reputation in Japan as one of the most politically connected and powerful companies in the United States. As Japanese companies were pressured from the United States to buy American, they were more likely to buy from Motorola. Motorola has come a long way since the day one of its executives visited a Hungarian minister who exasperatedly threw down a stack of business cards from a dozen different Motorola divisions and asked, "Which of these people am I supposed to talk to?"[13] Like most companies, Motorola wasn't set up to integrate stakeholder communications. Different business units pursued the same stakeholders independently of one another. Today the electronics behemoth has an integrated interface with every one of its critical stakeholders.

To be clear, integrated stakeholder communications is not about divulging the exact same information to everyone, but about being consistent. Different stakeholders have different communications needs: Customers want to learn about the value of service offerings, investors want to know about the company's overall performance, and employees want to find out about personal growth opportunities. World-class companies address each stakeholder's needs, without appearing disintegrated. Think of the way an individual communicates differently with his or her spouse, friends, and boss, while still maintaining a single personality. In much the same way, companies need to have a clear "personality," with easily recognizable traits that can be conveyed in all communications. By integrating communications to different stakeholders with a clear single personality, companies can adapt to each stakeholder's needs while still maintaining a sense of "self."[14] The road to integrated stakeholder communications takes the following course: identifying the "critical few" stakeholders, cultivating "symmetrical relationships" with them, and involving everyone in the entire organization in integrating communications with them, as explained below.

Identifying the "Critical Few"

All stakeholders are not created equal. As with customers, most important stakeholders are small in numbers but big in effect. For instance, most organizations will find that 20 percent of all journalists account for 80 percent of the media coverage of the company and 20 percent of all shareholders own 80 percent of the company. The 20 percent are, in most cases, the most cost-effective group to target with communications. A database can build patterns on how individual stakeholders operate in order to identify the "critical few" that really matter.

One approach of identifying the most critical stakeholders, developed by scholars Mitchell, Agle, and Wood, is to rank them in terms of their power, legitimacy, and urgency.[15] A major shareholder has *power*, the ability to influence the firm. A television news anchor has *legitimacy*, as someone with respect based on socially accepted norms. A recently laid-off worker has *urgency*, with a time-sensitive stake that is critically important to the stakeholder. But stakeholders who only possess one of these attributes are merely latent stakeholders. They warrant less attention, but cannot be ignored. A hotline still sits in the White House, as a reminder of the importance of keeping open channels of communication to a former superpower that has lost its legitimacy and urgency but still has power. Stakeholders who combine two of the attributes have to be taken more seriously. Take, for example, a disgruntled employee who appears on a television news show, thus combining urgency and legitimacy. Stakeholders with all three attributes deserve top management attention. One example is when the federal antitrust enforcer, a person in a position of power and legitimacy, filed suit against Microsoft. Companies should periodically review stakeholders in terms of their power, legitimacy, and urgency as a basis for prioritizing them and developing communications plans.

Cultivating "Symmetrical Relationships"

Once key stakeholders have been identified, world-class companies go out of their way to learn about their needs and accommodate them. Eastman Chemical Company stands out as a role model in this respect. It commissions regular phone surveys with neighbors around its sites. Director of Corporate Communications Rod Irvin explains that the purpose of the surveys is "to determine how we are viewed as an employer, and as a community citizen." A particular survey question revealed that the main concern among the community members was the odor from the chemical plants. "So we have put money into reducing odors, and are also looking at ways to completely eliminate them," assures Irvin, adding that the company has "definitely reduced odors over the last years." The surveys have played a critical role in expediting this progress: "We would have done it anyway, but we became much more aggressive when we saw some of those survey numbers back in the 1980s."

Eastman Chemical Company goes beyond surveys, by involving a "Community Advisory Panel" in its decision-making. Irvin portrays the composition of a typical panel: "There will be a couple of near neighbors, an environmentalist or two, a physician, an emergency response expert, one or two business leaders who are not connected to the company, and the principal of the closest school." The panel members serve three-year terms. They are treated to dinners at nice locations for their regular meetings, but are not paid for their services. One of the purposes of the group is to act as a sounding board for various company initiatives. "We pitch potential PR programs to them, we talk about our operations, we present worst-case accident scenarios to learn from the panel what the strengths and weaknesses of our emergency response are," explains Irvin. But more important than getting feedback on activities that Eastman has in the works is to keep a wet finger in the air on what's happening in the community and to build trust. The Community Advisory Panel helps Eastman identify emergent issues long before they would surface in a phone survey. It will learn about unfounded rumors that can be easily killed with proactive communication, or deep-rooted concerns that the company needs to deal with. The Community Advisory Panels have the ears of Eastman's senior managers, who take an active role in the meetings. "We give the panel full access to our senior managers," divulges Irvin. "At our main plant here in Kingsport, Tennessee, the plant site president attends almost every meeting, and there are times when, for example, the vice president of health, safety and environment is called in for a meeting." All of Eastman Chemical Company's U.S. plant sites have a Community Advisory Panel, and they are being considered at international plant sites as well.

Rod Irvin cites a number of examples of how his company has changed its behavior based on input from the Community Advisory Panels. Its community information has been completely restructured, for instance. "The panel said, you guys do a lot of great things that you assume the community knows about; you're going to have to tell more of the good things you do." An example of the changes prompted by this insight is a new neighborhood newsletter. "The newsletter is based on what the panel thought we ought to tell people," states Irvin. All members of the Chemical Manufacturers Organization are mandated to have these panels, but few companies have made such great strides as Eastman Chemical Company.

The rapport between Eastman Chemical Company and its community stakeholders is a prime example of what Jim Grunig and other public relations scholars refer to as "two-way symmetrical" relationships. The relationships are "symmetrical" in the sense that both the company and the stakeholders accommodate each other's needs. In contrast, many Production Century companies still practice "one-way asymmetrical" communications, where they dispatch a barrage of company propaganda without even bothering to learn about the concerns of the stakeholders. More enlightened Production Century companies will practice "two-way asymmetrical" communications, where they will survey the audience to hone the message. Complaints about the odors from a chemical plant would be met with a public information campaign focused on the fact that the odors aren't dangerous to people's health. With Eastman's "two-way symmetrical" approach to communications, it puts engineers in high gear to actually fix the problem. The company is adapting its own behavior to serve the needs of a key stakeholder.

Enlisting the Full Support of Part-Time Communicators

World-class companies enlist the support of managers and employees who interact with stakeholders on a daily basis. All employees are "part-time communicators" who talk to friends and neighbors who might own shares in the company; who interact with people in the local community whose environment is being affected by the company's presence; and who vote for legislators who can take actions that will affect the company. Research studies clearly indicate that people inside an organization are the primary source of information for external stakeholders.[16] At a minimum, employees need to be kept informed about any late-breaking news affecting the company. The fastest way to discourage employees from becoming company ambassadors is to release news of an important business development to the public before it's communicated to employees. In these days when employees receive news in real time through television, radio, and the Internet, companies cannot wait for the next edition of the employee magazine. They have to communicate instantaneously with their global workforces. Xerox's media relations manager, Judd Everhart, gives an example of the woes that ensue when that doesn't happen. "We hired a CFO who was from Great Britain. And no one ever thought before the announcement went out that we should have told our people in London." The London paper started calling Xerox's U.K. subsidiary to ask about the new CFO. "The people at Rank-Xerox London were furious, justifiably so. We should have looped them in. It took something like that for me to realize that you really need to keep in mind who needs to know what, so you don't end up looking stupid."

Keeping employees informed is a good start. The next level is to utilize managers and technical specialists in the company as corporate spokespeople. "There was a time when ICL formally forbade any manager from talking to the press, and asked that any manager approached by a journalist refer them to the press officer," recalls Anna Birchall, press officer of D2D, at the time an ICL subsidiary. "Today, any manager can talk to the press. They are empowered to discuss anything they feel is within their boundaries." ABB shares this philosophy. "You rarely see the communication department at ABB making a statement to the news media about anything. It's the managers who do it. They have the knowledge of the issues and the credibility; they shouldn't hide behind any shelter," says the outspoken corporate communications director of ABB Sweden, Roger Johansson. "But they need the support of professional communicators. We do a damn thorough job of reviewing with the managers what rules to stick to, what to emphasize, what not to emphasize, and how they should do it." The reason for this strategy is that reporters increasingly are steering away from the official spokespeople of the PR department, in favor of what they consider "real people." Johansson and Birchall are *renaissance* PR managers, acting as a coaches, counselors, and confidants of their senior management colleagues rather than being mere mouthpieces. "It is my job to make sure my senior managers appear in the right contexts and know what the hell they are doing," concludes Johansson.

Getting managers and technical specialists to become press spokespeople requires a serious training effort. Most business schools neglect to provide this essential managerial survival skill. Instead, many progressive PR departments have taken it upon themselves to provide the training. Ericsson's public relations director for the U.K., Paula Wagstaff, asks the manager of each business area to pick a team of people who can talk to the media, and sends them on a weekend retreat led by a journalist. "They meet a journalist on friendly terms who gets them to understand what a journalist is trying to get out of an interview," says Wagstaff.

This type of training teaches spokespeople to frame issues in newsworthy ways and to break them down to sound bites that are delivered with passion and conviction. Per Vagner Rasmussen, public relations director of Danfoss, finds television training particularly important. "Most of our managers handle newspaper interviews pretty well, but being interviewed on television, that takes skills. We run extensive training seminars with our managers to give them the hands-on experience."

Saturn and Eastman Chemical Company go beyond using their employees inside the organization as part-time communicators. Saturn also enlists its independent dealers as spokespeople to the local media. Madison, Wisconsin, dealer Tom Zimbrick speaks of a recent trip to Spring Hill: "I went down to Spring Hill for our regular meeting with retailers in the Midwest. Every retailer brings a local media reporter from his or her area as their guest. We had a meeting in the afternoon, and then the next morning the retailers and media people went to build cars at the plant. No other manufacturer would even think about doing this." Using retailers as conduits to local media is an effective way to nurture these important relationships and secure media publicity that benefits both retailer and manufacturer.

Eastman is another example of a company using its "extended enterprise" as communicators to fight its causes. It mobilizes a grass-roots organization of retirees, spouses, and anyone else who will volunteer to influence important policy issues. "We send our grass-roots members in Tennessee a monthly newsletter when the state legislature is in session," says D. Lynn Johnson, vice president, government relations. "They have calls for action, such as letter-writing campaigns to congresspeople, a similar newsletter for members living in the western states, and a federal newsletter to all members." Most of the issues deal with environment, tax, and trade issues. "We know from our research that the most value we can add to the company is on these three issues." An "issue management process" helps the grass-roots organizations focus on key issues— issues that are important to support the company's overall goals. The goals are identified, policy statements are made, measures of Eastman's success with them are determined, and an action plan is laid out. "I put out a monthly activity report on an issue-by-issue basis, where we show on a state-by-state basis who is doing what," says Johnson, who also enlists support from trade organizations.

At the end of the day, building stakeholder relationships is not much different from building customer relationships. The same principles of trust, honesty, respect, consistency, and two-way communication apply. Identify the critical few, gain insight into their needs, and involve all your employees in exceeding their expectations at every point of contact. Companies cannot afford to leave stakeholder communications to happenstance, or to the judgment of a former local newspaper reporter in the public relations department. The traditional tools and tactics of public relations are no longer sufficient: employees are not satisfied with a newsletter and a lunch meeting; investors are not content with a glossy annual report; and the news media don't settle for a press release. These stakeholders all want better access, more opportunities to ask questions of the decision-makers, and more in-depth understanding of the company. As stakeholders are getting more demanding, all managers have to be comfortable around Wall Street, Main Street, and Fleet Street. They have to learn to withstand the scrutiny of special interest groups, journalists, and prosecutors. The survival of organizations in the Customer Century is dependent not so much on their ability to compete as on their ability to collaborate with their environment. Organizational evolution no longer involves the survival of the fittest, but "survival of the fitting." The winners of the Customer Century will be companies that treat key stakeholders as customers, because the stakes are tremendous.

Few companies have done a more splendid job of leveraging communications against different stakeholders than ABB, which is plotting its next-generation T50 campaign as this book goes to print. This time, the focus will shift from streamlining the operations to improving its knowledge management process. "To be quite honest, many companies have caught up with our lean manufacturing processes and empowered employees out on the shop floors," divulges Roger Johansson. He recognizes that for ABB to be viable in the Customer Century, the focus needs to be on "how to move from a production company to a knowledge company." While the content of the new change process may be different, you can be sure that the method of achieving it will stay the same. The three-punch combination of external, horizontal, and vertical communications that have served the company so well in the 1990s will now catapult it into the Customer Century. How to reach, motivate, and communicate with front-liners is the topic of the next chapter. It explores the second dimension of integration—"vertical" communications between senior management and front-line employees.

What to Do Monday Morning:

- Consolidate all available attitudinal, behavioral, and customer satisfaction data about individual end-user customers from marketing communications, marketing research, sales, customer service, and billing departments, as well as channel members and syndicated sources into a central database.
- Identify customers or customer segments with the highest potential lifetime customer value, based on purchase history, cost, "share of wallet," retention rate, and other customer and marketplace data, and tailor communications and service offerings to them.
- Assign senior-level executives P&L responsibilities for the relationships with key customers or customer segments, as a first step in aligning the entire organizational structure, processes, and reward structure around customers.
- Get a solid grip on customer needs through the ongoing analysis of satisfaction surveys, complaints, inquiries, field operations, market research, and other sources of customer information. Share these insights broadly within the organization and involve everyone in continual improvements and customization of products, service, and communications.
- Identify and prioritize the moments when customers come in contact with the company; train, empower, and support all front-line employees to better delight customers and integrate communications at all of these moments of truth. The test of success is if any randomly selected employee can answer the following questions:

✔ Who are the most important customers that you are serving, how is your job impacting those customers, and how do you get feedback from them?

✔ What is the key message of your company?

✔ Which customer satisfaction improvement team are you currently on?

- Analyze which *stakeholders* have the potential to add the most value or incur the highest costs to your organization. Identify their critical needs and try to accommodate them in mutually satisfactory ways.
- Assign ongoing responsibility to managers for cultivating relationships with the most critical stakeholders.
- Establish an advisory board with critical stakeholders.
- Train and support everyone in the organization and its value chain to become spokespeople or ambassadors of their organization.

Notes

1. Susan Fournier, Susan Dobscha, and David Glen Mick (1998). "Preventing the Premature Death of Relationship Marketing." *Harvard Business Review*, January–February, p. 43.
2. Sears estimates the cost of acquiring new customers to be twenty times higher than the cost of retaining them. Bickert, Jock, "A Look as We Leap into the Mid-1990s: Databases, Brand, and Common Realities," National Direct Marketing Institute for Professors, DMED, San Francisco, March 20, 1996, as referred to in Duncan, Tom; Moriarty, Sandra (1997). *Driving Brand Value*. New York: McGraw-Hill.
3. Reichheld, Frederick (1996). "The Loyalty Effect." Boston, Mass.: Harvard Business School Press.
4. *Fortune*, special advertising section, September 19, 1994.
5. GISTICS Inc. (1996). Strategies for Building Digital Brands, Apple Computer.
6. According to a presentation by Judith Kincaid, Hewlett-Packard, at @dtech97.
7. Stepanek, Marcia (1999). "You'll Wanna Hold Their Hands." *Business Week*, March 22, pp. EB 30–31.
8. Jones, Thomas O., and Earl Sasser, Jr. (1995). "Why Satisfied Customers Defect." *Harvard Business Review*, November-December, pp. 88–99.
9. Rackham, Neil, and John De Vincentis (1999). *Rethinking the Sales Force*, New York: McGraw-Hill.

10. Freeman R. E. (1984). *Strategic Management: A Stakeholder Approach.* Boston: Pitman, p. vi.

11. This case is drawn from "Motorola's Japan Strategy." *Harvard Business School Case Study, 9-387-093.*

12. "Motorola's Japan Strategy." *Harvard Business School Case Study*, 9-387-093, p. 5.

13. Hardy, Quentin (1998). "Unsolid State: Motorola, Broadsided by the Digital Era, Struggles for a Footing." *Wall Street Journal*, April 22, p. A1

14. For more information on "brand personality," read my colleague Lisa Siracuse's article "Looks Aren't Everything: Creating Competitive Advantage with Brand Personality." (1998–1999). *Journal of Integrated Communications*, pp. 10–13.

15. This is drawn from Mitchell, Ronald K., Bradley R. Agle, and Dona J. Wood (1997). "Toward a Theory of Stakeholder Identification and Salience: Defining the Principle of Who and What Really Counts." *Academy of Management Review*, Vol. 22, No. 4, pp. 853–86.

16. McCallister, L. (1981). "The Interpersonal Side of Internal Communications." *Public Relations Journal* 37, February, pp. 20–23.

3

SECOND DIMENSION

Integrating Vertical
Communications

Real communication takes time, and top managers must be willing to make the investment. I personally interact with five thousand people a year in big and small groups.

We formed a secret group to reorganize the marketing operations of this company. I don't understand how everyone in the company somehow found out what we were doing. It amazes me how much people in this company talk to each other.

—*Percy Barnevik, chairman, ABB*

—*McKinsey consultant (hired to assist a client during a change process)*

"Philips is bankrupt!" The words from Philips's CEO Jan Timmer echoed in the conference room where the top fifty managers of the electronics giant were gathered. They were shaking their heads in disbelief as their CEO waved a press release announcing the bankruptcy. The sound of harrumphs and clearing of throats grew louder in the old Dutch castle that Philips had turned into a training center. They all knew that Philips wasn't really bankrupt. The faked press release was a ploy to drive home the CEO's message of the urgency of Philips's problems. But it got the attention of his senior managers. Timmer outlined a scenario based on hard data of corporate debts, cash flow, and competitive benchmarking information, according to which, Philips would be out of business in two years if it didn't change course.[1]

Just a few months earlier Philips had shocked the financial world with a two-billion-guilder loss. Its productivity was at 20 percent below its competitors. The Dutch-based electronics powerhouse that pioneered the development of the audiocassette, video recorder, and compact disc had become slow, inefficient, and costly. Jan Timmer was the third CEO in a short period of time chosen to tackle the daunting task of turning the ailing behemoth around. Within months of his appointment as CEO, Timmer called together his top one hundred senior managers. Fifty top managers at a time retreated to the old Dutch castle during two weekends. They were invited to air critiques about everything that was flawed about the company. Nothing was sacred. The meetings would soon become legends in the company, referred to as the "Valley of Death" seminars. "We were in a crisis, which always helps; it avoids 'analysis paralysis,' the postponing of solutions," says Hayen, Philips's director of external relations.

The radical restructuring program that was developed during the two retreats was named Operation Centurion. Before the meetings ended, Timmer had agreements with division managers to set bold targets such as cutting in half the time to market of new product developments and dramatically cutting costs. The targets would be achieved through the closing of factories, the selling of several businesses, overhauling operations, redefining the core business, and shedding no fewer than 68,000 people by the end of the first year. And just as important, Timmer got a commitment from the one hundred managers to repeat the same sessions with their key managers. This was the beginning of a massive communications cascade to reach the hearts and minds of over 240,000 employees spread over fifty-two countries and working in some 272 business units. "What we said to these top managers was you go home and do exactly the same with your people, and those people in the business units participating in this will have to do it with their people. Everyone had to conduct and participate in these Centurion sessions," explains Hayen. "The purpose was to get in synch with this group of top one hundred managers. Once you had them, then the cascade started rolling." Hayen was the architect behind integrating *horizontal* communications with the top one hundred managers, and the subsequent *vertical* communications cascaded down the organization.

The participants in the first meetings set a cascade of vertical communications in motion. They were required to hold meetings every three months in groups of fifty, which were called Centurion I meetings, to translate the change process into more specific break-through objectives for product divisions and business groups. The message was that Philips had to lay off employees, cut costs, and divest unprofitable businesses to survive. But there was also a more positive message of renewed dedication to serving and growing customers. "It was important to do more than just restructure the company—we needed to revitalize it. We wanted to seek out new opportunities for growth and provide stretch goals for the entire organization," says Willem Guitink, vice president for management education and training for Philips. Fourteen thousand managers were brought together for these weekend retreats. The participants in these meetings had similar meetings, called Centurion IIs, to plan the implementation of Centurion I decisions. The participants in these meetings held Centurion III meetings. By the time the Centurion IV meetings were held, all 240,000 employees had partic-ipated. These meetings were both "top-down" and "bottom-up." Employees at all levels were encouraged to provide input and feed-back. Centurion IV meetings were "town meetings" run by the local manager and an outside facilitator, during which managers answered anonymous, uncensored employee questions. "The facili-tator wasn't shy. It showed employees that there was no manipula-tion," says Hayen. "Every manager had to stand up for his people and answer questions." The meetings gave birth to thousands of local improvement projects.

To create additional pressure for change, the company chose an unusual *external* communications strategy of not speaking with the media. It did not even try to dissuade the press from writing nega-tive articles and comments. Philips felt it helped to create a crisis atmosphere internally. "We dramatized the crisis. We did not react to the outside world. We let them give nasty comments because that put pressure on the inside," explains Hayen. It was a dramatic demonstration of "pain management," the conscious orchestration of information to inspire dissatisfied people to jump-start the change process.

During the Centurion sessions, a list of improvement opportunities emerged. A task force was assigned to each opportunity, staffed with people from different product divisions, different countries, and different ranks. Newly hired people were mixed with Philips veterans. They were asked to benchmark other companies, speak to experts, read literature, and come up with recommendations. Hayen describes this horizontal communication, vehicle: "We asked 'how long will it take you to come up with recommendations on the subject.' The task forces responded, 'half a year.' We said, 'fine, do it in a quarter of a year.'" The task forces dealt with issues ranging from inventory reductions and distribution channels to the rate of progress in R&D and management development. Hayen himself was on the task force that drafted a new mission statement for Philips.

Philips also implemented another drastic measure to facilitate open vertical communications. It closed all the factories for one day and conducted a worldwide meeting with almost all of its employees. They sat at round tables of six in their plants, sometimes thousands in the same location. A Philips plant in Singapore held 6,000 workers. The beginning of the day was devoted to three workshops in which the groups around each table discussed what they could do as individuals, departments, and as a company to not only turn the difficult financial times around, but to improve how they served customers. A trained facilitator led every table of six, helping them to develop concrete action plans for the months to come. Later, they watched the CEO give a speech transmitted live through satellite to large-screen videos to every factory, translated into thirty-seven different languages. The employee teams were asked to come up with one question for the local management and one for the CEO. Thousands of questions were sent to the headquarters in Eindhoven via phone, fax, and e-mail. Says Hayen, "We hired fifty people to take calls." About thirty of those questions were answered by the CEO during the hour and a half of the satellite linkup. The others were answered by mail within three weeks—all with a letter signed by the CEO. This process has been repeated every year since then.

Yet the formal communications processes only go so far in explaining the success of this turnaround. The real success story behind Philips's transformation is the role of brutally open and honest communication. A booklet that was distributed to all employees a few years into the Centurion process contained a slew of criticisms by employees and addressed their concerns. Examples of quotes were: "Why do Philips's managers always blame forces outside of the company when something goes wrong?"; "When will Centurion blow over?"; "Centurion? Is it still going on? Wasn't it enough with the firing of 45,000 people?" By being forthright with these kinds of comments, Philips took the responsibility for past years' half-hearted, short-lived, and failed restructuring efforts that left employees embittered and frustrated. Few companies in crisis have the courage to air the voices of their most jaded and bitter employees. But rather than hearing the cynical wisecracks behind their backs, Philips's managers decided to put them on the table for discussion.

The integration of vertical communication between senior management and front-line workers is now institutionalized at Philips. All managers spend three to four weekends a year at Centurion sessions, which are cascaded down the ranks. And they hold town meetings two to three times a year to relay communications up to senior management. Philips rode out the initial crisis and is today uniquely positioned as the only European consumer electronics player of its kind. The case is a dramatic display of the power of *integrated vertical communications.* This second dimension keeps the top brass in touch with the realities of the business, and employees in tune with the strategic context of their work. World-class CEOs are relentless in their "top-down" communication of a clearly defined mission in words and actions to align their organizations like geese in V formation. Messages are cascaded down the organization, and employees are reached directly via the Intranet. Employees and middle managers communicate up the organization through processes of "bottom-up" communication, transferring opinions, feelings, and ideas up the ranks of the organization. To support this infrastructure, a climate of open communication exists where killing the messenger is anathema.

**2nd Dimension:
Vertical Integration**

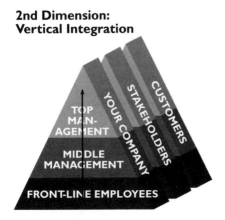

Figure 3.1. The second dimension of integrated communications: Integrating vertical communications between senior management and front-line workers.

The Vision Thing

Top-down communication starts with the communication of a vision of how the organization adds value to its customers that provides focus and a sense of purpose to the entire organization. The vision needs to be anchored in the values and philosophies that a company stands for and the mission or purpose of the company. These values need to be translated to clear brand promises that are communicated to customers and stakeholders. Examples of brand promises are: "A different kind of company, a different kind of car" (Saturn); "The world on time" (FedEx), "Providing superior solutions for the plant floor" (Allen-Bradley); to be "The Document Company" (Xerox); and to "Become Europe's leading contract electronics manufacturer"(D2D). These statements are not only communicated to customers, but were prominently featured wherever I turned in the company buildings. They hang as framed pictures in the lobbies, the coffee rooms, and in the offices. They are on the covers of the annual reports and the employee magazines. The managers I interviewed even pulled out cards from their shirt pockets that stated their vision, mission philosophy, and annual goals. Saturn's public relations manager, Greg Martin, explains the significance of the cards: "Everything we do is done in the context of those three cards. It pretty much ensures that everybody sings off of the same song sheet; everybody is in tune." Although these statements are typically simplistic, they do indeed help energize and focus everyone in the organization. Besides, other people are going to sum up your company in a few words anyway, so you might as well do the job for them.

Making the vision and the corporate brand promise pervasive inside and outside company walls is not a priority for most traditional managers. Fred Cahuzak, communications director of Ericsson Netherlands, caused quite a stir with his suggestion to take its mission public. At the end of a long meeting with the senior management team, during which they finalized the mission, objectives, and goals, he said, "Fine, now I will design posters with our mission to put in the hallways of all our facilities." He could not begin to describe the look of bewilderment and incredulity on the faces around the table. "It caused a riot among the senior managers. They said that they didn't want all our visitors to be able to see what our objectives were. After all, the mission has been kept secret for seventy-five years." But Cahuzak argued successfully that "You cannot ask people to follow a strategy if it's kept secret." Today, not only the mission is on display in the hallways of Ericsson Netherlands: "We post monthly sick leave average, revenue, cost and profit, for everyone to see, including visitors. It was quite a shock for the senior managers." In addition, his employee magazine features both successes and failures in achieving the goals.

Hewlett-Packard's corporate communications staff ensures that its vision is consistently communicated by using an elaborate "major messages" binder, which is structured around its seven corporate objectives: profit, customers, fields of interest, growth, our people, management, and citizenship. This binder is a reference point for all of the important issues that are communicated on a daily basis. It contains the proper wording for messages that, if communicated poorly, can damage the company's reputation. It gives employees a foundation to work from so they are never caught off guard in any given situation. "We took profit," explains Mary Ann Easley, "and we said, 'What do we want to say about profit? What is the current situation in the company with our profitability?' So we have the message, submessages, and then evidence or proof to back it up." The binder also outlines specific messages regarding the company's financial performance that HP hopes to convey to students, stockholders, and employees. No HP communicator is more than an arm's length away from their major messages binder. By establishing a limited number of corporate messages, communications professionals can ensure consistency in all communication. The key is to find messages that can transcend cultural and regional differences, and then adapt any submessages that apply.

Developing a Customercentric Vision

The challenge is to develop a vision that is specific enough to provide real guidance, yet is adaptable enough in today's rapidly changing environment. Some companies make the mistake of crafting exceedingly vague visions that offer the precision of "Make love, not war." On the other hand, a vision that is too detailed, focusing on particular products or technology, will only serve to maintain the status quo. The classic example of how a vision can paralyze, rather than propel a company forward, is Xerox's failure to capitalize on the personal computer. Xerox's Palo Alto Research Center invented the personal computer in the 1970s, along with its many features, including the mouse, the window concept and pull-down menus, and the computer networking system, Ethernet. These innovations could have made the company a bigger fortune than xerography. But Xerox decided against taking its wonder products to the market because they didn't fit with the company's copying business. It sat on them for six years, until a couple of teenage kids named Steven Jobs and Steve Wozniak commercialized them with the Macintosh. The rest, as they say, is history. Xerox had a Production Century vision that hampered its growth rather than fostering it, by focusing on products rather than customer needs.

The vision needs to be based not only on the firm's core competency—the bundle of skills and technologies that is central to its strength—but also on opportunities in the marketplace. And it needs to be a broadly phrased direction of the company rather than a detailed plan, expressed in terms of customer benefits rather than product features. When a division of Danfoss replaced its vision of "selling air filters" to one that involved "selling clean air," it became more of a service company that offered measurement and advice on dust prevention.

Once a customercentric big picture is developed, it needs to be condensed to succinct, pithy statements that can be communicated effectively. Xerox has boiled its vision down to four messages. "We have four core messages that we drive through the organization," explains Xerox's corporate communications director, Joseph Cahalan. The messages are "The Document Company," "Customer First," "Empowering Work Environment," and "Growth and Productiveness." Cahalan contrasted this approach with Xerox's message approach of just a few years ago, which earned the epithet "Partridge in a Pear Tree" among cynical employees: "We had one strategic direction, two vital objectives, three corporate-wide initiatives, four priorities, and five corporate values." Having such a litany of messages was synonymous with having no message at all. "We had fifteen messages, and depending on which manager was communicating with employees at a particular time, one of them was *the* most important message," says Cahalan. Today it's different. All internal messages are related to one of the four core messages. Icons have been developed for each of them. They are tagged on to all internal print and online messages as a visual reminder of which core message they're tied to. Employees are surveyed every six months about the familiarity, understanding, relevance, and credibility of the four core messages. Without a clearly defined and broadly communicated vision and strategy, employees have no basis for integrating communications about the company externally.

The CEO Is the CCO

The CEO and the senior management team play a critical role in communicating the vision. One CEO who has realized that he really is the "CCO," chief communications officer, is Xerox's Paul Allaire. He regularly reviews employee survey and focus group results with Corporate Communications Director Joseph Cahalan. "We spend a couple of hours going through it, then he presents it to the senior management team, which validates or changes the analysis and action plan." Cahalan argues that the responsibility of communicating with employees is ultimately the CEO's. "I'm seen as the coach, the enabler, the helper, but it's your [the CEO's] problem."

Beyond being in charge of the communications planning and evaluation, Xerox's CEO and top management team spend much of their time on the circuit delivering key messages to all employees. It culminates in a "communication blitz" every year. "It really starts in the beginning of February with the senior management meeting with about 150 of the top managers throughout the world," says Ann Silvernail, manager of employee and management communications. "And then we follow up by giving them a lot of materials for them to use as communication tools with their employees." Next, the chairman holds a live broadcast that goes to about ninety sites all over the world. He talks about the company's direction for the year. "This year, we had all eight of the corporate office members on the broadcast taking live call-in questions," says Silvernail. After the broadcast is aired, the chairman joins other executive vice presidents on a tour around the world to several major locations. This allows them to talk with employees face-to-face. Employees' perceptions are carefully surveyed after the communications cascade and again six months later to feed into the next year's planning cycle. In addition, Silvernail is privy to the calendars of the top six Executive VPs and is assigned to look for opportunities to add employee communications events to their schedules. "If, for example, an executive VP is going to St. Louis to meet a customer, I will check the timetable to see if there's an extra hour available to go to our St. Louis office and have a meeting with the employees," explains Silvernail.

ABB Atom executives share the same commitment to employee communications. The top three executives of its fuel division jointly participated in no less than sixty meetings with employees when it launched a new initiative. Says Kjell Morlin, "Rather than holding a structured meeting and talking at employees, the three senior executives stood up in front of the employees and not only allowed people to ask questions, but encouraged them to participate, criticize, and contribute their input." The ABB managers are following a precedent set by their venerated CEO, Percy Barnevik, who is now a non-executive chairman of ABB. During his tenure as CEO, Barnevik required that the eight members of the Executive Committee, including himself, held personal meetings with ABB's 25,000 middle managers, who in turn had to communicate with everyone else in the organization. "That's a gigantic task," Barnevik admits.[2] To accomplish it, he and his signature goatee flew around the world over two hundred days a year in permanent campaign mode to reiterate the direction of the company to ABB managers and employees. Barnevik was only half joking when he said, "I'm normally in my office two days a week—Saturdays and Sundays."[3] He never claimed that communication was easy. "Real communication takes time, and top managers must be willing to make the investment." The fast-talking chairman of the self-proclaimed "overhead company" ran ABB on a seemingly endless supply of adrenaline: "I personally have two thousand overhead slides and interact with five thousand people a year in big and small groups."[4] Oh, and did I mention that the value of the ABB stock rose an average of 30.5 percent per year, almost three times the stock index, during Barnevik's reign as CEO?

Communicating the vision with words alone will lead management down the path of management by "slogans and exhortations," an idea TQM guru Edwards Deming cautioned against. No matter how impeccably firm the rhetoric of top management is, or how frequently it's repeated, employees and stakeholders listen to their actions more than their words. It is management's actions that determine if the vision becomes a force of corporate unity or a source of employee cynicism. Xerox's internal research shows, for instance, that its key messages still aren't credible with many employees because, "They say that there is a gap between what managers tell them and what they can see managers doing," laments Cahalan. ABB chairman Percy Barnevik goes as far as arguing that "the most important thing of all, overshadowing everything else" when it comes to getting all employees to internalize the ABB values, "is for managers to live that way themselves." He gives an example: "If you talk about speed in action and you procrastinate on certain difficult decisions, you are not believable."[5] Few understood the need to walk the walk and talk the talk better than Motorola's former CEO, Bob Galvin. He grew tired of spending entire meetings discussing short-term financial issues rather than the quality improvement issues that were central to the vision of the company. Galvin decided to move quality improvement issues to the top of the agenda at every management staff meeting he presided over. And that's not all. After the quality reports were discussed, he got up and left the meeting. He argued that if quality was in place, the financial return would follow. He continued to do so for over ten years. The story grew to legendary proportions at

Motorola, and the agenda change was soon emulated at every business meeting throughout the organization. Quality quickly became Motorola's number one priority through Galvin's personal example.

Galvin slept, walked, and talked the company vision of quality, which paid off. In 1981 Motorola set out to achieve and did achieve a ten-time improvement of product quality in five years. It improved another ten times by 1989, and another hundredfold by 1991. Motorola estimates that it has saved over $11 billion since it embarked on the TQM journey. During the ten-year period when Galvin had quality on top of every agenda, the electronics giant experienced a fivefold increase in sales, a sixfold increase of profit, and a sevenfold increase of stock price. The word "whew" comes to mind. It is only slight hyperbole to say that all Motorolans would emulate every step Galvin took. He was well aware of his tremendous influence as Motorola's chief communications officer and institutional icon. Stories of Galvin's histrionics went a long way in establishing positive change. He proved that leadership in the Customer Century is about storytelling, about dramatizing events and creating corporate myths and legends that embody the purpose of the firm. Where leaders set a personal example, employees rally behind them, align themselves around their visions, and work to make them a reality.

Bob Galvin was able to instill Motorola's vision in every employee by being a powerful role model. Xerox also puts its money where its mouth is with a bonus system for both corporate performance and individual performance—multiplied with each other. If an individual manager's operations perform at 120 percent of the plan but the corporation as a whole is at 80 percent of plan, the individual gets only 96 percent of his or her bonus (1.2 x 0.8). But if both the individual and the corporation perform at 120 percent of the plan, the bonus is 144 percent.[6] Correlating compensation with effective communication sends a strong message about the organization's priorities.

Cascading Breakthrough Objectives

Guided by the vision, leading-edge managers focus their companies' efforts around a small number of breakthrough objectives that will move their organizations closer to the vision. Communicating these objectives effectively is key to achieving them. When objectives have been drafted, each senior manager sits down with the managers reporting to them to discuss how they can contribute to the corporate objectives. When second-level management has decided its objectives for the year in support of the corporate objectives, it initiates similar discussions with the third-level management. This way, the corporate objectives are "cascaded" down the management ranks of the organization, and translated into specific actions along the way.

Take Xerox, for example. Its customer satisfaction objectives find their way from the Connecticut headquarters via Rank-Xerox's European headquarters in London, through its Danish subsidiary, and down to the individual service representative in Copenhagen. The year I paid my visit there, the objective was to be number one in the market of printers and copiers, to have a minimum of 98 percent overall customer satisfaction, and no individual satisfaction under 50 percent. Rank-Xerox Denmark has cross-functional teams analyzing what "vital few actions" will have the largest leverage on the objective. "These vital few actions are different in different parts of the world, but they build up to the same objectives," explains Tom Kenneth, quality director of Rank-Xerox's Nordic region.

Hewlett-Packard is another devotee of this approach of cascading breakthrough objectives, or in HP lingo, "hoshins." The term is short for the Japanese term *hoshin kanri,* which translates to "policy deployment." HP imported this planning process from its Japanese division, Yokogawa Hewlett-Packard, which is one of the companies that has developed and perfected this strategic component of TQM. Every business unit, department, and individual at HP has set their own hoshins of how they can contribute to the corporate hoshins. Everyone's hoshins are summarized on a one-page Annual Hoshin Planning Table. For every hoshin, it lists the target/goals which are the means to achieving the hoshin, the strategy to accomplish the target, the owners who are responsible for each strategy, and performance measures of how to measure progress on the strategy. "It's an important way to coordinate my work," says Gene Endicott, Bay Area government affairs manager. "I think it's a very valuable exercise for the department to sit down prior to the beginning of the year, and ask, What kind of things do we need to work on to be more effective contributors to the company's vision and bottom line?"

Endicott explains the hoshin planning process: "We go away for two days as a department off site, and talk about what we want to accomplish over the course of the next year. And once we get on some agreement as a department of what our goals are going to be, then each section will meet separately to discuss how they are going to support that." Finally, everyone develops individual hoshin plans in collaboration with their managers. Through such rigor, the same objectives are communicated and acted upon by everyone in the organization. After having this system in place for several years, HP is now easing on the requirement for all business units to use the hoshin. "Some business units don't find it appropriate and they don't need to use it, but they all need to do planning around the corporate objectives," comments Mary Ann Easley.

If you think this sounds like good old "management by objectives," you've missed the point. The problem with MBO is that top management will go off on a retreat and dream up a wish list of thirty objectives and assign different—and often conflicting—objectives to different departments. Like a kamikaze pilot with a quota of five ships, the organization has more goals than it can realistically accomplish and no plans for achieving them. As a result, people in the organization play games with each other to meet numerical targets. In contrast, the Customer Century company will align the whole organization around a small number of shared objectives, and develop processes to achieve them. The other difference with this process is that it starts with bottom-up communications, from front-line employees up through the ranks of the organization. "I think it's important for people to dream about where the company will be six years from now," says Vagn Hesselager, employee communications manager at Danfoss. The vision and objectives of these companies are not just the brainchild of senior managers. They emanate from dialogue with the workers who are closest to the customers.

Finally, the difference from traditional approaches is that the goals are communicated widely and openly. One example of brutally honest and open communication is when Hewlett-Packard dramatized one of its hoshins, to improve order fulfillment, the time that elapses from when a customer makes an order until the customer receives it. It ran a series of articles in its employee magazine featuring disgruntled customers who didn't get their HP equipment delivered on time. Unlike most other employee publications that exclusively tout successes that the companies have had with their goals, HP's magazine gave the real story. The corporate communications department of HP believed in showcasing the truth to shake up everyone in the company and get them to realize the magnitude of the order-fulfillment problem. As it turned out, some senior managers weren't thrilled with the idea. "It irritated a couple of very high-level people who thought we were being too open," says Mary Ann Easley, employee communications director and PR manager. "It went ultimately to the CEO, who asked us to run it anyway." This type of support by the chieftain is a key ingredient in making integrated communications work. CEO Lew Platt recognized that HP had a serious problem, and the only way to enlist every employee's support in fixing it was to give them a sobering assessment of its seriousness and urgency. Through such candid communication, HP has earned its spot among the top ten on *Fortune*'s "100 Best Companies to Work for in America." [7]

Aligning such a titan as HP around a clear-cut vision and focused objectives is no small communications task. This fiercely entrepreneurial company of over 120,000 employees around the world is organized into small, largely autonomous product divisions. New divisions are spun off as soon as a new product is developed, in the interest of keeping units small, innovative, agile, and close to customers. Yet this sprawling organization is lined up behind a single direction through unrelenting and brutally honest two-way communications. Employees are invited to regular "coffeepot talks" to be up on the latest developments, and they are encouraged to air out opinions on the Intranet. "I think it is to the company's credit that people can get on [an electronic bulletin board] and say that 'I think the CEO makes too much money, what does everybody else out there think?' And they flame on for days or weeks or months about how much the CEO makes and if he is worth it," muses Mary

Anne Easley. This openness is part of the famous culture known as the "HP Way" that is holding the group together.

Cascading Ongoing Communications

The same cascading process is practiced for ongoing communications as well, as our friends from D2D will tell us. Its senior management team meets every other Monday morning. At the end of the meeting, it determines key messages, which typically deal with changes in the marketplace, company performance, and improvement information. Immediately after that meeting, the senior managers meet the people reporting to them over lunch to pass along the same message. The participants in the lunch meetings carry the process one step down. Before the last shift has gone home Tuesday night, the same message has traveled five management levels in less than forty-eight hours. At that time, every employee has participated in a "team brief meeting" where they have heard the same message in a small group setting and been offered the opportunity to give feedback. As Quality Manager Dayvon Goodsell explains it, "[The meetings] don't cost a lot of time or money, they are practical, manageable and achievable." To avoid distorting the message, every manager has a "brief sheet," a page summarizing the key messages. After the program had been in place for a while, D2D managers found the meetings to be too one-sided. The "team briefs" were renamed "team talk," and the brief sheets were revised to incorporate more questions to facilitate discussions. Managers were trained to become more concise and leave more time for discussion. "We wanted to emphasize that they are not briefings as much as opportunities for people to openly discuss various issues with their managers. Employees are encouraged to bring any issues out onto the table for discussion," says Goodsell.

Cascade Training

World-class companies use the same cascade approach for employee training, which is another important avenue for vertical communications. The most dramatic example of successful cascade training comes from Xerox. On the brink of bankruptcy in 1983, Xerox kicked off its quality management transformation with an elaborate three-year learning cascade. CEO David T. Kearns gathered his senior management team and held a six-day training session in total quality management. As part of the session, the senior management team went through two quality improvement projects, one to improve the effectiveness of the corporate management committee meetings, and the other to streamline quarterly operations reviews. Such a "just-in-time" approach merges learning and application. After that week, each of the senior managers led a one-week training session with the managers reporting to them, assisted by a professional trainer. It took three years and four million training hours, or 2,500 man-years, before everyone in Xerox was fully trained. This long time frame presented Xerox with a communications challenge because some employees were not going to get the training until several years after others were already practicing what they had learned. To cope, two hundred Xerox managers were enlisted to give two days of training and information to all employees during the first year, preceding the more thorough six days of training, which eventually cascaded down to everyone.

Another example of successful cascade training is at ISS, which brings the senior management team of one subsidiary company at a time to its Quality Management Institute, located at its Danish headquarters. "The senior management teams are taught the ISS approach to total quality management during two four-day sessions and one three-day session," explains Karsten Jenson from the ISS Quality Institute. "Later, the senior managers teach the people reporting to them here at the same facility." The training is cascaded down three levels, sometimes all the way down to the supervisory levels. Unlike the Xerox approach, ISS does not mandate the training to all its subsidiaries. "We can't go to our Finnish subsidiary and demand 'you should start TQM now!' Instead, we should be available to them when they say 'we are ready now, let's get going,'" says Jenson.

ISS and Xerox's experience is that training needs to start at the top. Research by Motorola supports this notion. It revealed that companies whose plant managers reinforced training reaped a $33 return for every dollar spent on training. In contrast, where managers did not reinforce training, there was a negative return on investment. The president of Motorola University, William Wiggenhorn, noted that Motorola used to make the mistake of "briefing at the top and teaching at the bottom." Management soon realized that it had to do it the other way around. The training is wasted if a work group comes back from a training session charged up and ready to implement new ideas, only to meet managers who don't know what the workers are talking about. Training at Motorola is integral with the business. "Motorola trains to solve performance problems. It doesn't just put a little red schoolhouse in the workplace," as labor economist Anthony Carnevale described it.[8]

Motorola makes extraordinary commitments to training, thanks to its former CEO, Bob Galvin. He was voted down eleven to one in 1979 when he proposed to his board of directors that the firm should make a commitment to training its workers. As CEO and the largest shareholder, Galvin decided to defy the board's decision and plunge ahead. Today, Motorola spends an average of $200 million per year on training—a figure that is actually twice as high if you include the salary and benefits employees receive during training.[9] Motorola University has grown beyond the walls of its Schaumburg facility, with thirteen sites around the world. By 1996, a full-time faculty of four hundred and a part-time faculty of six hundred offered upwards of nine hundred courses in twenty-four different languages. The average Motorola employee receives fifty-seven hours of training every year. Executives who are concerned about the cost of training and the down time in production should consider that Motorola's employee productivity has improved 204 percent over a nine-year period as a result of its training. "We figure if we can outlearn our competitors, we can beat them every time," argues William Wiggenhorn. The research behind *Fortune's* list of the one hundred best companies to work for reveals that the average time invested by these one hundred companies in the education and training is forty-three hours per year—over six working days per employee.

The most hard-core devotee of training is Saturn. Ten percent of every Saturn employee's salary can actually be held back if all employees do not complete ninety-two hours of training every year. "The neat thing is that suppose I do my ninety-two hours of training and someone else doesn't, I don't get my ten percent," says Public Relations Director Greg Martin. "Last year we had two people out of our eight thousand employees that didn't make their training hours." Although they prorated it to what amounted to four or five dollars, employees felt disappointed in the two (undisclosed) people who ruined it for the rest of them. Out of the ninety-two hours, about one-quarter of the courses are required: team building, consensus decision-making, conflict resolution, and creative thinking. "It is not a quick hit-and-run type of course where the effects last a week. It is ninety-two hours of training that keeps you continuously focused and motivated," says Martin. Most of the training is skill-specific. For example, the communications professionals are expected to take courses offered by professional organizations and report the number of hours they spend on each such course. Saturn offers a course catalogue for communications professionals featuring courses available internally and externally. "You spend money to maintain million-dollar machines, why not maintain people in the same respect?" asks Martin rhetorically. "We look at all people who do a job as a creative resource to help us identify ways to do that job better." Training is a key ingredient in successful vertical communications by giving everyone in the organization shared frames of reference, shared language, and a shared vision of the company's future.

The Power of the Cascade

What makes cascading such a powerful approach to planning and ongoing communications is that it gets every manager involved twice, first as a participant and second as a teacher. The focus in recent years on "delayering" the middle ranks of the organization and "empowering" the front line has turned middle managers of many organizations into silent resistors of change. Cascade communications enlists their support. When people see their managers' involvement, they know they mean serious business. An additional benefit of this communication method is that corporate planning and communications can be tailored to each part of an organization and delivered in a small interactive setting where employees can ask questions about how the news will affect them. Employee surveys show that employees prefer to get company information from their immediate managers or supervisors. "Our research has shown that the first thing employees do when they receive corporate messages is to run to their manager and say 'should we worry about this,'" says Xerox's Cahalan. His colleague at Allen-Bradley, Christine Zwicke, echoes this point: "As you know, employees want to hear major news face-to-face from their boss. Surveys have been talking about that for probably two or three decades now and we find that to be absolutely true." The Allen-Bradley manager believes a lot of fears and rumors can be extinguished before they're ignited by having managers sit down and talk to their employees and provide them with all the information they need. To support their efforts, the company provides managers with briefing kits complete with Q&A and feedback forms for questions they can't answer and for insight into areas that employees are most interested in.

Interestingly though, a *Newsweek* poll showed that most workers' biggest complaint was poor communication between themselves and managers. Sixty-four percent believed that this problem impeded their work.[10] Motorola is determined to change this. "So what we have said is that if people prefer to receive information from their superiors, then our role should be to provide the resource channels to those managers," says Steve Biedermann, director of employee communications. "The only way to make a company's vision and objectives sink in to employees is through face-to-face dialogue. It is a matter of managers sitting down with the people reporting to them perhaps armed with a supplemental videotape that provides a consistent message across the corporation."

Personal communication is getting more important for every new generation entering the workforce. Research that Ericsson's human resources director of Denmark, Anders Boysen, conducted showed that his younger employees were clearly disenchanted. "We invited all the young people to a meeting where we asked them about how to improve the work. Information and communication were the main issues. The young people didn't feel that middle managers were informative enough." Boysen is even finding that younger employees are listing this as their reason for leaving Ericsson during the exit interviews he holds. "Many times the reason for quitting is a lack of communication with their managers." Training and supporting line managers and supervisors to be communicators ensures that communication is based on the communication needs of employees rather than just on senior managers' self-interested needs to convey or withhold messages that may merely benefit them.

The obvious risk with the cascade is that information will get stuck at the middle-management level, distorted and drained of content. Analogous to the "telephone game," there is always the risk of distortion when information is passed along multiple channels. To avoid this problem, the cascade can be supported with a videotaped message from the CEO to start the meetings, facilitators who help guide the meetings, and presentation slides and talking points to be used by the leader of the group. But more importantly, managers need to be provided with the information, time, resources, and training to communicate effectively. Ericsson makes communication skills a key criterion in hiring and promoting its managers. It even puts communication-challenged managers on a separate career track. Young aspiring employees are offered a choice between two career tracks: management or technical specialist. Both routes are of equal status and salary. Employees attend seminars that explain the tracks, in which great emphasis is placed on the communication skills required of people who choose the management track. "The problem we had was that middle managers were skilled engineers that have been promoted without much consideration to their communication skills," states Anders Boysen. He now administers rigorous assessments using psychologists and Ericsson managers to profile employees and counsel them on the appropriate track to choose. Once people with the right communication skills have been selected for the management track, they are provided ongoing communication training. "We base promotions on communication skills like never before," says Boysen. Ericsson's investment in dual career tracks has paid off in multiple ways. Not only does the company get the most communication-skilled people for management jobs, the techies are allowed to grow and excel in their technical fields without the burden of managerial responsibilities and the hassle of interacting with other human beings.

Virtual Vertical Communications

Communication cascades of face-to-face meetings need to be supplemented with instantaneous digital communications. One of the largest business units of Hewlett-Packard, for instance, is accelerating vertical communications with a web-based news service called The Edge. The sales force of HP's Software and Services Group receives late-breaking news every day on its screen savers. Whenever the computer is idle for a moment, the five most important news items for the day will appear on the screen. "Our technical supplier, PointCast, calls it 'unobtrusive push,'" explains Bill Hornung, managing editor of The Edge, and gives a background: "We researched our salespeople and found that their most pressing need was to get consistent information to help proactively serve customers." Customer focus groups confirmed this finding: "knowledgeable salespeople" was their number one requirement of the sales process. The electronic news service was created in response to this need.

An editorial board of two writers and an editor convenes every day to discuss upcoming stories. "We go through what is happening in HP, the news releases we send out, and internal documents," says Hornung. His team also scavenges the marketplace for relevant information. "Our focus is on information about our main clients and competitors." The Edge features top lines of the major stories of the day. "It's very brief write-ups that can be read in thirty seconds," comments Hornung, adding, "It offers information that they need to know that day, and they can click to links to get more information." The salespeople will increasingly be able to customize their news updates, for instance, to get information about their particular client companies. The response from the sales force has been overwhelmingly positive. Says Bill Hornung, "Ninety percent of the employees use it daily, 72 percent use information from the service to help prepare for customer contacts, which is exactly what we hoped to accomplish." The system will be offered more broadly at HP in the future to reach all part-time communicators instantaneously, and get them to speak in one informed voice to the customers. The powerful combination of high-tech vehicles like HP's The Edge, and high-touch ones such as the communications cascade support each other synergistically in bridging the vertical communications gap.

Bottoms Up!

The more difficult challenge with vertical communications is to assure that untarnished information is relayed up the organization, giving senior managers direct access to the front-line workers who know the customers and the operations firsthand. Management thinker Russell Ackoff illustrates the absence of bottom-up communications with the true story of a team of workers that received an award for implementing an improvement that saved its company millions of dollars every year. Ackoff asked the workers when they got the idea for the improvement, and they responded, "Eight years ago." When a baffled Ackoff asked why they had waited for so long to suggest it, the workers responded, "The bastards never asked." At the end of the day, the responsibility for integrating bottom-up communications lands squarely on the mahogany desks of the "bastards" at the top. The triumvirate of the CEO, senior management team, and board of directors needs to instigate ongoing processes of both face-to-face dialogue and instantaneous online communications with employees. The litmus test of effective bottom-up communications is how long it takes for bad news to reach senior management. It used to take months in the Production Century. The best world-class companies now have it down to minutes.

D2D recognizes the value of bottom-up communications through "doughnut meetings." General managers call together a small group of seven to ten people in an area where they would naturally sit down and have coffee. They provide coffee and doughnuts and talk about anything and everything. The only D2D site that takes exception to these meetings is the one in Aston, U.K., which holds "scotch on the rocks" meetings instead! "We try to get a natural communication going so that people actually open up about what issues and concerns they have so we can better understand their problem," explains Dayvon Goodsell. During the conversation, the general manager asks questions of employees and encourages them to speak candidly. The key to the success of such meetings is that the managers remain open and honest. "People are not stupid, they see when there is a sense that there is a 'management speech,' or 'corp talk,' going on." This is a more formal way of practicing MBWA (Management by Walking Around), which was invented by HP founder Dave Packard, who described it this way: "Straightforward as it sounds, there are some subtleties and requirements that go with MBWA. It needs to be frequent, friendly, unfocused, and unscheduled—but far from pointless. And since its principal aim is to seek out people's thoughts and opinions, it requires good listening."

Another bottom-up communication device at D2D is an electronic suggestion system. "The objective is to change a thousand things by one percent instead of one thing by one thousand percent. It doesn't matter how small your idea is. The point is to take lots of little steps instead of a giant leap," explains Anna Birchall, marketing communications manager. E-mail is a powerful bottom-up channel at HP. Says Public Relations Director Mary Ann Easley, "The CEO gets e-mail messages constantly from employees—complaints, suggestions. All you have to do is write his name. He answers them personally or else he asks somebody that has the answer to respond to them." E-mail is providing a rapid bottom-up channel from the front line.

Bottom-up communication with new hires is particularly important because they provide an objective, outside perspective. When Jackie Karlsson was hired as marketing communications manager at Ericsson U.K., she was surprised to find that her new employer didn't take advantage of her previous job experience. "People come in with wonderful experience from other companies, and then get sucked in to Ericsson and we don't know what they have done before." She has changed that now, by instituting thorough induction seminars. "We are taking a step further now and looking at the whole induction process, how people are looked after in the first months," explains Karlsson. She is in the process of setting up a competitive intelligence system, with a comprehensive database of employees' work histories, including which employees used to work for specific competitors or customer companies in the past. These employees can then be contacted about areas they are familiar with and provide their input.

Employee satisfaction surveys are an important bottom-up vehicle. They allow upper management to act upon the ideas and suggestions of the people who are closest to the customers. They are also a leading indicator of changing customer satisfaction. Research by Xerox shows that when employee satisfaction increases, customer satisfaction increases with it.[11] Xerox has taken employee surveys to higher levels with its "360-degree feedback process," where every manager is evaluated by peers, superiors, and subordinates, thus facilitating bottom-up, top-down, and horizontal communications all in one. A human resource professional collects the feedback, analyzes it, and presents it individually to each manager in a constructive manner. Used correctly, it becomes a powerful means of communication in all directions.

Eastman uses informal surveys with a panel of workers, for ongoing bottom-up communication. Explains Martha Lawson, internal communications manager, "We have people that are called area personnel representatives and they know all the rumors—they know what people's concerns are. So I have an informal network of them." She continues, "It is not unusual for them to send me a note or call and say that 'we heard people voice concerns about this.' So that is another example of ways that we raise issues or concerns and make our management aware of them." She also conducts focus groups among plant operators. One example of an enlightening focus group session was related to one of the company's major corporate objectives, rapid globalization. "We had no idea that the operators were threatened by it—that they thought this meant they would lose their jobs. So we were able, through those focus groups, to quickly identify the concern and address it." These and other means of bottom-up communications tap into the creative powers of rank-and-file workers, treating them not as a cost to be controlled but an asset to be developed.

Driving Out a Negative Work AtmosFEAR

Facilitating bottom-up communications goes much deeper than the mechanical processes of meetings and surveys. It requires an open atmosphere, free of fear of punishment from speaking up. At Saturn, it's management's job to encourage employees to provide honest feedback and input. "We are trying to create an atmosphere where there is no such thing as a bad idea. You reward them for ideas and sometimes reward them for mistakes. 'Hey, we all thought that would work,' or 'It didn't work this time but we tried,'" reflects Don Hudler. Hewlett-Packard's Mary Ann Easley believes this type of openness helps make people more productive. "We are very honest to each other. There is almost no game playing. We are all much too busy to be bothered with that sort of thing. So, while we disagree pretty regularly on things, none of us minds giving up and saying 'I was wrong this time,' and moving on." Ericsson has taken a step toward more open communication by reversing the burden of proof regarding what information can be publicized and shared with all employees. Instead of assuming that all information is confidential and having to prove that it's not in order to publicize it, managers need to prove that something would be damaging to the company in order to classify it. Ericsson actually has a written policy which states that its 95,000 employees worldwide have the right to be kept informed of any relevant company information before or at least concurrent with the time it becomes public information.

Contrary to the conventional wisdom these days that lifelong job security is a thing of the past, it's a reoccurring perk among world-class companies that have found it to be the fastest route to dispelling any fears of speaking out. Their employees can communicate more openly and freely with the assurance that their opinions aren't going to put their jobs on the line. Hewlett-Packard's commitment to a non-layoff policy was put to the test during the 1970 recession when it had 10 percent too many employees. Instead of laying off one of every ten workers, everyone in the company took every other Friday off without pay. In the fall of 1998, HP made a similar request of middle and senior managers. Two thousand four hundred of them were asked to take a three-month pay cut to help the company cut costs. One of those managers, Marlene Somsak, feels it's important to take the good with the bad. "Most of us have been able to put nice down payments on homes and had great holidays as a result of the success of this company and we expect more of the same in the future."[12] Saturn and Federal Express have lifetime job guarantees as well. As this book is being written, Saturn is in the process of cutting down its production by 17 percent. But instead of laying people off, it is sending workers to training classes and improving manufacturing processes. The management of HP, Saturn, and FedEx have sent a powerful signal that they trust employees strongly enough that they commit to keep them for life.

W. Edwards Deming, the all-time quality guru, was an ardent advocate of creating trust by stamping out fear in organizations. He took a lot of heat for that position. But much of the critique stems from confusion about what kind of fear he was referring to. Intel's CEO Andy Grove points out in his book *Only the Paranoid Survive*[13] that fear—even to the level of paranoia—of competition and of not satisfying customers is healthy and keeps companies from growing complacent. But fear of being reprimanded for communicating openly is something entirely different. A "shoot the messenger" attitude will shut everyone up, paralyze the organization, and isolate managers. The only remedy against such fear is open debate and tolerance of criticism.

Without trust, problems and mistakes don't get discussed and addressed. "If we can trust our employees to build nuclear reactors, we should be able to trust that they manage their own work time," says Kjell Morlin, quality director of ABB Atom. He picked up an employee newsletter and read, "It is totally okay to make mistakes but it's wrong to hide them. They need to come up on the table so we can avoid them next time." Morlin grinned and asked me to guess who made the statement, then quickly answered his own question. "This quote is from Göte Knutson, a plant floor worker and twenty-five-year veteran of ABB Atom." That's how deep the commitment to open communication runs at this company. Everyone at ABB Atom knows that a company that never makes mistakes isn't trying hard enough. But a company that is repeating the same mistakes isn't communicating hard enough.

An audit of the communications climate is a good way of identifying barriers to open communications and setting a baseline for improvements. Quantitative and qualitative surveys of employees can include the following questions:

How well do immediate supervisors, divisional management, and senior management listen to ideas and suggestions and keep employees informed?

How open do you as an employee feel you can be to express your opinions without fear of punishment?

Do managers speak openly and honestly about issues even if it's bad news? The audit can help many managers realize how their rampant, subtle, or unspoken censorship is hampering open communication, killing fertile ideas, and silencing the voice of the customer.

No Perestroika without Glasnost

No example is more revealing of the power of open communications than the fall of the Soviet Union. Regardless of the present turmoil in Russia, Mikhail Gorbachev had it right: You cannot have perestroika (reconstruction) without glasnost (openness or transparency). The former Soviet leader brought about the fall of the communist regime by allowing freedom of speech. Once people were free to express their opinions and voice criticism, there was no turning back for the reform movement. Glasnost is as important for corporations as it is for nations. Yet few companies allow, let alone encourage, open discussions about problems. People report only the good news up and send management propaganda down the ranks. To the extent that even bad news reaches senior management levels, it has been so drained of content that any sense of urgency is lost, and most information that is sent down the organization is so sanitized that employees discount it. Most of what pass as employee communication publications are the equivalents of the Soviet newspaper *Pravda,* with a focus on corporate puffery and management happy talk, instead of information designed to build a broad base understanding of, and a debate around, the organization's goals. This Soviet-style approach to communication is still surprisingly prevalent. But change is underway. Tyranny is no longer possible to sustain at a time when communication is instantaneous. Corporate censorship is not an option anymore. Having experienced the fall of most dictatorships around the world, we are now witnessing the fall of autocratic corporations. Managers are beginning to open lines of communication and tapping into the reservoir of employees' latent ideas, talent, and commitment.

So if you find yourself in a meeting where your CEO stands up and yells "We're bankrupt!" the way Philips's CEO did, act surprised. Let it be your secret that he or she got the idea from this book. Whether one exaggerates their company's present situation the way Timmer did to light a fire under peoples' butts, or whether their company is truly in crisis, the secret is in facilitating open and honest top-down and bottom-up communications before one's company is on the brink of bankruptcy. Lines of communication between the periphery where the action is and the center where the buck stops need to be open, candid, and instantaneous. But that's just half the battle. The real payoff comes from communicating with the same speed and agility across departments, disciplines, and regions of the firm, which is the focus of the next chapter. It explores how world-class companies leverage the skills, expertise, relationships, and information of the entire enterprise through the integration of horizontal communications.

What to Do Tuesday Morning:

• Assign a team of people from different functions, ranks, and nationalities the task of creating the company's future by developing a vision and a brand promise. A draft should be presented to the senior management team and discussed with progressively lower levels of the organization before it's finalized.

• Use any opportunity to communicate the vision of the company, and the key messages, tone, look, and personality of the company's brand(s). Encourage senior managers to set personal examples that illustrate the vision, and communicate these corporate legends informally and formally through the organization.

• Set up a cascading process of personal communication by immediate managers and an infrastructure of electronic communications for direct communication to keep all employees informed about important company news.

• Set up a system of ongoing bottom-up communications through employee surveys, electronic communications, suggestions schemes, an open-door policy, and regular mandated management-employee meetings.

• Train managers to become communicators, and incorporate communication skills in hiring, evaluating, and promoting managers.

• Institute training in areas that are central to the vision of the company, which is cascaded down from the top, thereby securing commitment and involvement from all management levels.

> • Conduct an audit of the communications climate. Use a combination of qualitative survey techniques such as focus groups and one-on-one interviews, and quantitative survey methods to a larger number of employees.

Notes

1. Philips Semiconductors breaking with the past, 1996, case from London Business School, LBS-CS96-040
2. Kets de Vries, Manfred F. R. (1994). *Percy Barnevik: The Corporate Transformation Wizard. An Interview.* Fontainebleau, France: European Case Clearing House, p. 10.
3. Kets de Vries, Manfred F. R. (1993). *Percy Barnevik and ABB.* Fontainebleau, France: European Case Clearing House, p. 17.
4. Taylor, William, (1991). "The Logic of Global Business: An Interview with ABB's Percy Barnevik." *Harvard Business Review*, March–April, p. 104.
5. Kets de Vries, Manfred F. R. (1998). "Charisma in Action: The Transformational Abilities of Virgin's Richard Branson and ABB's Percy Barnevik." *Organizational Dynamics*, No. 3, Vol. 26, p. 6.
6. Allaire, Paul A. (1998). *Lessons in Teamwork, in Navigating Change.* Edited by Donald C. Hambrick, David A. Nadler, and Michael L. Tushman. Boston, Mass.: Harvard Business School Press, p. 119.
7. *Fortune*, January 11, 1999, pp. 118–44.
8. U.S. News & World Report, May, 1995, cited in Motorola B. Harvard Business School Case Study, 9-996-052.
9. Motorola B. *Harvard Business School Case Study, 9-996-052.*
10. *Newsweek* August 12, 1997
11. Carey, Robert (1995). "Coming around to 360-Degree Feedback." *Incentive*, March, pp. 56–60.
12. Taylor, Roger (1998). "Silicon Valley Shrugs Off Hard Times." *Financial Times*, August 1.
13. Andrew S. Grove (1996). *Only the Paranoid Survive.* New York: Doubleday.

4

THIRD DIMENSION

Integrating Horizontal Communications

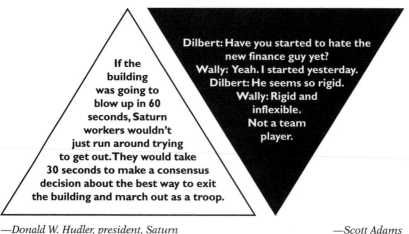

If the building was going to blow up in 60 seconds, Saturn workers wouldn't just run around trying to get out. They would take 30 seconds to make a consensus decision about the best way to exit the building and march out as a troop.

Dilbert: Have you started to hate the new finance guy yet?
Wally: Yeah. I started yesterday.
Dilbert: He seems so rigid.
Wally: Rigid and inflexible. Not a team player.

—*Donald W. Hudler, president, Saturn*

—*Scott Adams*

It was the second time the Rank-Xerox team got together. The six members had flown to its headquarters in Marlow, U.K., from six different European countries. The meeting was intense. The facilitator could hardly keep up with the notes he was making on the flip chart during the lively debate. Arms were moving, feet were stomping, heads were nodding, and faces were frowning, as ideas ricocheted off the walls. The team members became more and more fired up about an emerging marketing strategy to launch a new line of copying machines.

Everyone except Nicole, who quietly disagreed with the strategy. By the end of the afternoon, Nicole broke her silence. With a cracked voice and her hands slightly shaking with nervousness, she suggested an alternative strategy. The other team members sighed with frustration. They began twisting and turning and demonstrably looking at their watches. But the team leader asked everyone to pay attention. The facilitator made notes of Nicole's comments on the flip chart. Everyone knew that they had to come up with a consensus decision. Such are the rules at Xerox. Nicole had her veto power, like anyone else on the team. They knew that their job would not be done until they had arrived at a solution that everyone, including Nicole, would be comfortable with.

Holding her ground, Nicole continued to make her case more forcefully, now standing up. Slowly, the other members started to ask probing questions and began to nod in agreement. Two hours later, there was a begrudging consensus around a new marketing strategy—no mean feat for marketing people, a group of professionals known for their lengthy blather and strong egos. On the way out from the conference room, the teammates came up to congratulate Nicole for steering the team to a new strategy.[1]

Teamwork at Xerox

Teamwork is more than empty rhetoric at the Document Company. It is the modus operandi. But it wasn't always that way, as Xerox's corporate communications director, Dr. Joseph Cahalan, a twenty-five-plus-year veteran of the company explains. "It used to be that if I was in a meeting with somebody from Sweden and somebody from Brazil, and somebody in finance and somebody in the law department, we had a terrible time communicating, not because of language, but just because of very different thought processes, very different ways of approaching it." Today, everyone at Xerox is trained to use the same tools and methods. If there is ever any doubt in a member's mind, they just need to look around the walls of any Xerox conference room to see the framed posters featuring the "ground rules" for teamwork, the "problem-solving process," the "quality improvement process," and the "decision-making tools" (figure 4.1). Says Cahalan, "And those are almost second nature to people now. In fact, sometimes we will be just sitting around, dealing with something. And someone says, 'Wait a minute, hold it, what is the problem we are trying to solve,' which is the first step of the process." These structured problem-solving methods provide teams a road map to follow, restraining them from jumping directly from the problem to implementing a solution. "It gives you a common language, a common approach to dealing with issues. It has made an incredible difference," comments Cahalan. "You could talk for days at each other and not be able to get together. Now, within minutes, you may still have problems but everybody is addressing them in the same way."

Problem-Solving Process

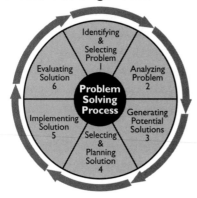

Figure 4.1. Xerox's six-step "problem-solving process," which is posted at every Xerox conference room around the world.

Another secret behind Xerox's teamwork success is to define every team member's role. Members of Xerox's teams are assigned the roles of *facilitator*, responsible for aiding discussions; *team leader*, directing the project; *scribe* to take notes; *timekeeper*, responsible for seeing that an appropriate amount of time is spent on each agenda item and starting and ending meetings on time; and—my favorite—*behavioral checker*, whose job it is to make sure that no one dominates the meeting, everyone's opinions are being heard, and everyone is an active listener. At most corporations, the only universal language is financial accounting. Companies like Xerox have developed a much more dynamic team- and process-oriented universal language. Xerox's chairman and CEO, Paul Allaire, finds that "effective teamwork harnesses creativity and unleashes brain power; it leads to better solutions, better decisions, and improved business results through more effective implementation."[2] And it's the engine of horizontal communications.

Integrated horizontal communications is at the heart of integrated communications, because few customers go shopping for a company with really innovative R&D, knockout finance, efficient operations, or creative advertising. Instead, they look for good service, leading-edge products, and reputable brands. What really matter to customers are the core processes—the chain of events in which value is added—that cut straight across functions and departments. Examples are: taking and delivering an order, bringing a new product to market, offering responsive customer service, and labeling the service offering with a brand customers trust. This process view requires a change in perspective, from a vertical to a horizontal view.

The problem with most organizations is that processes are not managed with the same care as functions. As a result, cross-functional processes are left to happenstance. The designers design a new product, engineers change it, operations makes it, the bean counters price it, marketing promotes it, sales sells it, finance collects payments, and customer service returns it. Integrated horizontal communications reverses this flow. It starts from the "outside in," feeding information about the customer's needs back through the value chain of order fulfillment, manufacturing or operations, and finally to R&D. This horizontal integration of the value chain becomes even more important for service providers like FedEx and ISS where meticulous timing is required and some steps are done simultaneously. The third dimension of *integrated horizontal communications* is illustrated in figure 4.2. It links and leverages skills, assets, and processes, by opening up a free flow of communications across departments, business units, and regions of the organization. It bridges the inherent conflicts between aligning the organization with customers and developing core competencies, between functional excellence and cross-functional synergies, between maximal coordination between business units and minimal corporate overhead, and between localization and globalization. The secret to horizontal integration is in establishing effective teamwork processes, facilitating "virtual communities of practice," and systematically rotating people among job assignments.

3rd Dimension:
Horizontal Integration

Figure 4.2. The third dimension of integrated communications: Integrating horizontal communications at all levels of the organization across departments, business units, and regions.

Linking Core Processes from the Top

Horizontal communications takes place at all levels of world-class companies, starting at the board level. The way the board manages horizontal processes and works like a team sets a precedent for middle management, which is where the brunt of horizontal communications rests. It's the middle managers who support the front-line units by making the collective resources and capabilities of the company available to them, and by continually keeping the knowledge flowing and growing in the company. Xerox assigns senior managers additional responsibilities for core processes of leadership, human resources, customer and market focus, and quality management tools, on top of their daily functional responsibilities like marketing and finance. The Document Company has forty-two measures for horizontal processes that senior managers are accountable for. Figure 4.3 shows the processes and how they are linked. "The CEO chose three of the process to champion: diversity, communication and empowerment," notes Cahalan. "So it automatically elevates communications to the place where it should be." Combining vertical and horizontal structures enables an organization to enjoy both the depth of specialized knowledge that vertical structure facilitates and the synergistic collaborative thinking that horizontal structure provides.

Horizontal process responsibilities need to be assigned at both senior and middle management levels. Take the case of John Jakobsen of Danfoss. In addition to being the company's quality manager, he is a "gatekeeper" for quality function deployment, a

Xerox Management Model

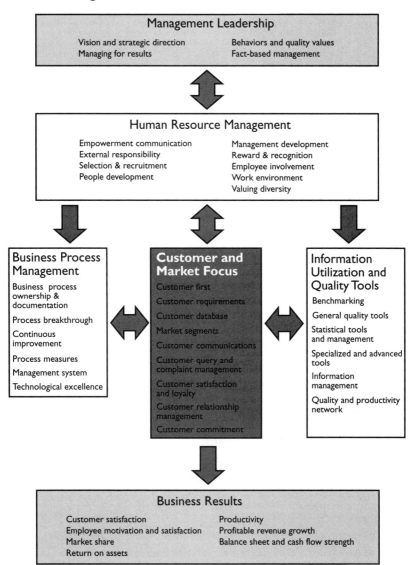

Figure 4.3. The horizontal management processes at Xerox.

method of addressing customer needs in new product development. The task of being a gatekeeper involves disseminating and implementing a core competency that cuts across departments. The senior management team of Danfoss developed an interest in quality function deployment several years ago. It assigned a team of managers from different business units to learn more about it. Later, quality function deployment was elevated to a core competency. "I had spent the most time on it so I was named the gatekeeper," says Jakobsen. "That's how methods and technology are introduced to Danfoss." Other middle managers at Danfoss are gatekeepers for engineering areas that have applications for all the business units. Stainless steel technology, for instance, is so important that it has four gatekeepers. Each gatekeeper is supported by a team of people from different business units. In addition, the gatekeepers have senior officers as their "sponsors." Jakobsen explains, "If the gatekeeper can't get through with his message, he can go to his sponsor and say 'You have more stars on your shoulders, can you help me make people listen to this?'"

Employees from different business units can convene in a building called "Room for Visions" at Danfoss's headquarters campus in southern Denmark to develop core competencies and other emerging areas that haven't yet been elevated to core competencies. "The rooms are equipped with computer group ware for teams to make notes or drawings together," says Vibeke Gustafsson, head of technology management. For example, one of the teams works on coordinating the company's Internet presence. Some of the team rooms are set up with computer group ware. The teams sometimes bring in professional artists to create visual representations of ideas. Using these methods, Danfoss has institutionalized horizontal processes of communication across functions and business units.

Teamwork—Like Riding a Bike

The team is where the rubber of horizontal communications really meets the road. Companies like Xerox and Saturn have found cross-functional teams to be the real engines of horizontal communications. Although they represent entirely different industries, they both manage teamwork in similar ways. Both of these world-class companies have discovered that teamwork is a skill that has to be taught and practiced by everyone in an organization. Unfortunately, schools and universities don't prepare people to work in teams. "In fact, as a variety of educational theorists have observed, most classroom experiences teach students the very reverse. From the earliest grades on, students learn to primarily value individual successes," reflects Brett Robs, a professor at University of

Colorado. As a result, most teams operate below the lowest IQ of the group. Companies like Saturn spend tremendous efforts on remedial teamwork training. The carmaker has found that teamwork training is most effective when work units go through training together. Saturn has teamwork training courses ranging from Outward Bound classes—where the team members help each other climb a thirty-foot pole, turn 180 degrees on a rotating platform, jump off and ring a bell—to courses on conflict resolution, consensus decision-making, assertive listening, transactional leadership, and team dynamics.

All of the world-class companies have similar teamwork processes that are engrained at every business level. These processes involve mutual respect, recognizing individual strengths and weaknesses, setting definite time limits for meetings, and keeping egos in check. Having set rules and guidelines streamlines projects from beginning to end. The mainstay of Saturn's team training is the four development stages of a team: forming, storming, norming, and performing.

1. Forming

The selection of team members with complementary skills is one of the most critical decisions of a successful project. Not only should all of the major areas of expertise be represented, there should also be diversity in terms of, for example, analytical versus creative skills. "If you select team members that are in your own image, you will not have the diversity you need in order to cover all your bases," comments Mike O'Neill, Eastman Chemical Company's communications director. "If you have people who think alike, you don't need a team." Before the team members are selected, there should be an assessment of what technical skills are necessary. The team also needs a clear mandate. A common problem with cross-functional teams is that they can't implement projects because they cut across the normal lines of authority. "The task force needs to be endorsed by senior management ... tied into support structures higher up," asserts former FedEx marketing manager Robert Hamilton. The team needs to be empowered to act on its plans. This is an essential element of successful horizontal communications. Cross-functional teams must be given decision-making authority and be allowed to see projects through from inception to completion.

2. Storming

Storming is the most emotionally turbulent stage of development, because although members have gotten to know each other, they have not yet come to trust each other. It's the time when leadership roles are established in the team. Rather than being a strong-willed despot, the leader's role is to facilitate group processes to make sure that the work in the team progresses according to preset timelines. "You don't have a team leader per se. You may have someone who has the coordinating responsibilities but everybody has an equal status among the team," says Eastman's O'Neill. His colleague, Martha Lawson, describes the role of team leader as a "steward of processes." The leader of the team is not necessarily the most senior person on the team, but the person with the best technical expertise and skills to guide the process smoothly and efficiently. The team leader task is rotated among all of the employees at Eastman. Says O'Neill, "And it is not like you have to struggle with other team leaders. They are going to be team leaders next week. They are pulling together, pulling for each other."

A number of the senior-level managers I interviewed told me about teams they were members of that were led by members several steps below them in the organizational pecking order. The leadership role may even be split up between a team leader who is responsible for the content of the meetings and a facilitator who is responsible for guiding productive discussions. The facilitator is not necessarily a permanent member of the team. Xerox trains a corps of facilitators at all levels of the organization who are called in to drive discussions during critical parts of team projects.

3. Norming

Having established a leadership structure that fosters collaboration, the team is then able to set up a series of ground rules or norms. While many of the rules concern issues such as regular attendance, being on time, and meeting deadlines, the most important ones focus on the decision-making process. At Saturn, consensus decision-making is the law. That doesn't mean that everyone loves every decision. But it does mean that everyone can live with every decision. Most world-class companies use some version of Saturn's 70/100 rule. Saturn's public relations manager, Greg

Martin, explains: "We ask that everybody is 70 percent comfortable with every decision. Once you get to 70 percent and the decision is made, you need to throw in 100 percent of your effort and enthusiasm into that decision to make it happen." Saturn also has a rule that in order to exercise your veto power, you have to offer an alternative solution. No team member is allowed to just stall decisions without offering alternatives.

Consensus building is a controversial issue with some people who find that it takes too much time and creates watered-down compromises. Organizations risk becoming mired in their own complex decision-making process of endless meetings. But the managers I interviewed strongly believed that "slower is faster," because if the group does not take time to reach a consensus, it is likely to overlook factors and be forced to go back and make extensive revisions. Saturn's president, Don Hudler, scoffed at suggestions that consensus decisions need to be more time-consuming. Drawing an analogy, he argued that if the building is going to blow up in sixty seconds, Saturn workers wouldn't just run around trying to get out. They would take thirty seconds to make a consensus decision about the best way to exit the building and march out as a troop! "We have trained people how to reach consensus decisions even under time pressure," Hudler explains. One time-saver is to focus on obtaining consensus on a broad framework and then let individuals or individual units work out implementation details. "What that eliminates," states Motorola's employee communications manager Steve Biedermann, "is a whole lot of wordsmithing and consensus building that doesn't buy us anything." Hudler sees a number of benefits of consensus decision-making. "It allows different people to put forth their strength and expertise. Often times it is the least likely person in the group that will come up with the best solutions. You have to put egos aside." And since everyone is involved in the process and has provided their input, the decisions are more likely to be implemented successfully. "When people feel they are a part of it, they will work harder for it to be successful," comments Hudler.

The other line of critique against consensus decision-making is that the teams gravitate toward lowest common denominators, rather than agreeing on great ideas. Teams start compromising, where 1+1=1.5, instead of seeking a synergistic solution where 1+1=3. The secret is in communication. Team members need good listening skills, which don't come easily to most U.S. managers, who usually don't find other people's ideas nearly as compelling as their own. Studies show that American managers put forward their own ideas nine times for every time they put forth someone else's idea.[3] Saturn and Eastman Chemical Company are both determined to buck that ratio. Saturn's ground rules for teamwork includes such tidbits as "checking egos at the door." Eastman's team leaders are taught to be sensitive to team members' personalities. "You'll have people that will always dominate and have others who are more reflective. The team leader makes it a point to probe the more quiet team members and encourage them to participate," explains Mike O'Neill. ABB chairman Percy Barnevik goes a step further, by arguing that "you have to encourage dissenters." This participative leadership approach helps unleash people's potential, harness their energy, and multiply their talent by involving everyone in the team.

4. Performing

The forming, storming, and norming stages are necessary preludes to the final performing stage when the team begins to kick butt. All team members come prepared and in time for every meeting. They agree on a clear, realistic agenda in the beginning of each meeting, which indicates how much time should be spent on each agenda item. The agenda also distinguishes brainstorming, information, and decision items. Information items are kept brief. Some units of Ericsson even have "stand-up meetings" every morning. Participants are not even allowed to sit down during these ten-minute meetings, to keep them brief and emphasize that the purpose is to share information. When brainstorming is on the agenda, on the other hand, plenty of time is scheduled and no one is allowed to criticize anyone else's ideas.

There is no shortcut to the performing stage. Any team that tries to skip any of the previous three steps will find itself caught up in them later on. But through training, teams can zip through the stages in a meeting or two. Without these hard-earned skills, teams may never get there, no matter how good their intentions. Through the rigor of team communication, companies can effectively draw on multiple talents and perspectives. The team process is not just a political tool to create "buy-in" with key players, but is a powerful way of creating value and communication horizontally in the organization.

Bringing Everyone on Board

A common problem with team projects is that a single individual or small group creates the project objectives and strategies and brings in team members as needed to flesh out these decisions and execute them. As a result, the teams go through the forming, storming, norming, and performing stages again and again—having to repeat them every time new people are brought on board. As Robert Linder, video production manager from Allen-Bradley, puts it, "If there is anything that is the most important thing, it is you have to start the process early. You can't bring people in later on, because any decision at all—even a decision that seems very minor [in the early stage] can have very large effects on the outcome." Although the process of reaching consensus around goals and strategies is not simple, it is better to involve everyone early on and deal with differences of opinion at that time. "That's the time to resolve issues," says Jerry Houston, marketing communications director at Allen-Bradley. "Disagreements about fundamentals at a later date can bring work to a standstill." Just as importantly, when team members are involved in all of the decisions right from the start, they are more committed to the project and its goals. "No one wants to be just an implementer and think that I am this tactical moron that doesn't get to think big," notes Hewlett-Packard's marketing communications director, Arlene King. Bringing everyone on board right away makes them feel like cathedral builders rather than stonecutters.

A case in point of early involvement of all communications functions is the planning that took place at Hewlett-Packard for the launch of a new laser printer. Traditionally, the sales promotion professionals got involved about eighteen months before the launch of a new product because of its longer lead time. The advertising people didn't get involved until six months before the launch, and marketing public relations three months later. As a result, sales promotion experts developed sales support material that they "threw over the wall" to the ad department, which developed an ad campaign that was in turn "thrown over the wall" to the PR people who would crank up a media event. This sequential approach effectively prevented any synergies from occurring between the disciplines. "In sales promotion we would think of a four-page brochure that the ad people couldn't condense to a one-page ad," notes Dorothy Fitzgerald, sales promotion manager. Marketing communications was an afterthought, which wasn't sufficiently integrated with other pieces of the process. However, in the particular launch of a new laser printer, a team of advertising, sales promotions, and public relations managers got involved about eighteen months before the launch. They spent several days off-site with the product development team, "to immerse themselves with research so they could almost speak as in-depth about the product and its customers as the product manager," comments Arlene King. This early involvement gave marketing communications specialists input to strategic decisions of target audience, key message, and positioning. They found that the product development team had defined the target audience too broadly. "This is frequently the case that product managers want the product to be all things to all people and you end up with a laundry basket of messages," claims Lori Ode, advertising manager at the Laser Print Division, "so we helped them to focus the ideas."

The team spent about two months working on the communications strategy, meeting as a team two to three times a week. It then presented its draft of the creative brief at a joint meeting with its advertising and sales promotion agencies, which developed the creative ideas of the advertising and the sales promotion together. This strategic role of marketing communications was new to HP. "In the past, if we were trying to sell sushi, we would market it as a cold dead fish," admits Bojana Fazarinc, corporate marketing communications director. Developing all communications pieces concurrently this way, rather than sequentially, facilitates better integration. It is the only way to develop great big ideas that will work well in all promotional channels.

Working as a team from day one sets the stage for a zero-based approach to any problem. "I think before any decision is made, before there is any preconceived notion of what this will look like or even what the objective of it is, you have to get all the people together that are going to participate," says Robert Linder. "You need a blank sheet of paper and a stated objective, and then whatever tools make the most sense is what needs to be used. In other words, the discussion doesn't start off with 'I have written a script, would you like to read it?'" That is not to say that the team should not build on past experience, but neither should it build plans on erroneous assumptions and conventions. One way to transfer learning from one project to the next is to involve the entire team in a thorough and honest evaluation, which is then communicated broadly in the organization. HP teams always go through a debriefing process for every project so they can learn from their mistakes and identify actions worth repeating. Arlene King explains the rationale for these sessions. "You sit together for a day after the project, you complain about us and we complain about you. We discuss what went well and what we need to do better. How can we learn from it?" After these grueling sessions, the team members all go out for dinner to celebrate their achievements as a reward. Says King, "What I hope to accomplish is that information gets cross-fertilized to the other people [who are not on the project team]. So that if you learn a real nugget about the advertising method in that particular project that didn't go well, the other people in advertising will think 'gosh, I will never step in that hole' because they learn from others' mistakes and proceed differently on future projects." This process has helped turn HP into a learning organization that constantly seeks to share knowledge and improve itself, while still starting each new project with a clean slate.

Celebrating Teamwork

When it comes to creating a corporate teamwork culture, Motorola and Xerox are in a league of their own. They don't just practice teamwork, they celebrate it. Xerox organizes a huge "Teamwork Day" once a year, simultaneously at its main manufacturing facilities in El Segundo, Dallas, Rochester, and London, where outstanding teams receive recognition and their stories are told. The event is broadcast live on the company's internal network to about 30,000 Xerox employees at ninety-five sites around the word. Managers get to participate only by invitation from employee committees that oversee the event. "It is a huge deal; it is almost like a Xerox holiday," assures Cahalan, who describes it as "a cross between a professional conference, a trade fair, and a revival meeting."

Motorola has followed Xerox's lead. As many as five thousand teams involving 65,000 of Motorola's 142,000-plus employees take part in the qualifying contests leading up to its version of Team Day.[4] "It's a recognition tool," says Steve Biedermann of Motorola. Every team gets twelve minutes to present a project, and teams are judged by the results they accomplish as well as the creativity of their initiatives. The winners go to a "division-level" competition and later to a "sector-level" competition. The finalist teams go to the "World-Wide Total Customer Satisfaction Team Competition" held in January of every year. There is a carnival atmosphere at this one-day event. It's led by a master of ceremonies who is assisted by a puppet named Max Databurst, Motorola's "assistant director of enthusiasm for total customer satisfaction." The show features teams from all across the world with names like the "Administrators," "Document Doctors," "The Oriental Express," and "The Boys from Bangalore." Many wear national costumes. A judging panel, made up of Motorola's top fifteen executives, awards gold and silver medals. Each team is responsible for its own presentation. Some teams introduce themselves with a video. "In a sense, we're teaching everyone in the company to become a communicator," says Biedermann. The results of the improvements are flashed on an electronic bulletin board. The winners of last year's contest, "The Green Tray Packers," wore green football jerseys. They developed standardized packaging trays for sending pagers to customers and a database for packaging requirements.

While the event is good humored, the teams' achievements are no laughing matter. The winning team alone created a cost savings of $6.1 million. All of the projects presented are based on meeting one of the company's five corporate initiatives. Recently, the competition has been extended to Motorola's suppliers. Fifty-one supplier teams competed in three regional competitions. The three winners faced off in a national competition the day before the big event of Motorola's team day.

Recognizing good teamwork doesn't have to be as grandiose as the Motorola or Xerox events. D2D, with just two thousand-plus employees, holds regular events where the president gives bronze, silver, and gold medals to individuals or teams. Anyone in the company can nominate anyone else for the awards. "We try to encourage the right sort of behavior we're looking for," comments Quality Manager Dayvon Goodsell. He is careful to point out that it is more about celebration and recognition than competition. There are no limits on the number of prizes and there's no money involved—just gifts worth $50. "We don't encourage competition where people are letting other people down. They are helping each other to improve. We don't allow situations were people snipe and say he doesn't really deserve it," adds Goodsell. ABB Sweden's corporate communications director, Roger Johansson, subscribes to the same approach of exploiting early success stories: "The heroes are important. We publicize success stories as widely as possible." His staff writes stories about successful team projects in the employee magazine and has published the book and magazine of case studies described in an earlier chapter. Putting a strong spotlight on the successful team experiences is an important part of facilitating a corporate teamwork culture.

Clearly, teamwork is the ultimate vehicle for facilitating integrated communications. It facilitates conversations across areas of expertise, cultures, and ranks. It allows organizations to integrate processes and develop new insights. Facilitating systematic teamwork requires a shift in mind-set, away from the American tradition of rugged individualism. Such a shift is particularly difficult in marketing and communications departments, where notions of individualism and self-made stars remain prevalent. But companies like Xerox, Motorola, and Saturn demonstrate that successful teamwork is possible if senior management is committed to training everyone in teamwork skills, rewarding successful teams, and setting examples by practicing teamwork in their own daily work.

Learning How the Other Half Works

An effective way to institutionalize horizontal communications is to deliberately move managers across functions, business units, and countries. This practice enables world-class companies to transfer experience, facilitate personal networks, and build pride in the company rather than just the occupational and technical specialties. "You don't just associate yourself with a particular function, a particular business unit, so I don't personally feel that I'm a 'Motorola cellular guy,' or a 'Motorola corporate guy,'" reflects Motorola's investor relations manager, Edward Gams, who has rotated through the corporate audit department, two-way radio unit, cellular infrastructure business, and cellular handset business. Giving employees the opportunity to perform various functions is mutually beneficial for the individuals and the employer. By rotating jobs, employees get a genuine sense of what's involved in other positions and departments. Production Century companies typically cast their employees in one role to perform very specific functions. The employees are never made aware of what other individuals are doing or how various departments should work together toward common goals. World-class companies, on the other hand, encourage individuals to explore many different areas. It helps the employees develop a greater respect for their coworkers, and encourages an exchange of information among various departments. "In our marketing department we move people from the technical side of marketing, to branding, to product management, to market development, to dealer relationships," says HP's Fitzgerald. We're talking anything from short-term job switches for a few weeks or months to long-term rotation. Public Relations Director Per Vagner Rasmussen argues that his thirty-four years in different positions at Danfoss have been invaluable to his job: "The advantages are knowing the company and knowing its people on a personal level." For example, when Rasmussen gets requests from journalists, he knows exactly which Danfoss manager to put them in touch with. "We know each other very well from rotating through different positions. It's a big company, but still one family."

World-class companies have formal processes to redeploy employees within the firm to encourage rotation. Some even have internal employment agencies. Employees of Eastman Chemical Company, for instance, can fill out a form that indicates what other types of jobs they would be interested in doing. When there is a job opening, the agency looks through those forms prior to looking outside of the company. "We just did four moves this month," exclaims Martha Lawson, employee communications manager. "We moved one of the guys who worked for the company newspaper into a speechwriting job; we moved a person from one of the plants who has some writing experience into the employee newspaper job; and we moved a media relations representative to be editor of an employee publication and the editor of the employee publication into the media relations job." Like Eastman, Ericsson favors internal recruits. "If I have a choice between an internal candidate for a communications position with 80 percent of the qualifications of the best external candidate, I pick the internal candidate," says Corporate Communications Director Nils Ingvar Lundin (who later moved on to assume the same position at one of Ericsson's owners, Investor), explaining: "Communications professionals need to know two things, communications *and* the Ericsson organization." The Ericsson acumen makes up for the lack of communications skills.

International rotation is becoming increasingly important in the face of a more global marketplace. "There is no substitute for line experience in three or four countries to create a global perspective," argues ABB's plain-speaking chairman, Percy Barnevik. In his experience, managers who are cross-trained in multiple countries "don't passively accept it when someone says, 'You can't do that in Italy or Spain because of the unions,' or 'You can't do that in Japan because of the Ministry of Finance.' They sort through the debris of cultural excuses and find opportunities to innovate."[5] Tough talk aside, Barnevik has a goal of developing five hundred global managers, which he thinks is an ideal number to run a company of ABB's size. American companies are slowly warming up to this idea. But a staggering 25 percent of American managers in overseas assignments are called home prematurely, which is a rate four to five times higher than that of European managers in foreign assignments.[6] Of course, sending out expatriates within technical disciplines like engineering or finance to different corners of the world is far easier, because a knowledge of local culture and language is not as critical. The international transfer of people in marketing and communications, however, is still very rare, even among world-class companies. But the need for global integrated communications is providing the impetus for a growth of communications expatriates.

The impediments to job rotation are deeply embedded in Western traditions. In contrast to the Japanese, who tend to stay loyal to the same company throughout their careers but change occupations within the company frequently, most Westerners remain loyal to their occupation throughout their lives, but change employers. Lateral moves are commonly viewed as a demotion— someone is "kicked sideways." Therefore, moving people horizontally has to be done with caution. It can only be successful if the people involved perceive the rotation as a growth opportunity, and are rewarded for switching jobs. ABB gives people a "rotation bonus" of $50–70 a month to anyone who agrees to take another position. All available positions are announced internally. Kjell Morlin doesn't think his company is going far enough, though. "I have argued that we should have an internal drafting system."

Is job rotation expensive? You bet. "But the flip side of that is, it could be expensive not to," proclaims Eastman's corporate communications director, Mike O'Neill. "Ten years from now, if you have the same people doing the same thing and you don't have the good thinking or new ideas that might occur. One good idea can save thousands of hours." World-class managers like O'Neill enable their people to experiment and explore other areas. In return, employees stay with their company for a longer period of time when they see growth potential through job rotation.

Beware of the danger of overdoing job rotation. Companies risk missing out on the fresh perspectives provided by externally recruited employees, and instead get run by an incestuous elite who are so inbred that no one would be surprised to see them with an eye in the middle of their foreheads. Another danger lies in rotation that is done too frequently—not giving people enough time to settle into a position. Says O'Neill, "You need to give people, when you are rotating, enough time to understand the basics of the organization in order that they can lend to the improvement of that operation. If you do it every year or every two years, that may be too quick." Danfoss's employee communications director, Vagn Hesselager, finds that rotation every five years is optimal. "That's a company policy. After half a year to a year, you are up to a certain level and you keep that level for about four to four and a half years. Then it goes down."

O'Neill cautions that it's important to train and prepare people for their new jobs while still allowing them to start fresh and make changes: "So, you have to say, 'here is the concept, here is what we are trying to do.' But not get into too many details that could cramp a person's innovation." The upshot: Any company that can manage systematic job rotation without overdoing it, and while combining it with appropriate training, will find it to be one of the most powerful ways to integrate communications across departments and business units.

The Impact of Office Architecture

There's more to open internal communications than the structure and rigor of formal horizontal and vertical communications. Unlike what most communications professionals would have you believe, the buzz in the hallway is where real communication takes place in any organization. The thick informal personal networks that exist in any organization are much better equipped to handle coordination than any formal mechanisms. Informal communication can be encouraged through the right physical layout of the office. As Winston Churchill once said, "We shape our buildings. After that, they shape us." Tom Holland, FedEx's former managing director of investor relations and currently managing director of finance in Asia, believes physical closeness enables more relaxed interactions. "Proximity to each other is important because if it is too much trouble to walk by, you miss a lot. Because you don't want to call people over the phone and ask 'how is it going, anything new?' So dropping by is always necessary. The phone is not as casual." The physical arrangements of the office might seem like a trivial issue, but in fact, one study found that if people are more than ten meters apart they have only a 8 to 9 percent probability of communicating at least once a week, versus a 25 percent chance at five meters.[7]

Companies like Hewlett-Packard and Saturn have literally done away with all office walls to encourage communication. "The only doors you'll find here are the restroom doors," notes HP's Dorothy Fitzgerald. Instead of being hulled up in individual offices, everyone works in a Dilbert maze of cubicles where there are plenty of shared spaces that enable teams to get together at a moment's notice. HP pioneered the open floor plan in the 1950s, when carved paneling, corner offices, and mahogany desks were fixtures of the corporate office scene. The HP offices are designed to fit around work processes, not the other way around. "Actually, when we moved into this building," shares Mary Ann Easley, "the CEO had a cubicle too. A bigger one that had a sofa in it, but still a cubicle," continues the public relations director, gesturing around her un-adorned cubicle area. Not surprisingly, some reactionaries still mourn the corporate aristocracy of the Production Century. "After a couple of years, our salespeople started to complain about bring-ing in CEOs of other *Fortune* 500 companies who have offices on Park Avenue. The outsiders come in here and think the CEO of HP is not very important," says Easley. As a result, they built something a little fancier. "But still, by corporate standards, it is very modest, and in fact, it doesn't have doors either."

The open-door policy at HP is both literal and metaphorical. Employees are encouraged to communicate freely with anyone in the company. Saturn has the same philosophy. "Many of us had worked our way up to corner offices and secretaries. We had to give all of that up to come to Saturn," notes Don Hudler, president, from his cubicle, which is literally not much larger than that of his secretary and other coworkers. His public relations manager, Greg Martin, adds, "You don't have these people that sit in these glass-encapsulated offices behind these desks, with a sixty-year-old lady protecting them. I can just pick up the phone and ask any senior manager 'Do you have five minutes?'" This philosophy of doing away with status symbols like "the corner office," and level-ing the traditional communication hierarchies where senior man-agement is off limits, plays an integral role in successful internal communications.

The Digital Architecture

Computer connectivity is developing with such unprecedented speed and unstoppable momentum that "digital architecture" is quickly becoming as important as office architecture in integrating internal communications. Intranets, internal websites for employ-ees, are emerging as the universal platform of choice. Ericsson has no fewer than 1,500 websites on its Intranet. Many of them are organized vertically around organizational units. But others are horizontal in nature, creating "communities of practice" within the company, which is a critical element of horizontal communications. A community of practice is a group of people who are informally bound together by facing the same type of problem. It's not necessarily a team or an officially identified group. They might just be performing the same job function in different parts of the organization, working on the same task, or serving the same customer. "We have sites about ISO 14001 in Ericsson, about our Internet products, standards for wireless, and business intelligence where you can find information about almost anything," explains Anders Wennersten, manager of corporate technology. He also uses e-mail notification to encourage information sharing in topic areas that cut across the organizations horizontally. "Any employee can register on any topic site and receive updates through e-mail whenever there is late-breaking news in the area." Wennersten has found that this combination of the "push" channel of e-mail and the "pull" channel of the Intranet site is the wave of the future: "We have seen a large increase in the number of people who are signing up for these services and clearly think it's the future of getting information relevant for one's job."

"I'm a big believer that the Intranet is revolutionizing employee communications big time," exclaims Cahalan. His Xerox has 400,000 hits per month by employees on its Intranet site, the Web Board. Employees of the Document Company are invited to the Web Board with these words: "Pull up a chair, take a look around and make yourself at home. This is our meeting place, a friendly home in cyberspace, where Xerox employees can work and learn, grow and share, talk and laugh together—regardless of where we're located—around the corner or around the globe." Cindy Casselman, manager of strategic communications, explains: "In my mind, this is going to be the place people go to get their mail, find out what's going on, communicate with others, and do their work."[8] Xerox's sales reps can cruise from the Web Board to the FIRST Knowledge Base to get instant answers to customer questions, and to share best practices and expertise. The repair people swap stories of how particular problems can be fixed by storing them in a database called Eureka. This repository is built bottom-up through the online conversations among the tech reps who are asking each other questions, identifying problems, and devising new solutions. The annual value of the database is estimated at $100 million.[9] Such virtual support is particularly important since Xerox's sales and service staffs don't share offices. It also gives them a sense of confidence and empowerment to be able to solve problems at a moment's notice and have important information at their fingertips.

Whenever Xerox's CEO, Paul Allaire, makes a speech, it is made available on the Xerox Intranet the same day. In addition, the speech will be supplemented with commentaries by Wall Street analysts—positive and negative. This CEO is not as concerned about putting a Xerox spin on the news as on encouraging candid dialogue. "It really democratizes communication," says Allaire, who is a regular participant in a chat line on the Intranet.[10] Using an Intranet-based collaboration tool called Docushare, Xerox researchers are able to share lab results from experiments all over the world, employees can contact others and use them as sounding boards for ideas, or they can get instant feedback from other units. Xerox's Intranet creates an atmosphere for learning and information sharing. Says Dan Holtshouse, director of corporate business strategy, "Perhaps the most powerful aspect of the Web Board is its ability to organize employees into communities of workers, built around common interest and common practice, rather than work-groups organized around a task or location.... There's no central control, so it's better for worker communities."[11]

Intranets put global access to thousands of documents, presentations, software packages, policies, and training materials at the fingertips of employees twenty-four hours a day. Information hidden in drawers, binders, piles on desks, in-baskets, out-baskets, and wastepaper baskets becomes unlocked and available anywhere and anytime. It can be easily searched, cut, and pasted into memos, presentations, sales pitches, marketing tools, and training modules. Employees can communicate with the person who produces the information and see how particular information relates to other information via hyperlinks. Intranets empower people to make suggestions, share ideas, and learn from colleagues. All this without the hassle of telephone tag, or the inconvenience of meetings and traveling. It leverages the organizational intelligence and facilitates organizational learning. In addition, Intranets are an effective way for managers to keep a finger on the pulse of employees. Managers can correspond with people over e-mail and listen in on discussion groups on the Intranet. They can practice virtual "management by wandering around" in today's far-flung international organizations without moving their butts.

Only Hewlett-Packard's rivals the size and scope of Xerox's Intranet. In describing HP's Intranet, Mary Ann Easley exalts, "It's if not *the* largest Intranet in the world, certainly one of the world's largest." HP's Intranet has created an explosion of information sharing among employees. More than four thousand HP sales reps can download and print over ten thousand documents, saving them an average of five hours per week. In the R&D arena, it has reduced the number of different design versions in new product development from as many as eight to a single product. Anyone in the company can search for all company information, including white papers, office memos, product information, and competitive briefs. Steve Beitler, HP's manager of investor communications, takes a realistic approach to having the information he needs. "This is a huge company. I cannot be current and thorough on every topic. But I know where to find the information. In a place this big, knowing how to find out is more valuable than knowing." The costs of printing and distribution saved are usually more than enough to cover the Intranet investments. Studies are showing payback periods ranging from six to twelve weeks and return on investments well over 1,000 percent on Intranets.[12] A newfound spirit of community and learning is spiraling in the virtual quarters of Ericsson's, Xerox's, and HP's global networks, giving a new meaning to the role of horizontal communication.

Reaching Workers Offline

A problem with Intranets is how to reach workers who don't work in front of a computer. Ericsson considers this to be only a short-term problem, as it's in the process of outsourcing most of its production and is left with a mostly white-collar staff. Other world-class companies have developed ingenious ways of reaching blue-collar workers with digital media. Manufacturing workers at Xerox who don't have Intranet access can call an 800 number to get the latest company news from Radio Xerox. Saturn uses good old-fashioned television. The carmaker can reach all of its 360 retailers and over eight thousand employees with live broadcasts through an internal satellite television network. The weekly newscast, *Saturn Windows*, keeps all Saturn "team members" abreast of company news and advertising and other marketing communications programs. It is also used to communicate late-breaking news. "Say for example," explains Greg Martin, "before we announce that we may have to recall some of our cars, we will go on a broadcast to the retailer and tell them what is happening." A typical scenario in such an event, such as a car recall, is that all dealerships will get a message through the computer network. The e-mail will say what time there will be a broadcast. The dealers will gather in a conference room at their dealerships and turn on the satellite channel of their television sets to watch the live broadcast. The Saturn plant workers in Spring Hill, Tennessee, and the staff workers at the headquarters in Troy, Michigan, will be watching as well. The Saturn president will explain in detail why cars are being recalled, how dealers and Saturn employees should respond to questions, and how the recall will be administered. The remarks are followed by telephone calls from retailers and employees. As Martin aptly describes the format, "It is sort of like *Larry King Live*."

Philips reaches workers offline with interactive kiosks available to all employees. "In every factory you have an interactive kiosk, in every lunchroom, in every hallway," comments Guum Hayen, director of external relations. Employees can participate in interactive sessions through the kiosks and, for instance, learn about business management through running a fictitious company or learn about best practices from Philips's Deming Award–winning Taiwanese subsidiary. "All electronic media has its place," argues Mona Malmquist, Philips's Scandinavian communications director. "We use the computer network for immediacy, satellite television for live broadcasts, and the CDs for in-depth information." The future of electronic employee communications is in the morphing of video and Intranet technology, allowing two-way full-motion video on everyone's desktop.

Surviving Hypercommunication

The new climate of hypercommunication has created its own problem: information overload. The average employee receives 2.3 million words in routine communication in a three-month period. That is on top of the 178 voice and electronic mail, faxes, and mail messages that the average person sends and receives each workday, interrupting them three to four times an hour.[13] Add that to the average of seventeen hours per week senior managers spend in meetings and an additional six hours preparing for them.[14] Not to mention the four thousand marketing messages they are drenched with every day when they join the ranks of consumers outside of work. People like Rodney Irvin, Eastman Chemical Company's public relations manager, are struggling with this balancing act of encouraging open communication while not getting overwhelmed by it. "I have a sign, 'On deadline, please do not disturb,' as a courteous way to say, 'Stay out of my office.' But that is a very fine line because you want to foster people talking to one another, you want the two-way communication."

The traditional fix of the problem is to control and restrict the flow of information, which is the justification of bureaucracies. Now, you don't have to go to Washington to realize that bureaucracies aren't the answer to any problem. The only viable solution is to develop more effective processes of both vertical and horizontal communications. Vertical communication from the top needs to be tailored to the needs and preferences of individual employees, and messages have to be carefully labeled for content, audience, and urgency. For instance, Danfoss classifies employee information in "need to know" and "nice to know" categories. Explains Vibeke Gustafsson, head of technology management, "If a department is moving, everyone needs to know about where they can reach it. Then there is the "nice to know" information that gives background and meaning to that move. Employees who don't care to read that can skip it."

The deluge of horizontal communications needs to be managed with better work habits. E-mail users need to learn to use the cc function more judiciously; managers need to eliminate rambling meetings that lack agendas or goals; and road warriors need to replace some off-site meetings with video or phone conferences.

Everyone needs to learn to process information faster. Intelligent agents will play an increasing role in helping people to sort and screen their way through the dense thickets of information. Xerox, for one, is hard at work on developing artificial intelligence technology, which summarizes multipage documents into a paragraph or half a page.

But the most important skill in managing the rising tide of hyper-communication is to use both high-tech and high-touch communication when they are most appropriate. Online communication needs to be used for speed and access. Human communication needs to be used for problem solving, idea generation, and hashing out conflicts and disagreements. Many companies do the opposite, which is inefficient at best and devastating at worst. Using personal meetings to recite information is a waste of people's time; using e-mail to criticize people can create abysmal conflicts. There is probably no other place in the world where the human nature reveals itself in more nightmarish permutations than at the keyboard of a computer. In the solitude of their offices, people tend to resort to their most primitive instincts by sending rude and insulting e-mail messages. Psychiatrist Edward M. Hallowell makes the parallel to the anonymity of driving an automobile, where normally stable people can behave like crazed maniacs.[15] Because of the absence of body language, voice intonation, and facial expressions, e-mail messages frequently get misconstrued or forwarded to the wrong people. Misunderstandings get compounded and conflicts erupt. People have lost their jobs and companies have lost clients over quarrels created by heat-of-the-moment e-mail exchanges. Meanwhile, a lot of valuable face-to-face time is wasted on communication that could be handled more expeditiously online. We don't need Dilbert to remind us of how much of our workdays are spent listening to monologues that could be conveyed more effectively in a memo.

The future calls for a better balance between high-tech and high-touch communications. Human and virtual communications need to work in tandem to reinforce each other and optimize horizontal communications.

Whose Responsibility Is It Anyway?

The responsibility to facilitate horizontal communications has slipped between the department chairs of most organizations. It's woefully ignored by most employee communications staffs, which usually focus narrowly on top-down vertical communications. At companies where employee communication resides in the HR department, the focus turns frequently to communicating benefits issues. Where it's organized in the corporate communications department, it tends to err on the side of too much corporate propaganda, with videos and magazines that include every utterance by the CEO. Neither the news reporters of the communications department nor the number crunchers from HR are very concerned about the role employees play as part-time marketers, which recently has prompted some marketing departments to get into the game of "internal marketing." Although well intentioned, these efforts are typically limited to teaching workers to recite marketing slogans. The fact that 44 percent of all marketing directors don't even share their marketing plans within their marketing departments, and 68 percent don't share them with other departments, suggests that most marketing directors aren't serious about internal marketing.[16]

None of these departments typically understand the value of cross-functional and cross-business unit communication. In some companies, the quality department has championed such horizontal communication. Total quality management offers a common language, tools, and approaches to improve communication among people in different parts of the organization. It supports communication through storyboards (posters with visual presentations of quality improvement projects in progress), team meetings, and job rotation. Unfortunately, most TQM departments are limited in scope to communication among plant floor work groups. In recent years, IS/IT departments have championed horizontal communication among white-collar workers under of the banner of "knowledge management." They have broken new ground in using computer networks to exchange information. The technical expertise of the IS folks is a critical component in managing knowledge exchange and horizontal communications.

Regardless of where the responsibility for employee communication resides in your organization, it's important to draw from all these disciplines. Communications, human resources, marketing, TQM, and IS departments all bring important perspectives. Their collaboration is needed to reinforce consistent brand messages, leverage knowledge, create synergies, and reap the advantages of scale and scope of the entire organization. From the Rank-Xerox conference room where Nicole had the courage of her convictions to speak up, to the virtual communities at HP's Intranet, horizontal communications is forever transforming the face of business. Nowhere is that more evident than at FedEx. The next chapter gives an in-depth look at how this company puts all of the dimensions together to help deliver in the Customer Century.

What to Do Wednesday Morning:

- Identify the core processes that matter most to customers. They typically include—but are not limited to—service delivery, branding, and product development. Appoint senior managers to be responsible for managing them.
- Set up a rigorous training program and guidelines for effective teamwork, using the forming, storming, norming, and performing stages as a foundation.
- Develop an open office architecture that is conducive to horizontal communications.
- Develop the internal electronic infrastructure whereby employees can communicate with one another. Set up "virtual communities" for information sharing across units and geographic borders.
- Set up an internal employment agency with the mission to redeploy employees more effectively within the firm and encourage rotation. Give preference in promotions to employees who have rotated among different functions, businesses, and countries.
- Identify areas where high-tech and high-touch communications are most appropriate. Train and empower employees to be effective high-tech and high-touch communicators.

Notes

1. This story is a fictional illustration based on an interview with Tom Kenneth, Rank-Xerox Denmark

2. Allaire, Paul A. (1998). *Lessons in Teamwork, in Navigating Change*. Edited by Donald C. Hambrick, David A. Nadler, and Michael L. Tushman. Boston, Mass.: Harvard Business School Press, p. 113.

3. Imai, M. (1986). *Kaizen—The Key to Japan's Competitive Success*. New York: McGraw-Hill.

4. Klaus, Leigh Ann (1997). "Motorola Brings Fairy Tales to Life." *Quality Progress*, June, pp. 25–28.

5. Taylor, William. (1991). "The Logic of Global Business: An Interview with ABB's Percy Barnevik." *Harvard Business Review*, March–April, p. 94.

6. According to a Study by the Center for International Briefing.

7. Allen, T. J. (1967). "Communication in the Research and Development Laboratory." *Technology Review*, October–November.

8. Schultz, Beth (1996). "Xerox-Wide Web." *Network World*, July 15.

9. Stewart, Thomas A. (1998). "The Cunning Plots of Leadership." *Fortune*, September 7, p. 166.

10. Ibid.

11. Shachtman, Noah (1998). "Group Think—Employees Are Shattering the Traditional Corporate Structure With Intranets." *Information Week*, June 1.

12. Beng, Lim Say (1997). "There's a Gold Mine Out There on the Web." *Business Times*, June 7, p. 3.

13. Markels, Alex (1997). "Memo 4/8/97, FYI: Messages Inundate Offices." *Wall Street Journal*, p. B1. Based on the *The Pitney Bowes Managing Corporate Communication Study*, conducted by the Institute for the Future, the Gallup Organization, and San Jose University.

14. Tobia, Peter, and Becker, Martin C. (1990). "Making the Most of Meeting Time." *Training and Development Journal*, August, p. 34.

15. Hallowell, Edward M. (1999). "The Human Moment at Work." *Harvard Business Review*, January–February, pp. 58–66.

16. Williams, Juliet (1996). *Strategic Management Resources*, Dec. Cited in Don E. Schultz and Jeffrey S. Walters, *Measuring Brand Communication ROI* (1997). New York: Association of National Advertisers.

5

AN INTEGRATED CASE STUDY

Delivering Results Overnight

Customer satisfaction begins with employee satisfaction.

Pointy Haired Boss: I've been saying for years that "employees are our most valuable asset." It turns out that I was wrong. Money is our most valuable asset. Employees are ninth.
Dilbert: I'm afraid to ask what came in eighth.
Pointy Haired Boss: Carbon paper.

—Frederick W. Smith, chairman and founder, Federal Express

—Scott Adams

"Mr. Smith, I have an international question about explaining our service to Europe ..." The question blares from the stereo speakers of a large television set in the center of a Federal Express lunchroom.

Men and women in FedEx uniforms munch on their sandwiches with their heads turned to the television screen as they watch the familiar face of Fred Smith, the venerated founder and chairman of the company. The white-haired figure on the screen sits in a studio setting resembling the *Larry King Live* show. With a pensive look on his face, he waits patiently for the caller to finish her question. He then leans forward and gives a rapid-fire response about how particular international deliveries should be handled. Just as suddenly, he slows down, lowers the pitch of his voice and concludes, "I'll ask Tom or someone on his staff to draft a response that he can get to all of our customer service representatives by tomorrow morning about how to handle such requests. Is that okay with you, Vicky?"

Vicky confirms that she is happy with the response.

This is the typical scene at every one of the 1,200 Federal Express offices in the United States and an increasing number of offices around the world which are reached by *One-On-One*, a call-in show on Federal Express's closed-circuit television network. Any employee from around the world can pick up the phone and speak live on the air to the company's chairman. The calls are not screened. When Fred Smith gets a question he does not know how to answer, one of his senior managers will call in to respond on air. In this sense, the programs serve as corporate town hall meetings where employees and senior managers have an open dialogue and re-solve problems. This is one of many ways in which FedEx facilitates open communication.

The Quintessential IC Company

Among integrated communications companies, none stands taller than Federal Express. Perched at the pinnacle of *Fortune* and Yankelovich Partners' "Corporate Equity" study (based on a survey of 7,750 *Fortune* subscribers) and the first service company ever to win the coveted Malcolm Baldrige National Quality Award, FedEx epitomizes Customer Century management. And it all started with a Yale undergraduate by the name of Frederick W. Smith, who wrote a term paper in which he pointed out that the passenger routes used by most air freight shippers were not appropriate for freight distribution. Packages were "hippety-hopping around the country from city to city and from airline to airline before reaching their destinations." Air freight would work better in a system specifically designed for it, rather than being part of the passenger service, he argued. The paper was awarded only a C because the professor believed the idea was not feasible. The term paper idea evolved into a quintessential integrated communications company, which currently delivers some three million packages a day to 211 countries around the world. The following discussion shows how the 3-D model presented throughout this book applies to a single company—one that is primed to deliver in the Customer Century.

Snaring Customers in the Web

Federal Express is more than a physical network of jets and vans for package delivery; it's also a digital network of bar code scanners, computers, and databases for information delivery. One key to FedEx's success is making customers an integral part of this network. Here is how the system works: When a package is picked up, the courier passes a small cordless scanner over its bar code. The information is beamed via satellite to a central database in Memphis. Every time a parcel changes hands, from a van to a plane, to a sorting facility, to a truck, it is scanned and the information in the database is updated. The FedEx proprietary computer network keeps track of each one of the daily three million shipments at all times.

In 1982, FedEx decided to link its high-volume customers straight to its mainframe computer by providing them with their own computer terminal, electronic weighing scale, bar code scanner, and printer, at no charge. This "PowerShip" computer equipment allows customers to print package labels, order courier pickups, make payments, and track packages en route. It adds convenience to customers while saving FedEx major costs. Without the PowerShips, FedEx would today need an additional 20,000 employees to pick up packages, answer phone calls, and key in airbill information.[1] In the mid-1990s, FedEx offered its smaller and less frequent customers free software that performs similar services. It helps customers create FedEx labels, schedule pickups, and track shipments through modem connections. IBM and Apple have even begun to incorporate this software in their personal computers. By 1997 FedEx had nearly 100,000 PowerShip systems installed and an additional 440,000 customers using the "FedEx Ship" software on their own computers. Two-thirds of FedEx's shipping transactions came from these online services. The problem was to incorporate the last third of low-volume customers into the computer system.

Enter the World Wide Web. Today customers anywhere in the world can log on to fedex.com and find out exactly where their parcel is at that moment within the maze of planes, vans, handlers, and sorters. The site is a seamless part of FedEx's computer network. Customers can access shipping rates, schedule pickups, print airbills, and send e-mail to the recipient of the package, all from the website. The system is also used to collect payments online. No fewer than 315,000 packages a day are tracked on the site.

The Internet system is an incredible win/win situation for all parties. It clearly allows customers greater convenience and control over their shipping by relieving them from the busywork involved in filling out address labels or getting on the phone to learn about the status of a package. "They can let the machine do the printing and the tracking while they do other things," comments Robert Hamilton, formerly manager of automated systems marketing. The annual cost savings so far: an estimated $8 million per year. And most importantly for FedEx, it creates ongoing relationships with profitable customers by making them integral parts of the system. "The biggest thing is to generate loyalty for the customers and make it difficult for the competition to go in with twenty-cent lower rates," states Hamilton. Mike Janes, former VP of electronic communications and logistics marketing, says it's only the beginning. "We will continue to add more transactions, more effective ways to do business. Ultimately our objective is to literally have every aspect, other than the physical pickup and delivery, accomplished through the website."[2]

An increasing number of companies are tapping into FedEx's on-line system to outsource their entire logistical processes to FedEx. Many of them are direct marketing firms. For instance, mail-order megastore Insight Direct has developed one of the most sophisticated logistics systems using FedEx as its primary resource. The company is using FedEx to handle all aspects of inventory and distribution.[3] Says Joel Borovay, Insight's senior VP of operations and logistics, "FedEx is a solid organization that has a premium level of service . . . that's why we are totally integrated with them." Insight is one of over one hundred companies that can sit back and collect the money while FedEx does all the heavy lifting of invoicing, warehousing, order fulfillment, and delivery. Such partnerships make it possible for FedEx to meld itself into an inseparable part of its clients' business operations, and serve the customer's customers. In the process, FedEx has contributed to the explosive growth of mail-order retailing by helping to overcome one of its largest handicaps versus retail stores, the immediacy of receiving purchases.

Living and Breathing the Lives of Customers

Every morning when Federal Express employees come to work, they learn how the company as a whole performed the night before, as the "Service Quality Indicator" (SQI) flashes on their computer screens. The score is also reported in the daily telecast to employees. The indicator measures how the company has performed on the twelve criteria that customers rate most important, weighted in proportion to their level of importance to them. For example, a five-minute-delayed package is a one and a lost package is a fifty. Damaged packages, missed pickups, and problems with invoices fall in between. Fred Smith calls it "our hierarchy of horrors." FedEx has a 99 percent on-time delivery rate. Among the 1 percent of late packages, many are delivered at 10:31 A.M. instead of 10:30, a difference customers rarely even notice. But Fred Smith is adamant about bringing all of the scores down to zero. "As Smith is fond of pointing out, would you be pleased if the banks sorted 99 percent of your checks correctly? Would you be pleased if one in a hundred flights you will be on would go down in flames?" says Hamilton in his best Smith voice. FedEx is constantly trying to devise ways to attack root causes of these failure points. Twelve "quality action teams," headed by different vice presidents, are each responsible for bringing down one of the Service Quality Indicator criteria.

In addition to the corporate SQI, many divisions and departments have developed their own SQI scores. The call centers, for instance, track the number of calls answered after twenty seconds, calls abandoned, transfers, holds, and service levels for each half-hour increment during a twenty-four-hour period. As a final reminder of the centrality of customers, each paycheck has the following statement printed visibly through the cellophane window: "A satisfied customer made this paycheck possible."

In addition to measuring the operational drivers of customer satisfaction, FedEx keeps a constant pulse on customer satisfaction. "Our research is indispensable for the company," says Robert Hamilton. "It is impossible to conceive FedEx operating for very long without having a mechanism like that. This is a way to be as proactive as possible." Customer satisfaction is monitored every business day of the year, through eight hundred monthly telephone interviews, comment cards at over one thousand service centers, and other studies. "We ask them a whole slew of questions, everything from how do they like our drop box, to what they think about the courier. It's probably the best satisfaction study there is," says Gayle Christensen, managing director of marketing communications. Top-line reports of the surveys are widely distributed throughout the company at the end of every month. A more comprehensive report is compiled twice a year. Sharing customer satisfaction information enables organizational learning and keeps everyone coordinated and focused on key customer needs. A case in point of how the results are promptly addressed is in claims services. "Our research showed that handling claims on the first day boosts satisfaction rate dramatically," explains Michael Glenn, senior VP of worldwide marketing.[4] To resolve more claims the first day, customer service reps are empowered to handle claims up to $300 in value.

An additional way to stay connected with customers and stakeholders is through the use of "strategic communication audits," which are conducted twice a year to measure how well long-term major strategic communication initiatives and key communication vehicles are achieving their objectives. A combination of mail surveys, focus group sessions, and audience observations are used to evaluate how well employees and outside stakeholders perceive the timeliness, credibility, relevance, and interest of each publication and television program. The customer satisfaction surveys and communication audits are important for integrating inbound customer and stakeholder communications. Explains Robert Hamilton, "We are all interacting with customers in different ways. Everyone picks ups impressions from the same phenomena. The customer satisfaction surveys are vehicles by which a lot of significant learning is expressed. It keeps things more coordinated."

As much as FedEx measures customer satisfaction and communication effect, it recognizes the limitations of these surveys. In a way, the surveys embellish that old joke of: "Enough about me . . . what did *you* think of *my* performance?" The real juicy customer insights are gleaned from going out into the field to live and breathe the lives of the customers. Every FedEx manager above managing director is required to spend one day each month with a salesperson. Staff members below the managing director level are required to spend two days every three months making sales calls from a field office, or taking hotline calls in the customer service department. Gayle Christensen describes her experiences in the field: "I have a sales district out in the West Coast and I have already spent five days there this month. That gives us exposure to the day-to-day lives of our account executives and customers. I go out with a sales account executive to specific accounts where I can add some value." Through this in-depth experience in the field, FedEx's managers not only have a finger on the pulse of their stakeholders, they have an IV injected into them. They all view FedEx from the customer's perspective, feel the customer's pain, and anticipate their future needs.

Mining the Database

Vast information warehouses filled with data on four million customers enable FedEx to compare all of the costs involved in doing business with a particular customer or customer segment with their profit contributions. Chances are that your name is in it, if you have sent a FedEx shipment within the last two years. This up-to-the-minute information is at the fingertips of sixteen customer segment teams. Each one of these teams is responsible and accountable for anywhere between 10,000 and a million customers. Their analyses reveal which 20 percent of the customers account for 80 percent of the profit and which ones end up costing FedEx money. The company has an internal system that rates customers as the "good, the bad, and the ugly." Explains Sharanjit Singh, managing director for marketing analysis, "We want to keep the good, grow the bad, and the ugly we want nothing to do with."[5] So far, FedEx has closed unprofitable accounts that shipped 150,000 packages a day.[6] A new system of pricing packages based on the distance they travel will take care of most remaining unprofitable customers. Every company has unprofitable customers, but few have the system to track them and drop them or make them profitable.

The most valued 20 percent of FedEx's customers are profiled in detail by the sixteen teams. The transaction information is matched with demographic information about the client company's industry, revenue, and number of employees. The analysis is used to "clone" high-profit customers, by going after new potential customers who share the same characteristics. Prospective customers are sent a business reply card that asks information about the customer, what they ship, where they ship, how shipping decisions are being made, etc. An incentive is offered for filling out the card. Salespeople who are consultants trained to examine logistic processes and suggest improvements follow up the hottest leads. The marketing department is also tapping into its army of couriers, using them as half-time salespeople. Under a program called "Finders Keepers," couriers receive cash awards when they identify prospects for the FedEx sales force to follow up.

This is a dramatic departure from the past when FedEx's marketing department was organized in product teams that tried to reach everyone in broadly defined demographic segments with the same message. In the old order, the product managers tried to find more customers for their products. Today, FedEx's customer managers and their teams are trying to sell more services to their existing customers. Their teams are matching marketing expenditures with expected customer value. In other words, the more a customer is potentially worth, the more is spent on trying to get or grow its business. These cross-functional teams have line responsibility and accountability for all interactions with their assigned portfolio of customers.

As a result, FedEx has improved its return on marketing investments anywhere from four- to fivefold. Customers benefit too, from not being bothered with mass-mailed offers that are not relevant to them. "The bottom line is the customer gets better, more relevant, more timely, more meaningful information with which to make the basis of a decision. It enhances the value of that customer for FedEx and, in turn, provides value to the customer," comments David Shoenfeld, FedEx's senior VP, marketing, U.S. and Canada.[7] The database marketing approach is now applied to European markets and key Asian markets as well.

People-Service-Profit

The real success story behind FedEx is the way communications is integrated with its 140,000-plus workforce. "We are totally candid about every subject, and making available any information requested that is not personal, privileged, or controlled by government regulation," says Roy Golightly, employee communications director, explaining the importance of top-down communication. He emphasizes that the company is just as serious about bottom-up communications by "involving each employee as an invaluable team member in all corporate activities, up to and including the development of corporate strategy." This commitment to employee communication is premised on the corporate philosophy of "people-service-profit," upon which the company was founded. Explains Fred Smith, "When employees are placed first, they will provide the highest possible service, and profits will follow." FedEx sets a "people objective," a "service objective," and a "profit objective" every year. Every employee knows at the beginning of the fiscal year what these three objectives are, and every manager is accountable for specific objectives based on these three corporate objectives. And that's not all. If the company does not reach the annual employee satisfaction, profit, and service quality goals, the top three hundred managers lose their entire bonuses, which are about 40 percent of their salaries. By putting its money where its mouth is, the board of FedEx sends a clear message to employees and managers that customers and employees are in charge of the operation. "It probably sounds trite, but the people-service-profit credo really is embedded in the culture," attests Gregory Rossiter, public relations managing director.

To further show the importance of the people-first philosophy, FedEx has a "no-layoff policy," guaranteeing all employees lifetime employment. The company has adhered to the policy since its inception with only one exception—when it shut down its inter-European operations. When it discontinued ZapMail, a failed effort to provide fax service, all 1,300 employees were placed in positions equal to or better than the ones they had. A job bank was established to give the highest priority to ensuring that the transition was a smooth one. In addition, FedEx guarantees employees their original salary for eighteen months when they are assigned a lower-paid position in the company. FedEx's management recognizes that its workforce doesn't just deliver letters and packages, it delivers the FedEx brand to the marketplace. By caring for employees and keeping them informed, external communications can be enforced by employees in their daily contact with customers.

Integrating Vertical Communications—Bit by Bit

Integrating vertical communications in a sprawling operation with stations, courier vans, and loading docks literally spread everywhere is a delicate task. In the early years of the company's history, this was handled through what became known as "The Family Briefing." Small teams of corporate officers left the Memphis headquarters twice a year to meet employees and their families on picnics and luncheons, usually on Sunday afternoons. The senior managers talked to employees about the company's problems, progress, and prospects.

The meetings became such an important part of communications that FedEx began televising them to several locations in 1977. Today, the company owns one of the world's largest private satellite television networks. It reaches virtually all its North American employees through an elaborate satellite system that connects with 1,200 sites in the United States and Canada, and sixteen sites in Europe. The Far East and Latin America will soon be covered as well. The programs are automatically taped and replayed on television monitors in all Federal Express break rooms continuously throughout the day by an automatic video playback system. So whenever a FedEx employee has a lunch break, he or she can catch the latest company news. Federal Express Television, FXTV, broadcasts three to four hundred programs a year. It has a daily broadcast called *FedEx Overnight*, which is an overview of how many packages were delivered the previous night, the Service Quality Indicator of the day, weather forecasts, and other pertinent information that might affect the day's operations. The program also features the latest company news, such as advertising campaigns, new services, or management appointments. In addition, FXTV carries weekly programs dedicated to various specialist functions. *Sales Line* gives the sales force the latest information on sales strategies and revisions of service offerings. *Front Line* addresses the needs of the couriers, and *Customer Service Today* is targeted at customer service agents. But the most interesting programs are the live broadcasts with the chairman and senior managers that were described in the introduction of this chapter. "Fred Smith addresses the key issues facing the corporation and some of the employees' concerns through the live phone calls," reflects Golightly. How many other chairmen would face questions live in front of a worldwide workforce of over 140,000 people, without any preparation? "The benefits of FXTV is of course that it is timely and consistent. We can discuss the impact of our latest financial result within hours of the announcement, clear up rumors before they are widespread, respond to crises instantly, and answer burning questions while they are still hot," explains Golightly. "It is a very powerful, stimulating medium. Most of our employees have grown up in the television age."

Digital communications is taken to new levels with a sophisticated internal Intranet site, from which employees can get new software, interact with colleagues in chat groups, and access the personnel manual. In addition, an interactive training system with full-motion video is used to teach the company's 45,000 couriers and customer service agents about areas such as customer-contact methods and new services.[8] The training can take place at the end of a shift, during slack periods, or whenever employees can fit it into their schedules. "Our strategy is to ultimately do just-in-time training when employees need it, wherever they are," explains Keith Brewer, manager of corporate headquarter systems.[9] Management is also able to measure the performance of employees during the training.

The infrastructure to reach the worldwide workforce simultaneously and regularly keeps everyone focused in the same direction. "Everybody knows what the main goals of the company are so they can operate with a big picture in mind," says Hamilton. "If you have heard the chairman say in the latest internal TV interview, 'the big thrust for this year is going to be international.' Well, then if you're serving on a task force that is considering international aspects of some project, you are going to know that it is important and worth your time." And the goals are not based on spur-of-the-moment decisions made at the latest management retreat. They are long-term and closely tied to the people-service-profit credo. The deeply embraced and consistently communicated direction helps make FedEx the consummate integrated communications company.

Integrating Vertical Communications—Face to Face

High-tech wizardry such as satellite newscasts and computer networks aside, the main form of vertical communications at Federal Express is personal communication between the front-line workers and their immediate managers. "The single important principle to realize about management communication is that it is two-way and it is a process. Our department certainly puts out a lot of communication products, but we are more interested in the process of communication rather than products. Employee communication is the right of the employees and the responsibility of the managers. Communication is not an extracurricular activity for managers after all their other duties are done," notes Golightly. A large part of a manager's job is to identify and satisfy the information needs of their work groups, which requires constant interaction with employees.

All managers are required to participate in forty hours of management training per year. A large part of these courses deals with how to communicate more effectively with employees. Managers' communication skills are assessed every year by their own employees. An online employee satisfaction survey pops up on all employees' computer screens to be filled out anonymously. A "leadership index" is calculated based on the survey. "Eight of the ten items on the survey measure managers' communication activities with employees," says Golightly. Managers are mandated to present survey results to their employees and develop action plans together with them to improve weak areas. The overall results are benchmarked with other companies that administer the same survey. FedEx has consistently obtained above-average ratings.[10] To put teeth in this "survey-feedback-action" system, managers who score below a certain level are put in a purgatory called "critical concern group." They are required to accept support to become better leaders and communicators and retake the survey again after six months, running through the same feedback-and-action drill. "We will work with the manager and employees to find out why the scores are so low and give the manager an opportunity to improve their scores," explains Golightly, who believes in giving people a fair chance. "But," he adds, "if you continue to be critical and ineffective for two years in a row, you are probably not going to be a manager at Federal Express much longer."

Another effective approach to bottom-up communications is "skip level meetings." Golightly explains: "If one of my people wants to have lunch with my boss, or if I want to have lunch with Fred Smith, all we have to do is to pick up the phone and call. It gets rid of the fear factor and makes employees feel that their input is valued." A "Guaranteed Fair Treatment Policy" gives employees the right to take grievances straight to top management without fear of retaliation. If the immediate manager and the next-level manager do not resolve the issue to the employee's satisfaction, he or she can take it to a board composed of senior managers, including the CEO. This board meets every two weeks and is known for having reversed decisions made by lower-level management.

A long-term approach to promoting bottom-up communications is to elevate front-line workers to management ranks. Federal Express has an elaborate process in place for promoting salaried workers within the company to management positions. Any employee who is interested in becoming a manager is invited to attend a one-day class called "Is Management for Me?" Says Golightly, "They take the employee through the trials and tribulations and the pressures and expectations of being a manager." The participants who decide that they want to be considered for management positions go through an extensive process of evaluation by their peers and managers, as well as training and interviews. Once candidates become managers, they are put through an intensive management training program at FedEx's "Leadership Institute" in Memphis. Communication skills are heavily stressed in all of the classes. When a position is open, it is first posted within the company. "Only when there are no qualified applicants from within the company do we search outside," concludes Golightly.

The dedication to employees is evident in every detail of FedEx's operations. Its planes are named after the children of employees. The week before Christmas you will find the top brass sorting packages at the super hub in Memphis. Before changing the design of its uniforms, FedEx conducted thirty focus groups with employees in fifteen cities worldwide. FedEx pays employees well and plows 10 percent of its profit into a profit-sharing plan. Anyone working as little as seventeen hours a week gets health coverage and perks including free rides in jump seats on company planes.

To be sure, FedEx hasn't been immune to strife among its employees. In the fall of 1998 its 3,500 pilots threatened to strike after negotiations became bogged down over compensation, retirement, and scheduling issues. A strike would have wreaked havoc on FedEx's Christmas shipments and its reputation for reliable service. FedEx was determined not to take customers by surprise. As soon as the conflict surfaced, customers were informed about it on FedEx's website. "Long before there was even the slightest hint of a concrete fear, we went out on the site," explains David Shoenfeld, senior VP of marketing.[11] When the conflict heated up, daily updates appeared on the first page of fedex.com. As it turned out, FedEx's management got unexpected help from the rest of its employees. In a spontaneous outpouring of company loyalty, six thousand FedEx employees turned out to demonstrate in support of their employer outside of its Memphis headquarters! The rally developed into a cross between a revival meeting and a homecoming parade, under the banner "Absolutely, Positively, Whatever It Takes." FedEx officials insisted they had no role in organizing or financing the rally. Suppliers to Federal Express, including a local ad agency and a shuttle-bus operator, donated services.[12] Two days later, the Pilots Association called off the pending strike vote and agreed to accept an earlier contract offer.

This wasn't the first labor contention in the company's history. In 1997, an upsurge of disgruntled employees began to rally around the unions, claiming that FedEx was not paying its workers enough and that jobs were being subcontracted or eliminated. The same year, two FedEx workers and a fired employee filed a lawsuit that is still pending alleging that FedEx violated federal law in trying to stifle the Teamsters' efforts to organize workers nationwide. FedEx denies the allegations. Another disgruntled employee developed "FedUp," a rogue site that slams the company in every direction. The headline reads, "When working at FedEx has irrefutably, undeniably become the pits!" It's little wonder that you will find a handful of employees foaming at the mouth and climbing the walls of their padded cells at a company of FedEx's size and magnitude. But the company perseveres and is still considered one of "100 best companies to work for in America," according to *Fortune*[13] and thousands of other FedEx employees.

Integrating Horizontal Communications

Communications are integrated horizontally at FedEx through a number of cross-functional task force teams. "You cannot think about making a change even in your own department without thinking of the widespread impact that you are going to have," reflects Golightly. "It is kind of like dropping a pebble into a pond. The pebble might be small, but the ripple effect goes as far as the pond goes." Any change requires the involvement of a cross section of people with diverse expertise from different departments. "In this company introducing something new is so complex, not like introducing a product for a shelf somewhere, because the courier in Des Moines has to know just as much as the courier in Paris. So it is a huge communication issue," explains Gayle Christensen. And since communication is so integral in new project development, there is always someone on the designated task force who is responsible for communications. "And that person then goes off and pulls together his own communications team, which would consist of whoever needs to be on it, be it PR or marketing."

Horizontal communication is further supported by job rotation. For instance, the employee communications director, Roy Golightly, worked for twelve years in the marketing department. Golightly gushes about the benefits of his marketing background: "I have a much better understanding of the process that they use in marketing and I have a much better understanding of the impact they can have on employees." He uses his marketing background to make the employee communications department realize that it too has customers, the employees. Golightly's predecessor, Tom Martin, went on to become public relations director. He found that his stint as employee communications director sensitized him to the need of employees to be informed about any news before or simultaneously to breaking it to the news media.

As FedEx has evolved from a U.S.-centric to a multinational and now a global business, horizontal communications across borders has become a high-priority issue. The international communications professionals at FedEx hold regular conference calls. Tom Martin explains the process. "On a monthly basis I have a planning session in which I get all of the international communicators from around the world on a global videoconference. We have live video from Singapore, Brussels, and Hong Kong, and by telephone we link in Canada and Latin America. The headquarters employee communications and PR staff participates too, and we discuss what is being planned for the next month." The result of these efforts is a very dynamic worldwide planning effort. Says Martin, "We talk for easily an hour to an hour and a half. And then we supplement that by talking on a more regular basis by the telephone with our international communicators, and we also use electronic mail." Integrating horizontal communications with videoconferencing, e-mail, and cross-functional teamwork helps communications staff cross-pollinate ideas and experiences from different parts of the world to make them global assets of the company.

Integrating Stakeholder Communications

As you might have guessed, FedEx sets an example in integrating stakeholder communications as well. A great case in point is when ABC's *20/20* produced an unflattering report about Federal Express's handling of hazardous materials. FedEx was notified only a few hours before the program was going to be aired. One and a half hours later, well before the start of the *20/20* program, its satellite television system beamed out a program to all employees in which company officials discussed the charges that *20/20* was going to make against Federal Express. The managers explained the company's policies and training to prevent problems with hazardous shipments. This gave employees the opportunity to respond to questions about the TV program from customers, neighbors, and friends the following day. Reflects Golightly, "When the *20/20* thing happened, we knew that it was going to be a big PR story. Employee consideration was a priority over the public relations consideration. Because we wanted our employees to know what was happening, why it was happening, what the truth was, and what they could do about it."

The release of the quarterly earnings report is also a study of carefully choreographed communications to multiple stakeholders, as Tom Holland, managing director of investor relations, describes. "I prepare the press release and I fax it out to media and financial analysts by the hundreds simultaneously. And then we have a conference call with about sixty financial analysts who follow us. All the participants in this conference have the faxed earnings release in front of them at that time. I get the chief financial officer to sit in, and we talk about the quarter, what happened, and then take questions from the analysts." At the same time, the press release is sent out through electronic mail to all Federal Express's employees, and through the wire services to news media. After the investor conference, Holland says the next step is to contact the media. "We do a media conference call about an hour later. We talk with the *Wall Street Journal* and some of the trade publications." Holland goes on to explain, "It is important to have the conference with the investor analysts first, because the media will usually call the analysts just to get a quote, 'is it good or is it bad?' That's why we make sure we have already talked to the analysts." By carefully timing communications to multiple stakeholders based on how they interact with each other, FedEx manages to project consistent messages.

Policymakers comprise another high-priority stakeholder group for FedEx, because the company operates in a heavily regulated environment. Federal Express played a significant role in making air freight part of President Carter's deregulation of the airline industry, which put an end to the passenger airlines' monopoly on air freight. Fred Smith and other senior officials attended fundraising dinners and gave speeches tirelessly. He mobilized its employees and customers in letter-writing and telephone campaigns against congresspeople and enlisted top-notch Washington lobbyists. At one of Fred Smith's numerous testimonies to congressional committees he tore apart the 250-page Aeronautics Act of 1938. "No other CEO has such a strong presence on Capitol Hill. Smith is, more than anyone, responsible for airline deregulation," argues Bill Margaritis, VP of corporate communications. Brian Clancy, a cargo industry consultant, adds, "When it comes to

Washington, those guys wrote the book."[14] The legislative victory is still considered to be the most important factor behind the success of Federal Express. Lately, the company's focus has turned to international regulatory barriers. The company has aggressively challenged any obstacle to the "open skies" of air cargo.

FedEx's stakeholder relationships extend to charity organizations as well. It has formed a strategic alliance with a number of organizations, including the American Red Cross. When a national disaster strikes, FedEx transports containers of cell phones, faxes, and radio equipment to the disaster site, needed for the Red Cross's Quick Response Team. "By sending planes to deliver needed supplies to Chinese flood victims last summer, FedEx cemented its relationship with the community while demonstrating its quick response and global capabilities," says David Drobis, CEO of FedEx's PR firm, Ketchum, adding, "The company seized an opportunity to do good, while gaining added visibility for its value proposition."[15] FedEx also uses its international delivery expertise to aid the Red Cross in the tracking and reuniting of families that have been separated due to war or natural disasters. The company makes a difference in the world by contributing its unique delivery, logistics, and warehousing expertise and capabilities to a broad range of stakeholders. In the process, it's reinforcing its promise of "The World on Time."

Using Managers and Employees as Spokespeople

A cross section of FedEx managers and employees are spokespeople for the company in addition to their normal duties. Few other companies feature their managers as frequently on television. For instance, Greg Rossiter who worked for Procter & Gamble prior to assuming his position as public relations director of FedEx, attests that "we probably do more TV interviews in a month than P&G does in a year." He attributes this to the heavy dose of broadcast interview training that all FedEx managers receive, and the ongoing practice they get from appearing on its employee television. It also helps that the FXTV studio is accustomed to feeding live and taped interviews of senior managers to television stations around the world.

Not only are managers used as spokespeople, but front-line

workers are enlisted as well. A large number of the workers get a break from their chores of sorting packages in the Memphis sorting hub every five weeks to be tour guides for a week. The tour starts at midnight and is open to anyone. "Visitors are always impressed with the enthusiasm that these regular front-line workers show," says Myron Lowery, who's in charge of the hub tours. The tour is the starting point of FedEx's own management seminar, which is held every other week. The one-day seminars feature presentations by FedEx managers and have been included in *Business Week's* list of "Meccas for Management Training."

FedEx managers and employees speak at external conferences as well. An in-house speaker's bureau fields all requests for FedEx representatives to speak at conferences that run the gamut from local Rotary Club meetings to industry conferences on topics from quality management and logistics to Internet and technology. Three hundred FedEx employees, ranging from front-line workers to the CEO, volunteer to give presentations. They have all undergone rigorous training. "Last year we accommodated 129 of 224 requests, at no charge other than travel expenses," divulges Sandra Munoz, who's in charge of the speaker's bureau. The purpose of all these activities is to reinforce FedEx's corporate reputation and build relationships with new and existing customers. Even though the focus is on long-term brand building, there are some short-term payoffs. For instance, the sales department is provided a list of all participants in the seminar who indicate on the evaluation form a predisposition to use FedEx for deliveries.

The Transparent Corporation

"From the very first days of FedEx's history, it has shared with employees, customers, and other stakeholders the good news and the lousy news," rejoices Hamilton. The company talked openly about such fiascoes as the ZapMail fax service, and the large-scale inter-European operations into which the company sank hundreds of millions of dollars before dismantling the business. FedEx is an example of how "transparent" companies have become as we approach the Customer Century. Nothing is secret anymore. Both senior managers and the company are in fishbowls. "The information gets cast so broadly within the company that even the courier will have heard about any big thing going on," notes Hamilton.

FedEx's keen sense of integrating high-tech and high-touch communication channels with employees, customers, and key stakeholders goes a long way in explaining its tremendous business success. It has pioneered new communications technologies. It was the first in its industry to use television advertising with the classic "when it absolutely, positively has to be there overnight" spots. It invested in its satellite network to keep all employees up to date long before most companies had any such infrastructure. It integrated customers in its computer system back in the PC stone ages and bronze ages of the early 1980s, long before the advent of the World Wide Web. Yet FedEx has never gotten carried away with its high-tech marvels. It uses good old-fashioned personal communication by its 140,000 "part-time communicators" to integrate communications vertically, horizontally, and externally. "We don't look at communications to be just the PR department's job or the employee communications department's job. It is a shared responsibility, just as budgeting or personnel management or anything else," says Hamilton with glee. As a result, FedEx has an army of die-hard employees around the globe, who are "bleeding purple" for the delivery company.

The bottom-line effects of FedEx's integrated communications are as unquantifiable as they are undeniable. When communication has been integrated into the way a company does business, its benefits can no longer be isolated and measured any more than it would be possible to measure the benefits of putting on one's pants in the morning. But there are other bottom-line numbers that speak volumes about FedEx's success. How about a tidy fivefold revenue growth between 1985 and 1996, from 2 to 10.3 billion dollars? In the five years prior to the writing of this book, its earnings per share rose from 2.11 to 5.39 dollars, and return on equity from 7 to almost 13 percent. Not a bad return on integrated communications. Directors of marketing and communications need to take note of FedEx's success, because they carry the burden of championing the integrated communications efforts in their organizations. Communications and marketing professionals are facing the challenge of redefining their roles and acquiring a new set of skills that will help them earn a seat at the management table, as we'll see in the next chapter.

What to Do Thursday Morning:

- Link primary customers and retailers straight to your corporate mainframe. Give them access to their own account information, and let them do ordering, tracking, and customer service online.
- Create partnerships with business customers in the spirit of becoming an integral part of their operations.
- Set up a system of measuring both customer satisfaction and operational quality based on customer priorities. Track them on a daily basis, communicate the results widely, and involve everyone in the organization in improving the scores.
- Organize the marketing department in customer teams (rather than product teams) and base marketing expenditures on expected customer value of individual customers. Track unprofitable customers, and drop them or turn them profitable.
- Train all senior managers and selected lower-level employees in presentation skills and use them systematically as spokespeople on plant tours, seminars, conferences, and media interviews.

Notes

1. U.S. Department of Commerce (1998). *The Emerging Digital Economy*.
2. Bunish, Christine (1998). "Web Execs: Site Payoff Goes Way Beyond ROI." *Business Marketing*, August 1, p. 25.
3. Costa, Dan (1997). "Special Delivery: Insight Direct and FedEx Master Strategic Logistics." *Computer Shopper*, Vol. 17, No. 3, p. 92.
4. Pastore, Richard (1995). "Special Delivery." *CIO*, August.
5. Judge, Paul C. (1998). "What've You Done for Us Lately?" *Business Week*, September 14.
6. Grant, Linda (1997). "Why FedEx Is Flying High." *Fortune*, November 10, pp. 156–60.
7. Loro, Laura (1997). "FedEx Mines Its Database to Drive New Sales." *Business Marketing*, March 1.
8. Tapscott, Don (1997). *The Digital Economy*. New York: McGraw-Hill.
9. Haber, Lynn (1996). "Corporate Giants Test the Waters." *Communications Week*, March 18.

10. Lovelock, Christopher H. (1990). Federal Express Quality Improvement Program. Case by the International Institute for Management Development.
11. Harrington, Ann (1999). "The E-Corporation." *Fortune*, May 24, p. 124.
12. Blackmon, Douglas A., and Greg Jaffe (1998). "Die-Hards Rally behind FedEx in Contract Talk." *Wall Street Journal*, p. B1&B4, November 18.
13. *Fortune*, January 11, 1999, pp. 118–44.
14. Baird, Woody (1999). "First FedEx Work Contract in Place, More to Come?" The Associated Press.
15. Drobis, David R. (1999)., "Communication: The Essential Ingredient in the Value Equation." *Ragan's Public Relations Journal*, March/April, p. 14.

6

INTEGRATING COMMUNICATIONS PROFESSIONALS

From Support Function to Business Driver

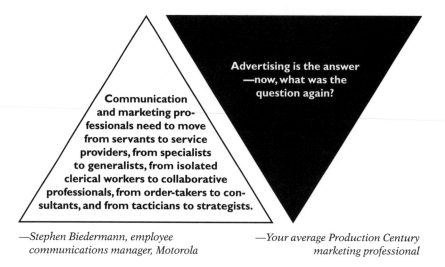

Communication and marketing professionals need to move from servants to service providers, from specialists to generalists, from isolated clerical workers to collaborative professionals, from order-takers to consultants, and from tacticians to strategists.

Advertising is the answer —now, what was the question again?

—Stephen Biedermann, employee communications manager, Motorola

—Your average Production Century marketing professional

"My job is to get Allen-Bradley to appear as one company in the marketplace, and combine and leverage our resources," ventures Edson Allen, reflecting on his role as VP of strategic communications. He is faced with the challenge of aligning the work of communications staffs at Allen-Bradley's four separate business units, which develop and manufacture plant-floor automation products, such as pushbuttons and sensors for industrial computers. "The need to integrate communications is obvious, since the different units are making products designed to work together, which a lot of times are sold to the same customers," says Allen. But the job of Edson Allen is a lot like running a cemetery: he has a lot of people under him but cannot make them do anything. Allen doesn't have official authority over the individual marketing and communications departments outside of corporate headquarters. They report to their business line managers in the interest of being integrated with the business and close to the customer, and have only a "dotted line" matrix reporting relationship to the corporate communications office. Yet Edson Allen has developed an effective participatory approach in the absence of a central authority.

One mechanism to integrate the work of the different marketing communications departments is the company's "Communication Handbook." "It provides all the tools to create integrated messages," explains Allen as he flips through his bible, which contains design rules and message guidelines with suggested key words and phrases to use in printed materials, along with a descriptive paragraph about the company. But in addition to prescribing the outcome of the communications, it also issues guidelines for the processes of developing them. "Until you get a process down on paper you really don't have a common understanding," argues Allen, who has established flowcharts for everything from placements of feature stories to video production projects. Common to every flowchart is one of the first process steps where the team sends drafts to Allen's office. "We promise a turnaround of twenty-four hours, during which we review how the communication pieces are integrated with each other and if they comply with the graphic design and message guidelines." Sometimes his department suggests adding a paragraph in the copy about Allen-Bradley as a company. By incorporating a review at the early stages of the development process, it's easier to make changes, before too much money and too many egos get invested.

Another powerful way in which Allen-Bradley standardizes the process of developing communications materials is by making all communication teams ask the same questions at the outset of any project. The teams are asked to follow a particular "message development worksheet" when they are planning any communications project. This is composed of a series of questions about objectives, goals, audiences, etc. The questions compel communicators to have strategic discussions about what they want to accomplish and how their particular projects will be integrated with other communications initiatives in the company, such as: How can we remind customers of the scope of the company behind our solution? Is this part of a larger communications effort? Are there other products or materials we can leverage? And most importantly, how will our solution help the customer grow more competitive?" Edson Allen explains the significance of this last question. "No matter what we are working on, if it is an ad, a piece of literature, or a press conference, we should always be asking this question, 'How are we helping our customers become more competitive through superior solutions?'" He continues, "It's a common denominator for every message. Any time a customer or prospect sees a message from Allen-Bradley, we like them to take away, 'My God, those people understand my business.'" Getting this slant on every message about Allen-Bradley and its products elevates the perception of the company. Allen focuses the integration efforts where they matter most, in the early planning stages of any project.

Rubbing Elbows with Al

But all the flowcharts and worksheets in the world couldn't replace the face-to-face meetings that Edson Allen's department hosts regularly. Communications professionals from all business units convene regularly in a number of "councils." There are councils for public relations professionals, trade show specialists, designers, technical writers, etc. "The product division managers nominate a representative to each council," explains Allen. Public Relations Director Christine Zwicke is responsible for the PR council meetings, where public relations professionals throughout the company can connect with one another. She has broadened participation to other professions in the company: "At the last PR council meeting, we brought in VPs of sales and VPs of marketing from all our different product groups, so we can talk about how we can take a long-term view together. The meeting ended up being very well attended, and now these marketing people are saying, 'We have this to talk about, let's take it to the PR council.'" The PR council meetings started off as very effective forums for information sharing but have increasingly turned into strategic planning sessions. Says Zwicke, "Bringing communications, marketing and product development people together makes them realize that there are exciting stories to be told, there are ways to leverage what they are doing, package messages and help build the image of the company, and help build the credibility in areas that would never have been thought of." The results speak for themselves, adds Zwicke. "The upshot of these meetings is that we are having more people talk, more cross-functional exposure, more face-to-face exchange of ideas, and more brainstorming."

The trade show council successfully illustrates Allen-Bradley's participatory approach. "Years ago we had a man on my staff who was in charge of trade shows, and he did everything," recalls Allen. "There were a lot of questions from the business units like 'How did we pick this show?' and 'Shouldn't we be in this show?' So back in 1983 we set up a trade show team with representatives from all the business units and turned it over to them." One of the members of this team, Jerry Houston, marcom manager of the Power Group, explains the new order: "We look for points to leverage. So, for example, if I have one business that is going into the paper market with a series of products, we put together a unified look in a paper industry trade show booth." All the Allen-Bradley business units that sell to the forest industry will get together with a joint display that shows the products working together and develop shared promotions. Concludes Houston, "It's beautifully orchestrated."

The most dramatic improvement of integration came from the council in charge of customer inquiries. Edson Allen describes what the process was like before. "When the secretary got around to it, she sent out literature that was requested, and it could take thirty to sixty days." Once a month, a list of their addresses was sent to the district sales offices. "At that time it was worthless, most of the leads were cold and the salespeople didn't call them," sighs Allen. Since leads are a dish best served warm, a council was formed to reengineer the process. The team designed a timely fulfillment processes managed by an outside vendor, which provided the sales force with leads while they were still simmering. "This council now only meets once a year to fine-tune the process, and the vendor does the day-to-day work," says Allen. The responsibility of integrating communications is turned from head-quarters to the business units, which work collaboratively to opti-mize their joint efforts.

Uniting Yugoslavia

Now, fast-forward five years. When I checked back with Allen-Bradley before this book went to print, the integrated communica-tions model had been put to the test when parent company Rockwell brought home three sisters after going on a shopping spree. Allen-Bradley was all of a sudden one of four companies in the new "Rockwell Automation" unit. Edson Allen had retired and the new marketing regime was faced with the task of integrating four companies with very distinct cultures, three of which had cen-tury-long histories. Joining the four brands of Allen-Bradley, Reliance Electric, Dodge, and Rockwell Software under the new umbrella of Rockwell Automation was a task that the new senior VP of branding strategy, Barclay Fitzpatrick, likens to the joining of Bosnia and Serbia into a Yugoslavia. "There was suspicion and mis-trust in the newly acquired companies." He concedes that "it looked like about fifteen different companies, made up of twenty-eight distinct business units, each with its own P&L, each with its own marketing budget, and with twelve different agencies." To make matters worse, the customer databases were "like an elec-tronic attic," with different files in different formats hidden in every corner of the organization.

Fitzpatrick and his colleagues went to work on integrating the brands in 3-D. The first step of *vertical* integration was to secure buy-in from senior management. They took a radical approach: "We collected all our ads in one spot, in what we called the War Room, and pasted them on the wall, along with ads from the competitors." The CEO and his senior management team were brought to the War Room for a demonstration of how competitors like Snyder, ABB, Siemens, and Cutler-Hammer were achieving much better consis-tency than the Rockwell companies. "Once they saw that we looked like fifteen different businesses by comparison, we were able to get the directive that this must change," recalls Fitzpatrick.

Having secured buy-in of the top dogs, the next step on Fitzpatrick's agenda was to facilitate *horizontal* integration among the marketing communications professionals who would lead the branding efforts. The result? The formation of the Integrated Marketing Communication Council, the union of representatives from all the separate and discrete councils of PR, marketing, etc. One marcom professional from each of the twenty-plus business units was chosen as a representative on the council, which is not just a discussion club but a decision-making body. "We established a *Robert's Rules of Order*," explained Fitzpatrick, referring to the bible of standardized meeting procedures. The rules define what is needed to pass the vote. For any decision that has international ramifications, for instance, a certain number of votes from non-U.S. members are required. Explains the gregarious VP: "We don't use them bureaucratically, but it gives us a foundation on which to rely when parochialism rears it ugly head."

Fitzpatrick took senior management's directive from the War Room exercise to the Integrated Marketing Communication Council. The message was clear. It was no longer an option for the team to achieve consistency and integration. "However, *how* we did it was up to us. So people felt empowered about how to achieve the direction," notes Fitzpatrick. The combination of a clear decree from the top and a cross-functional team in charge of execution of the integration is important to him: "What is required is a combination of consensus and direction."

The first step by the Integrated Marketing Communication Council was to facilitate *external* integration by surveying a cross section of customers from each business unit. The council was intimately involved in designing the research, analyzing the data, and developing brand promises. But that was only the first step. "We then took our competitive research and created the brand promises we thought our competition wanted to communicate and asked customers to critically compare them with ours. We used their feedback to refine our brand promises," says Fitzpatrick. Finally, the group developed a set of brand promises for the product lines "that were linked but distinct, and which consistently beat their relevant competitors." The team selected a single agency, from a shootout among all twelve incumbent agencies, to develop a new corporate identity. The four different brand names were kept, but their logos were adapted and placed in an ellipse surrounded by

Rockwell Automation as the endorsement brand. The advantages of engaging the business unit professionals in this process were twofold, as Fitzpatrick explained: "We were able to result in something that was very powerful, that everyone also was 100 percent committed to."

Having developed the brand strategy, the Integrated Marketing Communication Council didn't waste any time reengineering its planning processes. The Communication Handbook was, for instance, transformed into the "Marketing Communicator's Assistant Software." Communications professionals now develop a digitized agency brief by following a tutorial that takes them through a series of questions. The user is asked which brand they are promoting, upon which a drop-down menu appears, from which they can pick among predetermined messages for that brand. The user is also asked to input the dates when the activities will start, and the program offers certain milestones for the planning process. "For example, a problem in the past was that they came to the PR firm asking for a press release in twenty-four hours. Today, the timeline suggests that they start thirty days ahead of time, and shows each of the steps they need to go through during that time," explains Fitzpatrick. The new software is an essential tool in integrating the planning process of global communications.

Edson Allen and Barclay Fitzpatrick are living proof that integrating communications professionals across disciplines, business units, and countries is not best achieved through command and control, but through consensus and direction. In a frenzied time of megamergers and acquisitions, the challenge Rockwell Automation faced resonates with a large number of companies today. Just about every industry is coalescing into a handful of global giants that have to develop multibrand strategies. Rockwell's success is a testament to the adaptability of the 3-D integrated communications approach.

Losing Touch with Customers and Senior Management

Marketing and communications staffs are caught between a rock and a hard place. On one side they are facing increasingly cynical consumers, global markets, and demanding stakeholders. On the other side, they are facing ever-increasing standards of accountability and leaner budgets from their organizations. Many professionals are ill-equipped to handle the squeeze because they have lost touch with both sides. All they know about their customers is the sterile profile offered by their research firms, decribing a thirty-one- to forty-eight-year-old person with a college degree, one testicle, one breast, and 2.4 children. Many marketing and communications managers are equally out of touch with their CEOs and senior managers. The top brass want to know what returns they are getting on their marketing and communications investments and how this will help them achieve their business objectives. But their marketing and communications directors tend to talk about their *output* and *expenses*, instead of *outcome* and *revenues*. They talk about attention scores and media budget, instead of customer-retention rates and return on investments. In their defense, it should be noted that Production Century CEOs bear a large part of the responsibility for the problem, by relegating their marketing and communications staffs to the tactical back rooms or even dismissing them as superfluous overhed.

The lack of accountability has made marketing and corporate communications notoriously inefficient. Currently, marketing accounts for 50 percent of corporate costs—up from 20 percent after World War II. In contrast, manufacturing and operations expenses have gone from 50 percent of corporate costs after World War II to today's level of 30 percent, as seen in figure 6.1. These reductions are attributed to automation, TQM, and just-in-time. Meanwhile, management has downsized, rightsized, reengineered, and outsourced itself to a level of 20 percent of total corporate costs, down from 30 percent.[1] While other corporate functions are becoming more cost-efficient, marketing and corporate communications is the last bastion of unmanaged cost.

It's not an exaggeration to argue that marketing is teetering on the brink of obsolescence. It was created for an industrial-based management system for the purpose of influencing consumers, instead of creating value. At a time when the Production Century model is becoming outmoded by the new integrated, customized, and relationship-oriented imperatives, marketing and communi-

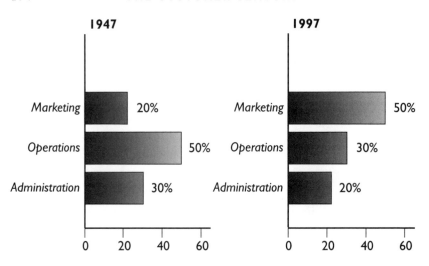

Figure 6.1. Marketing's bloated share of corporate budgets today compared with half a century ago.

cations needs to reinvent itself. In fact, the term "marketing" has so much Production Century baggage that many world-class companies are not even using the term any longer. The marketing and communications professions have reached the proverbial fork in the road. One road is the management of communications *processes*, which leads straight to the senior management table. The integrated communications "process owner" is responsible for developing a comprehensive measurement system of customer and stakeholder relationships, counseling the CEO, and connecting the marketing and communications professionals at different business units with each other. The other road is the responsibility of communications *functions*. It leads down the path of managing technical support functions of databases, customer and stakeholder research, and production of communications material. Marketing and communications professionals need to develop structured and streamlined processes for them and consider partnering with outside agencies.

Measure for Measure

The first order of business for every aspiring world-class corporate marketing and communications director should be to implement an integrated measurement process to keep a pulse on effective *external* communications. "Marketing needs to be reengineered to listen as much as it talks," argues Rockwell Automation's Barclay Fitzpatrick, echoing a comment I heard time and again from communications professionals. Communications departments are notorious for spending most of their time and resources on outbound communication. Many of their staff members have hardly encountered a real customer. What little inbound communication usually takes place is a crude measure of the communication effect of isolated activities or campaigns for the purpose of legitimizing their expenses. Advertising luminary David Ogilvy put it best when he described the mainstays of marketing and communications research as being "used like the drunkard uses the lamppost, for support rather than illumination."

The pervasive measurement tools used by most marketing and communications departments are social-scientific methods dating from the 1950s—opinion surveys, readership studies, copy testing, reach and frequency analyses, cost per thousand calculations, and press clipping counts. These measures of how loud companies scream in the clamor of commercial messages aren't exactly the fabric that strategy-building insights are built on. They are based on a century-old theory of how information is transferred to consumers, called the "hierarchy of effects," which measures how people think, feel, and act on a message. There are endless permutations of this message-effectiveness model, AIDA (Attention, Interest, Desire, and Action) and DAGMAR (Defining Advertising Goals, Measuring Advertising Results) being two of the most popular. Every self-respecting research firm and communications agency has its own in-house version of the model. They live and die by it, because it is logical, sequential, rational, predictable, linear, and one-way—from the producer to the consumer. It makes communication seem like engineering. The researchers' drones interrupt the lives of regular people at home with their phone calls and tidy lists of questions. The numbers get crunched and customers are divided into neat little segments, cohorts, and clusters. The audience is targeted with a mass-monologue of seductive advertisements that they are expected to uncritically absorb like androids, fall in love with, and act upon.

There is only one little quandary: the last fifty years of intense research have disproved the think-feel-act model over and over again.[2] Personally, I have always suspected this to be the case by observing some of my wife's purchasing decisions. For instance, in the five seconds that lapsed from the time she saw the house we now live in to her purchasing decision, I am convinced no rational thought processes occurred, although she later spent a great deal of effort justifying her decision in rational terms. We remain quite happy in the house, and an increasing number of consumer researchers are now concluding that it is not my wife who is abnormal but the communication theories. People don't necessarily think, feel, and act in an orderly sequence. And even if they did, the model is of limited use because it assumes that the job of communication is done when the buyer makes the first purchase. Then they are treated as another prospective buyer again. There's no measure of long-term relationship building. In fairness, survey data about the average knowledge and attitude among broad populations was the only information marketers had access to in those ancient pre–data mining, pre–scanner data, pre–frequent purchase club days. But today a wealth of purchasing and other behavioral data could be at the fingertips of any marketer.

The Production Century measurement model of communication effect is contrasted in Figure 6.2 with a new model for the Customer Century. The focus of the model is on the effect communication is having on relationships with customers and stakeholders on three levels.[3] The starting point is to measure how *customers and other stakeholders* add value to the *organization*—based on hard-nosed lifetime customer value analysis (as described in chapter 2). Having identified the potentially most profitable customers, the second level measures how well the *organization* adds value to the *customers and stakeholders*—based on satisfaction studies, in-depth interviews, complaints, responses from marcom activities, and other methods. It also includes measures of internal processes that have the largest impact on satisfying customer needs, such as time to market with new product developments, order to delivery cycle time, and defect rate. Improving these processes will improve the value provided to the customers and stakeholders, which will ultimately drive the value they provide the company. In other words, the more a company can delight and excite its customers, the more those customers will purchase and recommend the brand to others. The third level is the *reputation* of the corporation and its brand(s). Reputation is the estimation in which an organization is held by all its stakeholders. It describes how attractive the organization is perceived to be as a supplier, employer, investment, and citizen. While this cause and effect system might seem complex, it's important to keep the number of measures to a minimum and only measure the critical few factors that really matter at each of the three stages. And they need to be measured continually. "You need to be able to stay ahead of evolving trends and the impact they will have on customer needs, not just take snapshots once a year," says Fitzpatrick, who favors ongoing measures over the occasional survey.

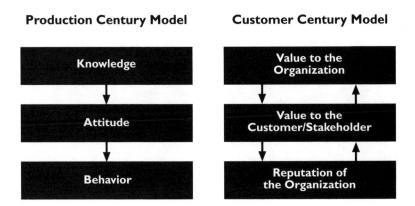

Production Century Model

Knowledge

↓

Attitude

↓

Behavior

Customer Century Model

Value to the Organization

↓ ↑

Value to the Customer/Stakeholder

↓ ↑

Reputation of the Organization

Figure 6.2. The Production Century model of communication measurement vs. the Customer Century integrated communication model.

Let's apply the model to FedEx, as seen in figure 6.3. For the *first*-level evaluation, recall from the previous chapter how FedEx measures profitability of its customers and grows its "share of mailbox" with them. By way of measuring how FedEx adds value to its most profitable customers, the *second*-level evaluation, it makes over eight hundred monthly telephone customer satisfaction interviews and analyzes responses of comment cards. It also analyzes complaints and conducts ongoing market research. Based on this information, it has identified twelve operational drivers of customer satisfaction, the Service Quality Indicator. The *third*-level evaluation of FedEx's reputation is measured through the company's "strategic communication audit." It includes mail surveys, focus group interviews, and observations, to ascertain how FedEx is perceived among critical stakeholders. These three carefully aligned levels of measures are widely communicated within FedEx to integrate its efforts and maximize the profitability of the entire company.

Integrated Communications Metrics

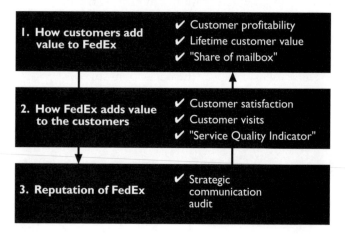

Figure 6.3. A three-pronged approach to integrated communications metrics, applied to FedEx.

New communications measurements such as customer profitability and "share of wallet" are not likely to be ready-made, nor very precise. Communications and marketing professionals need to work closely with accounting, customer service, operations, and other functions to develop the new measures since the financial data in most companies are organized around products and functions instead of customers and stakeholders. And the new measures will require both assumptions and estimates. No one is ever going to be able to calculate lifetime customer value with three decimal places. But isn't it better to calculate the right thing with a 20 percent margin of error than to calculate the wrong thing with a 2 percent margin of error? While traditional forms of communications measures focus on what's easily measurable, the new ones focus on what really matter.

Gauging the value of other stakeholders gets even more fuzzy than it does with customers. But it can be done, as is proven by Eastman Chemical Company's analysis of communications with the legislature in its home state of Tennessee. The company measures the percent of the bills for which it has lobbied successfully, and the translation of the dollar value of these bills to the company, as indicated in figure 6.4. The year prior to my interviews, the value of this first-level evaluation was $8.1 million. The second-level evaluation is done through "customer" satisfaction surveys of the Tennessee legislators. They are asked about the level of service that the company's government relations department provides and how well Eastman Chemical Company performs as a corporate citizen. Problems identified in the surveys are analyzed and key processes causing the problems are measured and improved. They might be indicators of the environmental impact that Eastman is having, as well as measures of communications activities with the legislators that the company values. The third-level evaluation of Eastman's reputation includes both qualitative methods like the community advisory panel, and quantitative ones like the neighborhood survey (described in chapter 2).

Integrated Communications Metrics

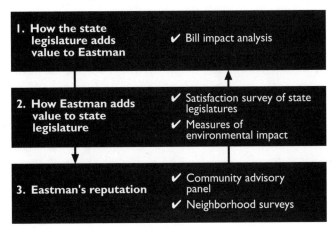

Figure 6.4. How Eastman Chemical Company measures communication with the Tennessee state legislature.

This system provides the basis for feedback, accountability, and communication of organizational goals. It forms a balanced scorecard that needs to be integrated into the organization's financial reporting and performance measurement system, rather than a stand-alone shadow of the traditional systems. While traditional financial accounting measures are a lagging indicator of corporate performance, or a look at the rearview mirror, the measures presented here are the leading indicators of future success. Making this three-pronged metrics the yardstick of performance is the surest way to make the entire company customer-focused.

Connecting with the CEO and Other Business Functions

Measuring relationships and reputation with key customers and stakeholders is only the first step in elevating the role of marketing and communications. But if marketing and communications directors are to assume the role of strategic counselors to management, they also need to measure the effect they are having on management. They need to meet regularly with their CEOs to help clarify their companies' strategies and reach agreements on how communications and marketing can support them, and what performance measures their progress should be evaluated against. Next, they need to listen to colleagues in other departments for how to better add value to the company. Eastman Chemical Company's Public Affairs department surveys the three departments that it impacts most directly. Says Lynn Johnson, director of the department, "We survey our internal customers—the benefits department, environmental department, and the tax group. We ask them how we are doing, what we can do better, and what their needs are."

Bill Margaritis, VP of corporate communications at FedEx, meets once a year individually with all of the company's senior managers to discuss their communication needs. "We have to understand what the business priorities are, in order to align corporate communications with them. Otherwise we will be relegated to a mouthpiece, a media impression generating machine," argues Margaritis. The corporate communications department of Motorola even surveys general managers on a regular basis. "The surveys are not only a good way to evaluate how well our department's services are received, but they also remind other departments that the PR department is eager to provide them with services," reflects Chuck Sengstock, corporate communications director of Motorola, now retired.

When it comes to finding ways to stay connected with managers of other functions in the firm, FedEx's investor relations manager, Tom Holland, is among the most ingenious. "I skunk out information anywhere I can," says Holland, who has obtained carte blanche to attend any company meeting, including board meetings. "I have the ability to go anywhere, read anything, sit in on any meeting, walk into anybody's office and take up their time. I have asked to get on all of the mailing lists. I get the notes from the board meetings and senior management meetings." But he gets his most valuable information from senior managers by working the hallways. "I sometimes drop by their offices, but I try to run into them in the hallway and strike up a conversation." Holland finds this access critical in order to be a credible spokesperson: "You have to give the comfort to the street that you know everything or can get that information."

While Holland has found unique ways of accessing other managers, Nils Ingvar Lundin of Ericsson has conditioned general managers to seek him out. "I get phone calls every day from managers in our organization who want advice on how a particular decision they are contemplating would be perceived by stakeholders." He has attained this role as a sounding board of business managers all across Ericsson through patient and aggressive networking. One avenue for doing that is teaching up-and-coming managers at Ericsson's management institute. "I think it's extremely important to meet all future managers at Ericsson and provide them with the information they need to get a good start," says Lundin, who also participates in media training of senior mangers: "Last fall, I was in the U.S. and China, as an instructor. I think it's important when we gather management groups for journalist training that I'm there in person to emphasize the importance of training and also to build relationships with the participants." While most other communications directors see their role as influencing outside stakeholders, Lundin is also uniquely able to influence the organization itself. He is a customer and stakeholder ombudsman, staunchly supporting their case when decisions are being made.

Lundin has learned that the success of marketing and communications professionals has less to do with how well they manage marketing and communications activities than with leading all other functions to embrace integration. They need to help their colleagues in finance, operations, HR, R&D, customer service, and sales to understand how their work directly or indirectly effects customers. Let's start with how the colleagues in accounting can become better part-time communicators. The problem with the accounting systems of most organizations is that they focus on cost rather than value, precision rather than relevance, the past rather than the future, and material assets rather than intangible values of customer loyalty. Teaching the legions of bookkeepers, clerks, auditors, and preparers of financial statements to become customer-focused is a tall order, but a necessary one. Only they have the information, tools, and expertise to help calculate the profitability of individual customers and customer segments. Marketers and communicators need to take on the controller's office as well. The role of the controller needs to transcend its futile analyses of balance sheet resources of plants, machines, and inventory and move into the analysis of relationship equity. While a handful of companies, including General Foods, Du Pont, and Johnson & Johnson have established offices of "marketing controller," the trend is still limited to a few companies where the controllers address primarily the efficiency of marketing expenditures rather than marketing effectiveness.[4] The controller ought to be controlling, monitoring, and auditing changes in lifetime customer value, the asset that matter above all others in the Customer Century.

The next target is the human resources department. It needs to rise above its well-orchestrated payroll and benefit administration chores and focus on the strategic issues of how to recruit, retain, and grow managers and front-line workers who are first-rate communicators. Marketers and communicators need to guide them in this direction.

R&D should be next on the hit list. Marketers and communicators should go down to the labs and invite the engineers out for a field trip into the real lives of the customers, to help them anticipate customer needs. Professionals in marketing and communications should get involved in every new product development team from day one to help R&D stay customer-focused and communicate externally about new products and services before the launch to generate interest and excitement among customers and stakeholders.

Let's tackle customer service next. Marketing and communications officers need to help overhaul its traditional performance metrics, which are based on minimizing the time spent on the phone with each caller. Instead, the reps need to give velvet-glove treatment to high-value customers and speak longer, not shorter, with them. If a high-value customer calls customer service, the rep should know about their last three purchases and any other contacts that they have had with customer service in the last six months. And while you're at it, don't forget to merge the call center, fax, and e-mail response units into a customer interaction center responsible for all queries. The center can develop databases with responses to commonly asked questions. In many instances, this database can be made available directly to customers on the website.

Next stop, the information systems department. These are the guys who are fluent in a language of bits and bytes, RAM and ROM, but don't have a word for "customer." Marketing and communications have to involve IS early as partners in developing databases and online infrastructures. It's a big mistake to merely send IS a list of specs that its department had no role in developing; or worse yet, to shortcut them by developing stand-alone websites and databases that are not integrated with the legacy system. Marketing and communications staffs need to work with their IS colleagues to reexamine how existing customer databases can be leveraged with data warehouses and website applications, and how the internal communication network can be turbocharged for more effective communication.

The final bastion for marketers and communicators to conquer is the sales force. The legions of sales glad-handers organized by geographic territory or client size, who are reciting product benefits and pushing boxes by pressuring customers into submission, have seen their best days. Instead, the sales approach needs to be adapted to the needs of each customer.[5] Price-sensitive customers in the market for commodity products need the option of low-cost automatic sales channels. Other customers might need the support of a skilled sales consultant with the diagnostic tools to analyze their needs and develop complete service solutions. Finally, some clients might seek a preferred supplier partner. In all cases, the sales force needs to look beyond the individual sales opportunity and manage the customer relationship. Salespeople need to be treated as professionals, and compensated with salaries. Commission is inherently antithetical to relationship building and should be, if not abolished, kept to a minimum or tied to customer satisfaction and retention rates. This new sales philosophy has profound implications for the role of marketing, which needs to transform itself from a supplier of sales material and leads to a partner that works with sales on customer-focused teams. Rockwell Automation is undergoing such a makeover as this book goes to print. Its four companies used to vie for the attention of the joint sales force. "Our salespeople were inundated with material. They threw away most it and when they later needed it they couldn't access it," sighs Barclay Fitzpatrick, and explains how Rockwell went to an Intranet-based database system instead: "We reengineered a push process to a pull process." The salespeople are now notified with an e-mail of new material that can be ordered through the electronic literature management system. Fitzpatrick's staff has also created PowerPoint presentation templates for the sales force, allowing the three thousand salespeople to customize presentations that all have the same look and feel. This new infrastructure allows the sales force more face time with clients, proving how the strategic use of technology can improve the more human elements of relationship building. Entering the Customer Century, the lines between marketing, communications, sales, HR, IS, accounting, and other functions are blurring. They are becoming integrated around customers, and orchestrated by marketing and communications professionals.

Connecting Marketing and Communications Professionals with Each Other

Being as closely integrated in the line organization as communications professionals of world-class companies are, it's important for them to also connect colleagues who serve similar functions across divisions. Bringing marketing and communications professionals together for a big-tent meeting is one of the most effective vehicles for cross-business integration. Motorola's Public Relations Council, for one, has met regularly for more than thirty years. "It has become the primary source of cooperation, coordination, information exchange, training, standards, and teamwork," says Motorola veteran Chuck Sengstock. In addition, he brought together his public relations, advertising, and employee communications councils to a "supercouncil." The meetings are held at one of Motorola's major manufacturing facilities and are combined with training classes. The supercouncil provides both professional development in communications and education about Motorola and the industry. Says Chris McClure, the company's former director of advertising, "We don't just educate them about the field of advertising and marketing communications, but also strengthen their knowledge of Motorola." Hewlett-Packard is taking notes. It's planning to merge its "ad council," "marcom council," and "direct marketing council" into a joint session that will culminate in an awards ceremony for communications achievements. Xerox already has such meetings in place. It organizes a "worldwide communication council" four times a year with representatives from virtually every communications function.

An important benefit of these council meetings is the opportunity for communications professionals to learn from each other by sharing best practices as well as mistakes. "Our network meetings with communications professionals ensure that everybody is moving in the same direction and understands what the other people are doing so we don't give our employees, public, or customers different messages and confuse them," explains Joseph Cahalan, Xerox's corporate communications director. Ericsson's manager of marketing communications, Birgitta Engart, couldn't agree more: "You exchange ideas and you find out what other people have been doing. So if a country has produced a particularly good brochure and they present it at the conference, it will be spread, and a few months later all the countries are using the same pictures and same material." She feels it's important to give the different offices some creative freedom and not have everything handed down to them from headquarters. The networking aspect of the meetings is helpful for day-to-day coordination. "You get to know your international

colleagues," says Fred Cahuzak, Ericsson's communications director of the Netherlands, adding, "I can call up Paula, my counterpart
in the U.K., anytime, and ask her questions; it's like she's next door."

An additional way for Hewlett-Packard to facilitate learning
across its business units is through an advertising and marketing
communications award competition. Explains Bojana Fazarinc,
corporate marketing communications director of HP, "Last year, we
had about five hundred entries in twenty-three categories. We try to
give it visibility. We bring in outside judges. We send out awards.
We send letters declaring the winners to general managers and
marketing managers." The judging categories include best integrated mixed media campaign, best consumer advertising, best
business-to-business advertising, a multimedia award, and more.
In addition to sharing success stories during the ad council meeting, Fazarinc takes the show on the road. "We develop a slide show
with samples of the finalists and winners, which circulates around
the world so that every business unit can have its own ceremonies."
And that's not all. "We also have exhibits set up at general managers' meetings giving some higher visibility to the communication
activities." This kind of sharing of best practices helps communications staffs at different HP units develop a shared professional
approach to communications. ABB Sweden has a similar award
festival with a panel of judges, including the president of the
National Advertising Federation and senior VPs of the company.
"Involving a high caliber of dignitaries raises the status of the communication profession in the company," reflects Lillemor Rolf,
director of marketing communications.

ABB Sweden has taken the learning aspect of its meetings a step
further by combining them with client visits. "We visit Volvo or SAS
to learn how they work with communication," Rolf says. The company is also offering formal marketing and communications classes
in collaboration with local universities for college credits, complete
with exams and research papers. "This type of training is important
because many of our communication professionals are engineers
who lack formal communication training," notes Rolf, who is now
helping ABB's Polish subsidiary set up a similar program. Motorola
is moving in the same direction by offering a three-day "Principles

and Practices of Public Relations" course led by top-notch university professors.

Typically, ideas for creating synergies and cooperation bubble up at large council meetings where subcommittees from different business units are formed and assigned to carry out specific tasks. Most of the actual coordination work takes place in these teams. Some of the teams are ad hoc to solve particular issues, and some are permanent. An example of a permanent team is Motorola's sponsorship team. It decides what events to enter and what business units will fund it. Another Motorola team is standardizing public relations measurements across business units. Almost every company has assigned cross-business unit teams to integrate customer databases and Internet efforts.

The development of Intranets and other forms of internal computer networks accelerates collaboration among communications professionals considerably. As Eastman's Rod Irvin would tell you, this is particularly important in times of crisis. "We have our crisis manual available on our Intranet. If we had an operational crisis going on in Malaysia, the headquarters group could follow it on the Intranet, without having to tie up telephone lines." Press releases and other informational material that will leave the company are edited online simultaneously by both the central public relations department and communicators at the sites. "It really cuts down review-approval time, because what happens a lot of times is that someone over at the site of the accident calls up, someone over here types up something, faxes it back, someone over there looks at it, makes changes, and you keep going back and forth." Today, all of these iterations happen online in real time.

Finally, a communications guideline book plays an important role in integrating the job of communications professionals, although these days it's more often an electronic file on the internal computer network than a physical book. In addition to the obligatory design guidelines of how to apply logotypes and which PMS colors to use, the guideline book should include key messages. It should provide boilerplate statements but also capture the emotional essence of the brand. Ericsson, for instance, has developed a "Global Brand Book" that describes in words and pictures the spirit of the brand to all communicators and other managers and employees. Danfoss also includes in its guidelines a three-step process to rename newly acquired companies. "It describes how at first they add the tag line 'member of the Danfoss Group' to the company name, next we switch to the Danfoss name in conjunction with the company name, and finally we switch over to just Danfoss," explains Torben Fich, director of communications and marketing. In order to get more than just a grudging commitment from communications professionals to adhere to the guidelines, they need to be involved in the development and continual refinement of them. This not only enhances quality, but provides the much-needed buy-in from the people who will live and breathe by the guidelines.

Along with shared guidelines, the processes and infrastructures of council meetings, training classes, award competitions, team projects, and computer connectivity play a pivotal role in aligning the efforts of communicators throughout the organization. They provide professionals the opportunities to develop personal relationships with each other, coordinate communications projects, share best practices, learn from each other's mistakes, offer professional training, improve the status of communication in the company, and become more committed to the organization as a whole. "It has created a camaraderie and spirit of cooperation and understanding that never would have occurred in a centralized organization," concludes Motorola's buoyant corporate communications director, Chuck Sengstock. Bringing together people in the company that are facing similar challenges helps to create an informal network, a "community of practice," if you will. Ties are formed every time colleagues communicate with each other, and they solidify over time to a surprisingly stable network, which is much better equipped at coordinating complex activities in times of rapid change than a formal hierarchy of command and control.

Needed: A Communications Pope

The collaborative approaches pioneered by the companies described on these pages require a new breed of marketing and communications managers. They need to counsel, mediate, support, network, acts as change agents, and add value to communications professionals in the business units. "It's more effective to motivate through training and highlighting good examples then to be a 'logo cop,'" contends Mats Rönne, marketing communications director at Ericsson, referring to the marcom directors whose sole role is to reprimand colleagues for not complying with the corporate identity. This view is shared by his counterpart at Motorola, Chuck Sengstock. He contrasts the new style with the old ways of relating to professionals at the business units: "We don't simply say we are going to be on your back, just watching over your shoulder. We say, we are here to help. We bring something to the party. We are adding value to you." Hewlett-Packard's marketing communications director, Bojana Fazarinc, has even developed a database to profile her "customers"—marcom professionals at the business units—to better meet their needs. "After all, they support the corporate overhead that keeps us here," notes Fazarinc. Her colleague, Mary Anne Easley, director of public relations, shares this view. "I don't have any authority over the communications professionals in the business units. I don't hire and I don't evaluate them. But I do have responsibility for networking those people."

An example of how the corporate communications staffs act as mediators is when Hewlett-Packard's computer division developed an advertising campaign with the theme "Think Again." The selling message was that computer buyers should not just go with the market leaders, but expand their short lists of computer suppliers to include Hewlett-Packard. This campaign message contradicted the communications objectives of Hewlett-Packard's laser and InkJet printing divisions, which were leaders in their respective markets—both had over 50 percent market share. Says Bojana Fazarinc, "Being a leader in printing categories, we didn't want people to 'think again.' Just buy HP and don't think of anything else." Fazarinc brought the parties together and solved the issue through consensus. "We were not saying, 'We at corporate tell you not to do this.' Instead we told them, 'Hear your colleagues, hear their case, give them a chance to provide a case for why they should do this,' and then hear the rebutting," she explains. The outcome of the mediation was that the computer division agreed to change the tag line.

Fazarinc's approach shows that companies don't need an authoritative "communications czar" to integrate communications, which is sometimes suggested. Instead, the communications leaders of these world-class companies are better described as "communica-tiona popes," who provide spiritual leadership without the formal authority of a virtual organization of communications profession-als around the world. Says Motorola advertising director Chris McClure, "More and more my role is turning into a role of a facili-tator of a team, working with all the different businesses."

The Support Functions: Process Makes Perfect

The focus so far has been on elevating the role of marketing and communications professionals to that of strategic drivers of the business. Needless to say, though, a large number of marketing and communications support functions still need to be performed. Speeches need to be written, databases need to be managed, web-sites need to be programmed, and commercials need to be shot. Like all other areas of business, these business processes need to be continuously improved to cut down cycle time, drive out cost, and enhance quality and integration. Saturn's president, Don Hudler, cuts to the chase on this point: "If there is a problem with the way that things are going, the *process* needs to be changed—not neces-sarily the people involved." Quality guru W. Edwards Deming couldn't have said it better. He was relentless in pointing out that as much as 94 percent of any company's performance is determined by its processes—the way work is structured. Only 6 percent is determined by individuals. Yet most managers focus on the 6 per-cent of a company that individual workers can impact, instead of the 94 percent that the managers have direct control and responsi-bility over.

A case in point of a process improvement is Motorola's quarterly earnings report, which used to be an embarrassment for the elec-tronics giant. "It was already old news when it arrived in the stock-holder's mailbox, six weeks or more later," bemoans Chuck Sengstock. His director of corporate identity, Jim Winski, adds, "In addition, the costs of producing the reports were skyrocket-ing because the number of shareholders was doubling every year." To remedy the problem, a cross-functional team was formed with members from the legal, investor relations, and financial reporting departments, along with an outside design firm. The team began by flowcharting their current processes for producing and distributing the quarterly report. As indicated in the upper portion of figure 6.5, the public relations department wrote a news release about the quarterly report. Then the investor and public relations departments rewrote the release, designed it, and had it printed in a glossy format and stapled. Two weeks later the quarterly report was sent out to shareholders. Shareholders who owned Motorola stocks in their brokers' names, so-called street name accounts, had to wait another two months because the quarterly reports were mailed to the brokers in bulk, who then remailed them to their clients.

The Motorola team benchmarked the process against ten other companies. Benchmarking is the process of evaluating work processes with best-in-class companies for the purpose of organizational improvement. "Some of the benchmark companies were our industry peers, like Intel and AMP; others were companies with outstanding communication from other industries such as McDonald's and Coca-Cola," explains Winski. Based on the team's analysis of Motorola's own processes, how the benchmark companies did it, and its shareholders' needs, it redesigned the processes completely, as shown in the lower portion of figure 6.5. Under their new process, the news release with the quarterly earnings was fed straight into a QuarkXpress template with a prepared feature story, at the same time as the report was published. It was transmitted electronically to a printer the same evening and printed overnight. "We used a simpler printing process to make overnight printing possible," comments Winski. The report was mailed the next morning directly to all shareholders from lists of addresses, which were bought from a vendor, instead of going through brokers for the street name accounts. "As a result, we cut the cycle time from three months to forty-eight hours," says Sengstock proudly. Non–value added steps of rewrites, proofreadings, approvals, printing a glossy cover page, and stapling were cut. The new process slashed costs to one-fourth of original costs, producing a savings of $175,000 a year. Motorola realized that what shareholders valued most was getting their stock information on a timely basis—not whether or not the report was nicely printed or had a glossy cover.

The next year the team met again to reexamine the quarterly report. "It turned out that the success of the previous year was only an interim solution," reflects Sengstock. This time it recommended

Before

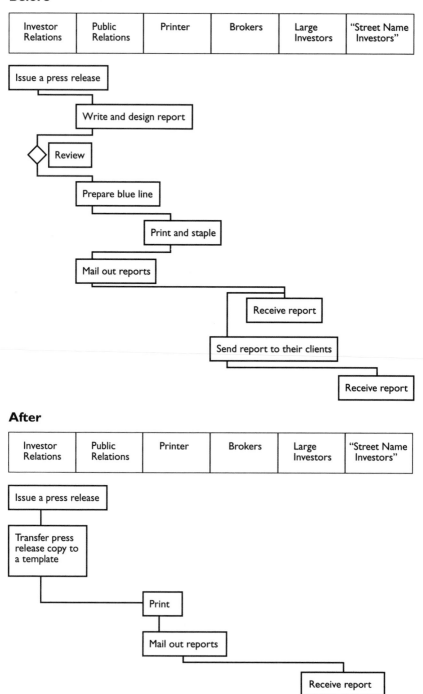

Investor Relations	Public Relations	Printer	Brokers	Large Investors	"Street Name Investors"

After

Investor Relations	Public Relations	Printer	Brokers	Large Investors	"Street Name Investors"

Figure 6.5. Motorola's process of producing quarterly reports before and after the process reengineering.

that the printed version be eliminated altogether and the report be made available on the Internet or by request via a toll-free investor-relations telephone service. "This change, along with a less costly annual report, ultimately saved us $800,000," concludes Sengstock. The time and cost savings of reengineering the processes are summarized in figure 6.6.

Integrating processes requires the rigor of actually documenting them, as displayed in the Motorola case. That's a difficult adjustment for many communications professionals, who are unaccustomed to defining work tasks in terms of process steps. The prevailing notion in the marketing and communications community is that the documentation of processes inhibits creativity and turns communications into assembly-line engineered work. After all, the purpose of manufacturing is that every product come off the line the same way, whereas communications processes have the opposite objective: to come up with creative original ideas. Chuck Sengstock describes his initial resistance to standardizing processes: "We said, 'We're different, we're creative, we're unique, we're in communications you know.'" He was, however, soon proven wrong and became an unabashed proponent for documenting and systematically improving communications processes.

Sengstock came to realize that there are a number of repetitive steps in any communications process than can be documented, standardized, and improved, without stifling creativity. "When you get into any kind of process, you find out that 60 or 70 percent of the time is non–value added, and maybe half of that is in waiting for something to happen, appointments to be made, phone calls to be returned, a supplier to perform, something to be done before something else can be done. So when you start looking at all these aspects, there is enormous potential for running things in parallel, eliminating the waiting time, cut the redundancy, three or four proofreadings, three or four approvals—those are unnecessary." Sengstock concludes that one approval and one proofreading should be adequate, and that is the way he attacks a major project. If everything marketing and communications professionals did was unique, they would not be able to build on their experiences. Even if the subject matter of a CEO's speech or a direct-mail piece changes, the techniques and mechanics of producing them do not.

Time Savings

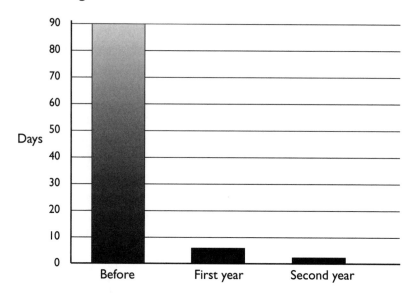

Cost Savings

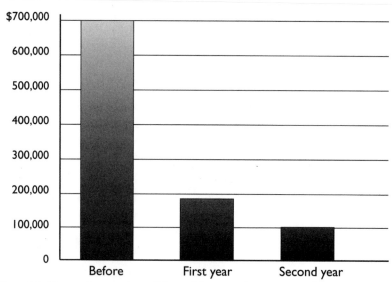

Figure 6.6. Time and cost savings of Motorola's process improvements for communicating its quarterly earnings report.

"Any job for which there is a learning curve is, in fact, a repeatable process and can be described and analyzed," says Richard Buetow, Motorola's now retired director of quality.[7] If the process steps are standardized, professionals can focus more energy on the creative content of each process step.

Anna-Karin Klinteskog, communications manager of Ericsson, notes another benefit of the structured processes she employs. "We have received status in the organization and a language to communicate in the organization in a way they understand," she says, referring to her engineering colleagues outside the communications department. She adds, "Communication tends to be about personal opinions and feelings." The process she developed for communications planning, however, "bases decisions on facts and the *customers'* opinions." Processes that are based on hard facts and structure lend credence to communications processes in the eyes of other company departments.

Sengstock and Klinteskog recognize that marketing and communications professionals have to catch up with the process improvements that colleagues in other departments have been doing for the last several decades. If Ford can cut the cycle time of assembling a car in half, why can't most public relations departments cut the cycle time of producing an annual report by even a day? If Motorola can achieve a six-sigma defect level (three defective products out of every million), why do most press releases and technical manuals have at least three typos per page? The old guard of marketing and communications is about to run out of excuses for not measuring and managing its processes to improve integration and provide consistently high-quality results.

The Internal Agency

A more radical approach to improving the quality, efficiency, and integration of marketing and communications support functions is to outsource them. In the face of this threat, Fred Cahuzak's communications department at Ericsson Netherlands is scrambling to demonstrate accountability by establishing client-service relationships. "We consider the marketing, human resource, and quality departments our customers. We develop written proposals for any project. They sign contracts and pay for our services," says Cahuzak. The internal clients are free to select outside suppliers instead. Danfoss pioneered this approach half a century ago, with an internal communications agency that now employs 140 people. "It probably has a 75 percent market share within Danfoss in the areas of technical documentation, user manuals, and marcom material," estimates Torben Fich, director of communications and marketing. "It works like any agency; Danfoss business units choose if they want to use it or not, and are invoiced for the services." But unlike outside agencies, it works exclusively for Danfoss. Fich makes no secret that he regrets this fact. "It would be nice if they could work with outside clients to give them opportunities to renew themselves and develop fresher creative ideas." He describes it as a "handicap," and ascribes "political reasons" for this policy.

Still, doubts are lingering in the boardrooms about the rationale for companies like Danfoss and Ericsson to keep marketing and communications service providers in-house. Many other business support functions such as payroll, security, and information systems are already being outsourced, why not the marketing and communications functions? The critical questions to ask in making any outsourcing decisions are: Can outsiders provide quality at a lower cost? Can it be done without the deep knowledge of the company that only an insider would have? Is the outside perspective and expertise of high importance? Many companies are responding with a resounding "yes" to all these questions when it comes to many support services like market research and the creation of speeches, brochures, and advertisements. Consider Kodak, which recently reduced its corporate communications staff from 420 to 37, largely through outsourcing.

Building an "Agency *Keiretsu*"

With a growing part of communications services outsourced, it is vitally important to form close-knit partnerships with a limited number of suppliers. A proliferation of different communications agencies can be a major impediment to integration, as Motorola has experienced. Chris McClure, director of advertising, was blunt about this problem: "We probably have two hundred agencies handling the marketing communications and advertising for our offices worldwide, and that's a nightmare. I believe we can bring the number down substantially and that would help with the uniformity." That's changing rapidly, as Motorola and other companies are trimming down their agency roster and forming intimate partnerships with a small number of suppliers to improve integration. It's only a slight exaggeration to compare these kinds of partnerships with the Japanese *keiretsu*, the dense partnerships between companies and their suppliers.

The consolidation of suppliers is primarily taking place within each marketing and communications function. World-class companies are turning to a single advertising agency, public relations firm, database marketing company, fulfillment supplier, sales promotion agency, web consultant, and market research firm. These suppliers sometimes have the responsibility for international regions, or even globally. It's an important first step to integrate within each discipline across business units and country markets. "You used to be able to pick up a magazine and find five different HP ads from five different business units that had a completely different, look, feel, and message about HP," admits HP's Fazarinc. She solved the problem by requiring all HP units to use a single advertising agency of record to coordinate the media placements.

An example of successful single-sourcing of public relations services to one global firm is Federal Express's relationship with Ketchum. FedEx used to work with a variety of PR firms. "We had a real hodgepodge of agencies. We worked with Ketchum and other firms in the U.S., Hill & Knowlton in Japan, and Ogilvy, Adams and Rinehart in Asia," says Tom Martin, FedEx's public relations director at the time. In 1994 it consolidated worldwide with Ketchum. Martin attributes the company's success in the trade battle with Japan (described in chapter 1) in part to its partnership with Ketchum's global network. "We could immediately assemble a team of people in New York, Washington, Tokyo, and elsewhere." He argues that FedEx would never have been able to orchestrate the press club performances in Tokyo, the media relations activities with Japanese newspaper correspondents in the United States, and the Washington lobbying if it was served by different PR firms in each country. Martin illustrates the problems he formerly encountered when he dealt with multiple public relations firms: "We'd get in a situation where two different public relation firms ended up going to the media on two different occasions pitching a similar story, to the same people, from the same company."

An additional benefit of using a single PR firm is that FedEx has Ketchum on call twenty-four hours a day if it needs emergency counsel or extra manpower. When FedEx had an airplane accident in New York, a senior Ketchum manager was on site to be FedEx's spokesperson an hour and a half before the FedEx corporate communications director got there. "We were praised for our rapid media response," notes Bill Margaritis, VP of corporate communications. During the UPS strike in 1997, Ketchum sent a planeload of people to Memphis to work in FedEx's PR department. In addition, FedEx tapped Ketchum's offices in San Francisco, Miami, Chicago, Los Angeles, and New York to deal with local and regional media inquiries. An additional benefit cited by Martin is that he receives more support from the senior management of Ketchum: "We used to be a $50,000 client for one PR firm in Singapore, and an $80,000 client in Tokyo for another. But by combining all of our business into a global network we are now a multimillion-dollar client around the world. And we get the attention from the highest level of the PR firm."

A few world-class companies are going a step further and consolidating a number of communications disciplines with the same supplier. Saturn is leading the way, as Steve Shannon, director of consumer marketing, explains. "Our advertising agency does a lot more for us than just advertising." Making a case for single-sourcing the different marketing communications services, Shannon continues. "So the more stuff you get under the same roof, the same people that are doing advertising are working on promotionals and doing other things, that makes everything look together, look the same, fit together."

When Saturn selected its agency, or, in Saturn parlance, its "communications partner," twenty-nine months before the first car went on sale, the choice fell on San Francisco–based Hal Riney & Partners. The agency gave strategic counsel in the early stages of the Saturn project. Its owner, Hal Riney, advised Saturn, for instance, to integrate the retailers by calling them "Saturn of [location]" and to integrate the car models by naming them Saturn SC and Saturn SL1, instead of separate descriptive names, in the manner of Honda Accord and Chevy Lumina. States Don Hudler, "Mr. Riney thought it was absolutely wrong to put anything but the Saturn name on it, and the more we tested and thought about it, he was absolutely right." Stressing the Saturn name this way was a key brand-building decision. The intimate collaboration with a single supplier offers Saturn the best of both worlds: the knowledge of its own operations that normally comes with in-house specialists, and the communications expertise and reality check of an outsider. The agency account teams entrench themselves in Saturn's business strategies and processes to give their client informed advice, yet through working with other clients and looking from the outside in, they are able to offer a fresh, unbiased perspective. After all, asking employees to dissect and describe their own organization is somewhat akin to asking a fish to describe the ocean. Often, an outside partner can provide a balanced perspective that companies need.

Publicis Hal Riney & Partners, as the agency is now called, continues to provide Saturn with an array of communications services. When, for example, Saturn's retailers are looking for salespeople, the agency develops and places the want ads. Hal Riney is a regular speaker at the annual business meetings of Saturn retailers. While dealers of most other car brands use their own agencies for local advertising, Saturn requires its retailers to use Publicis Hal Riney & Partners' services for all of their marketing communications needs. This not only benefits Saturn by avoiding the classic cheesy local TV spots that feature retail owners shoutingat the camera or wearing clown suits, but provides the Saturn retailers professional and effective marketing communications pieces that are in synch with national Saturn advertising and Saturn retail advertising elswhere. "Hal Riney provides the best service I have seen in all our eleven franchises," maintains Tom Zimbrick, owner of a Saturn dealership in Madison, Wisconsin. He feels the relationship with the agency is a cooperative one. "Hal Riney people act as our representatives. They really value our input and listen to us when we give recommendations, whereas other manufacturers are more directive: 'This is what we have, this is what we think, what do you think?'"

To build a partnership based on trust, both Saturn and Hal Riney have made a long-term commitment to each other. "If we were to rebid the job every year, there would be less trust in the system," argues Saturn's Steve Shannon. He makes every effort to make the agency personnel an integral part of Saturn's operations, including inviting them to participate in Saturn's employee training sessions. For instance, a team of advertising managers at Saturn and their counterparts at Publicis Hal Riney & Partners went through Saturn's Outward Bound course in team building. Shannon found that it helps to break down barriers and create a genuine bond "when you have climbed a thirty-foot pole and jumped off it into the arms of your agency counterpart."

The trend toward forging long-term relationships with a small number of global communications suppliers parallels the development in manufacturing. When Xerox turned to total quality management it reduced its number of suppliers from 18,000 to fewer than five hundred during the course of just a few years. The average *Fortune* 500 company has reduced its supplier base by half.[8] Xerox and other companies are forming long-term partnerships with a select few suppliers who don't merely provide supplies but also involve themselves in new product development and strategic consulting. As quality guru Deming put it, "I have yet to see a customer who has enough knowledge to work with one supplier. Don't tell me he has enough to work with two." In an environment where suppliers are bidding for every assignment, they don't feel the remotest sense of commitment or dedication to the customer. On the other hand, by becoming strategic partners, the suppliers become an integral part of the client's business and benefit in multiple ways from its success. A relationship founded on trust and mutual respect evolves. HP and Ericsson are even farming out their manufacturing to contract manufacturers such as D2D. It allows them to hone in on new product development and customer relationship building, while the contractor can offer them better quality, efficiency, and expertise at reduced costs in manufacturing.

Borrowing from contemporary manufacturing-supplier practices, progressive companies are now finding that the same logic holds true for communications suppliers. Marketing and communications directors have radically trimmed their supplier base and given more work to the survivors in return for better prices, better service, and closer integration. Birgitta Engart, manager of marketing communications, gives an example of Ericsson's relationship with Bates Worldwide: "We had something happening in central Europe so I just called my contact person at Bates, and he in turn called their local people in Central Europe and when our local people started asking for material, the local agency was already prepared with materials and films, etc." By working with one agency, Ericsson can get quicker responses and consistent collateral pieces for offices to use worldwide. In an increasingly global economy, companies are reaping the advantages of consistency in communications, speed of learning, and economies of scale and scope of a single global communications partner.

Having pared down the number of communications suppliers, the challenge is to get the remaining ones to collaborate with each other. "It is the cross-company communication we have to work on," comments Saturn's Steve Shannon. "No matter how few suppliers you have, it is hard to have just one, because of the expertise. That is why we have to spend a lot of time making sure that our suppliers communicate with each other. . . . Ultimately, we as clients have to make sure that that kind of interaction between suppliers takes place. My job is to create an environment where they can share information naturally."

The Problem with Monogamy

Single-sourcing communications services certainly has downsides. One of the most frequently mentioned problems is that few communications suppliers can offer first-class service in all disciplines and in every part of the world. Federal Express is careful not to force Ketchum upon any international office. "What I always tell our international communicators is that it's got to work for you at the local level, and if it doesn't, we're not going to push Ketchum down your throats," assures Tom Martin. FedEx in Canada has continued to work with its old PR firm, and Ketchum's Latin American offices were promptly fired. "Ketchum's Latin offices were a disaster," quipped one FedEx manager, adding that this hasn't hurt the overall relationship between FedEx and Ketchum.

Even as a number of communications agencies are beginning to offer first-rate services in most countries, few of them have yet made the transition from a multinational to a global company. They are still, for the most part, organized around international offices that each have their own P&L responsibilities. Only limited efforts have been made by some agencies to instead organize around global practice areas or clients. Most suppliers also lack effective processes of integrating their various communications services. While many of them have excellent design, advertising, database, and public relations expertise, they typically congregate in different departments or even different subsidiary companies. Few agencies have the processes, competency, infrastructure, and reward structure to integrate them well. That's why most world-class companies still keep control of the integration process in-house. Saturn is the early adopter in outsourcing the processes of integration to a lead agency. More client companies will probably follow its example as communications agencies themselves adopt world-class integrated communications.

Another argument against a monogamous supplier relationship is the perception that competition among suppliers helps "keep them on their toes" and makes them more efficient. Many world-class managers counter that competition also creates fear, dishonesty, and short-term thinking. They prefer instead to base relationships on trust and long-term commitment. If, for instance, a supplier who has to compete for every account runs into problems, the last person they would turn to would be the client. In a trusting relationship, the client would be the first person they would turn to, to work out the problem together.

Yet another problem with single-sourcing is the perception that clients are "putting all their eggs in one basket," making them vulnerable if the supplier experiences problems. These fears are certainly legitimate, but the people I interviewed pointed out that working with multiple agencies is a very expensive insurance against these risks. Not to mention that clients have a large responsibility in ensuring that the risks do not materialize. One of the leading total quality management proponents in Japan, the late Kaoru Ishikawa, argued that if the work of a subcontractor is unsatisfactory, the client bears 70 percent responsibility.[9] Any professional service is coproduced by the supplier and its client, and the success depends at least as much on the client side. That's why a number of world-class companies are following the advice of Mark Twain: "Put all your eggs in one basket—and watch that basket." The communications agency relationships might never get as intertwined as the Japanese *keiretsu*, where manufacturers typically own 20 to 50 percent of the equity of their largest suppliers, and many of the suppliers' managers have previously been employed by their customers. But companies like Saturn, Ericsson, and Federal Express have developed a Western-style "agency *keiretsu*" that will flourish in the Customer Century.

A Seat at the Management Table

As communication responsibilities are becoming dispersed across the organization and outside agencies, communications professionals need to rise to the occasion and assume a more strategic role. They need to integrate the various marketing and communications support functions, which are increasingly handled by outside specialists. But more importantly, they need to bring thoughtfully conceived agendas to the senior management table that address the strategic issues of business planning, resource allocation, priorities, and direction of the firm. Instead of asking what event to sponsor and at what cost, they should be asking which customer segments to invest in and at what projected returns. Instead of asking how to allocate money between advertising and product publicity, they should be asking how to allocate money between customer retention and acquisition. Instead of asking how to improve the number of hits to the website, they should be asking who their key stakeholders are and how to get more interactive with them. Instead of worrying about producing quick deliverables, they should focus on cultivating customer relationships.

A recent senior management meeting at Ericsson illustrates the need to have the senior communications director represented at the table. During a meeting at the Ericsson headquarters in the Stockholm suburb of Telefonplan, a division head announced his plans to lay off eight thousand workers.[6] Nils Ingvar Lundin responded, "That's okay if you want to be known as the 'Butcher of Telefonplan.'" He argued forcefully that a layoff of such magnitude at a time when Ericsson was raking in record profits would be a disaster to its reputation. After extensive discussions, the group decided to offer the employees positions in other Ericsson divisions. Shortly thereafter, all eight thousand workers were offered new jobs within Ericsson. A potential crisis was averted by a corporate communicationw director who acted as a policymaker rather than as an order taker. In the early days of the Production Century, Lundin would have been notified after the meeting with detailed instructions on how to draft the press release. More enlightened Production Century companies would have involved him in discussions about the timing of the announcement and the message strategy. In contrast, world-class companies like Ericsson take advice from the communications director during the strategic decision-making process itself. "Corporate communications directors should be members of the senior management team and report to the president," argues Lundin. "But that's nothing they can just demand. They have to earn their respect as effective managers first."

There is a lot of bemoaning in the hallways of marketing and communications offices of how CEOs "don't understand communications," when the real problem is that many marketing and communications professionals do not understand the intricacies of business management well enough to become part of the governing coalition. Few of Lundin's colleagues at other companies have reached the hard-earned place in the kitchen cabinet that CEOs turn to for strategic insights when their paradigm needs a shift, their core needs a competency, their organization needs learning, or their customer relationships need management. Being a player on the senior management team is necessary to plot an integrated "high-tech/high-touch" strategy, which will be explored further in the concluding chapter.

What Marketing and Communications Professionals Should Do Friday Morning:

- Develop measurements based on the three levels: how customers and stakeholders add value to the organization, how the organization adds value to customers and stakeholders, and the reputation of the organization and its brand(s). Make this the performance metrics of the entire company.

- Conduct an audit interviewing all senior managers and a sample of middle managers about how the marketing or communications department adds value to their functions and the company as a whole. Audit all professionals in the marketing/communications department as well. Analyze the gaps and develop action plans.

- Develop guidelines in words and pictures on the personality, look, tone, and core messages of the company and its brand(s), and process flowcharts for how to conduct communications planning and implementation.

- Form councils of marketing and communications professionals who share similar challenges in different parts of the organization, arrange regular meetings focused on dialogue, sharing of best and worst practices, and future plans. Assign cross-business teams to solve problems and opportunities that are identified by the council.

- Analyze which tasks need to be handled by a full-service firm, in-house, or a la carte (sourcing narrowly defined tasks to specialized firms) based on analysis of cost, quality, and importance of internal knowledge vs. outside perspective. Once the firm(s) is chosen, form a long-term partnership, based on the sharing of information, risks, and rewards.

- Bring thoughtfully conceived integrated communications and marketing agendas that address the strategic priorities of the company to the senior management table.

Notes

1. Sheth, Jagdish N., and Sisodia, Rajendra S. (1995). "Improving Marketing Productivity." In *Marketing Encyclopedia*. Lincolnwood, Ill.: NTC Business Books, pp. 217–37.

2. Dozier and Ehling conclude that "the problem with the domino effects model is that the last fifty years of communication research indicates that the model is wrong." Dozier, David M., and William P. Ehling (1992). "Evaluation of Public Relations Programs: What the Literature Tells Us about Their Effects." In James E. Grunig, ed., *Excellence in Public Relations and Communication Management*. Hillsdale, N.J.: Erlbaum, pp. 164.Larry Ligh reviewed over nine hundred advertising studies, conducted over nine hundred studies and did not find any evidence of the domino, or "hierarchy of effects" model. Light, Larry (1993). "At the Center of It All Is the Brand." *Advertising Age*, March 29, p. 22.

   Barry and Howard reviewed the research on hierarchy of effects and concluded that "no evidence currently exist supporting the contention that the sequential ordering of cognitive versus affective response to advertising communications ultimately matters in terms of what people purchase or consume." Barry, Thomas and Howard, Daniel (1990). "A Review and Critique of the Hierarchy of Effects in Advertising." *International Journal of Advertising*, Vol. 9, No. 2, pp. 121–35.

3. This three-pronged approach is based on Atkinson, Anthony A., John H. Waterhouse, and Robert B. Wells (1997). "A Stakeholder Approach to Strategic Performance Measurement." *Sloan Management Review*, Spring, pp. 25–37.

4. Sheth, Jagdish N., and Sisodia, Rajendra S. (1995). "Feeling the Heat—part 2: Information Technology, Creative Management Boost Marketing Productivity." *Marketing Management*, Winter.

5. This segmentation approach based on customer value is suggested in, Rackham, Neil, and John De Vincentis (1999). *Rethinking the Sales Force*. New York: McGraw-Hill.

6. This case is based on Klien, Ernst; Nilson, Ulf (1997). *Om Pressen Kommer*. Stockholm, Sweden: Bonnier Alba.

7. Buetow, Richard C. (1989). "The Motorola Quality Process." Speech, p. 13.

8. Rackham, Neil, and John De Vincentis (1999). *Rethinking the Sales Force*.

9. Ishikawa, Kaoru (1985). *What Is Total Quality Control?* Englewood Cliffs, N.J.: Prentice-Hall, p. 165.

7

INTEGRATING
HIGH-TECH AND HIGH-TOUCH

From the World Classroom
into the Customer Century

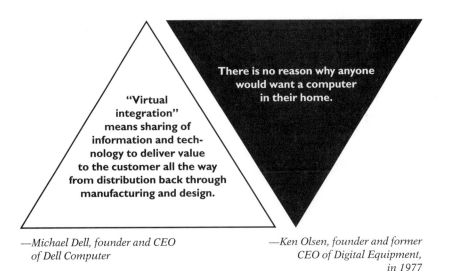

"Virtual integration" means sharing of information and technology to deliver value to the customer all the way from distribution back through manufacturing and design.

There is no reason why anyone would want a computer in their home.

—*Michael Dell, founder and CEO of Dell Computer*

—*Ken Olsen, founder and former CEO of Digital Equipment, in 1977*

The discovery of integrated communications is somewhat akin to the discovery of America. The American continent was only "discovered" for those who didn't know about its existence, not to the natives who lived there. In much the same way, integrated communications is new to the businesspeople who have been cultivated into believing that communications is a separate functional activity of the firm. The customers, on the other hand, are as native to integrated communications as the Native Americans were to America. They have always integrated their perceptions of companies and brands in their own minds, without making a distinction between an ad, a promotion, a sales call, or a service experience. They all blend together as representations of the same company or brand. That's why I have never been able to explain the significance of integrated communications to my mother. To consumers like her, it's an intuitive idea. It is difficult to argue against integrated communications. Yet it's rarely practiced by larger corporations. Wherever we turn our heads, we find companies that lack processes to integrate communications. Mercedes-Benz went from world-class to *A-Class* by flipping over a car and flipping off a number of journalists and customers in the process. The now successful Daimler-Chrysler had to learn to roll with the punches before understanding the value of integrated communications. That case and numerous others go to show that there's an obvious need to "discover" integrated communications and put it on the map for business leaders and marketing and communications professionals.

My own recent experience with MCI is another flagrant example of how far most companies have to go. I have been a long-distance customer for many years with MCI and put thousands of dollars straight into its bottom line. But the telecommunications company never bothered to communicate with me in any way other than through bills and an occasional solicitation to buy additional services. I finally responded to its offer to buy a cellular phone. The phone was sent to me two weeks later than promised and didn't work. I spent over half a day trying to get through to customer service, which was at first busy, then when I finally got through I was promptly put on hold for over an hour, and transferred to different departments. MCI finally promised to get back to me in forty-eight hours, but didn't didn't in fact do so until three months later when they called to ask why I didn't pay my bills. In the meantime, I had written the customer service manager threatening to move all my MCI business if the problem wasn't fixed. The letter was ignored and I took all my long-distance and cell phone business elsewhere. It took the company two months to react with a phone call from an MCI operator who tried to win back my business with a special offer. I was delighted to finally have a real person from MCI to talk to about my miserable experience. But my joy ended after about thirty seconds when the MCI operator hung up on me as I began to explain my misfortunes.

As an operator of a growing international consulting business, I represent a possible lifetime customer value of millions of dollars to MCI. It chose to walk away from that pile of money. Worse yet, the phone company has turned me into a customer terrorist who discourages others from becoming or remaining MCI customers. MCI obviously has no process of integrating communications across long-distance and cell phone divisions, and no vehicle for customer dialogue. And it's not for lack of a marketing budget. MCI lavishes more than $355 million on advertising every year, making it one of the world's largest advertisers. It would only take a fraction of that amount to set up an integrated process for customer dialogue. The company that started out two decades ago as a feisty young marketing maverick that despised regulations and took on AT&T has forgotten the marketing lessons that made it the nation's second largest long-distance carrier. MCI's disintegrated marketing has depressed the price of its own stock to a level that attracted today's maverick, WorldCom, to gulp it up. The case serves as a reminder that even if integrated communications is common sense, it's certainly not very common. I'm not bringing it up to simply bash this particular company. The problems with MCI are symptomatic of most Production Century companies. Confronted with the new business reality of the Customer Century, they are ending up like a deer frozen in the headlights—unwilling to open up a dialogue of vertical communications within the firm, unable to align horizontal communications, and incapable of building customer and stakeholder relationships. As a result, the average U.S. corporation loses half its customers in five years, half its employees in four years, and half its investors in less than one year.[1]

Integrated communications may not be a new idea, but it is a forgotten one. The companies featured in this book are not only rediscovering this idea, but taking it to new levels. They inhale every detail they can to learn about key customers, make systematic improvements, and address individual customer needs. They plan their entire business operations from the customer's point of view—from the outside in. In the process, they are redefining

marketing with a lowercase "m," to Marketing with a capital "M"—
from a discrete function acting as the sole conduit to customers, to
a state of mind of everyone in the organization. In doing so, they
will continue to set standards for other companies in the future.

Integrated Communications on Viagra

The need to integrate communications is in no small part propelled
by the revolution in digital technology. There is a convergence of
technical progress in database technology, online capabilities, and
mass customized manufacturing that is accelerating the integrated
communications revolution at an exponential rate. The change is
most visible in my children's generation, Generation N (as in
Netizens or Nintendo), which is the first group to embrace the
Internet with full force. This media-savvy and advertising-cynical
generation is finally abandoning the stalwart institution of the television. While, for the first time in history, television viewing is
plummeting among children, Internet usage is gaining momentum.
A majority of today's teenagers would rather give up their televi-
sions than their computers.[2] Where Generation N leads, the rest of
the population will follow. Internet traffic is doubling every one
hundred days, and traditional offline media are getting increasingly
fragmented. Currently, the U.S. television networks have only half
of the audience they had when Ronald Reagan was elected president. The last episode of *Seinfeld* drew only 75 percent as many
viewers as the concluding episode of *M*A*S*H*, and fewer viewers
than a regular episode of the *Beverly Hillbillies*.[3] The television audience of today is beginning to develop the demographic profile of
smokers: older, low income, and poorly educated. Magazine readership has become increasingly fragmented as well, with nine hundred new magazines launched in the United States in 1998 alone.
As media proliferate and audiences fragment, the cost of traditional advertising is going through the roof and its effectiveness is
in a free fall. The ability to influence customers with advertising in
the United States has dropped 30 percent in just the last ten years,[4]
and overwhelming evidence shows that much of today's advertising
has little or no effect at all on sales.[5] Every year, a quarter of a tril-
lion dollars are spent on advertising in the world; more than half of
that amount is estimated to be wasted.[6]

The rapidly declining effectiveness of traditional advertising is causing advertisers to turn to the Internet as their medium of choice. Many marketing departments and advertising agencies are still treating the Internet as "just another vehicle," with limited and impatient audiences. This view is on par with the horse-and-buggy operator criticizing the Model-T Ford for being too loud. It misses the whole point, because the Internet is not just a new medium, it's rapidly becoming a platform for all other media, and more. I listen to Swedish radio on a regular basis over the Internet from my Colorado home. Magazines and newspapers are already available on the Net and television is soon to follow. And that's just for starters. The Internet is becoming an information source, a communication channel, a transaction vehicle, and a distribution tool. It is the phone, the newspaper, the television, the shopping mall, the library, and the coffee shop. It is open twenty-four hours a day, 365 days a year, and is available in every corner of the world. The only reason to consider the Internet a "medium" is that it is not *rare* and not always *well done*. It is in fact subsuming all other media. The Internet is the new infrastructure of the addressable, interactive, one-to-one communication of the Customer Century.

Virtual 3-D Integration

While the rapid development of information technology drives integrated communications, the technology is still just a tool. Legendary photographer Irving Penn got it right when he took pictures of Ernest Hemingway, who commented upon seeing the pictures, "What good pictures you take, what camera do you have?" Penn replied, "What typewriter do you use, Ernest?" This comment is as astute now as it was then. No one has much advantage from technology itself. Most applications can be purchased by anyone off the shelf. The key to success is to use it strategically to integrate communications in 3-D.

A valuable lesson in how to invigorate horizontal communications with the Internet comes from ISS. The cleaning giant has developed a virtual Yellow Pages on its Intranet with information about the competencies of every individual in the company: "If you need expertise in cleaning auto shops in Austria, you can search for the people with that experience," says Alain Dehaze, business development director of ISS. The Intranet also features an internal benchmarking system called "Cockpit" to help keep everyone at the fifty ISS offices operating in Europe up to date on key clients. Key account managers enter information about their clients into the Intranet on a daily basis. "Country managers or key account managers can log on this Intranet site to compare their own performance with those of their peers," says Marketing Director Fred Nurskij, "such as how many new contracts have closed in the last month, bids and sales visits, and how they compare in profitability." To the extent that such information was ever documented in the past, it used to be put in a closet and never made available to anyone else unless, as Nurskij puts it, "Somebody had the same problem, asked the right questions, and happened to talk the guy who put the book in the closet." ISS is using this Intranet application to leverage learning in one place across all the twenty-nine countries where it operates. "Our Intranet is becoming a virtual university," concludes Nurskij, adding only half jokingly, "It is probably because we don't have an IS manager that we have been so successful with our Intranet." Instead, it's Nurskij and his marketing department that have developed the Intranet to support client relationship building, by making it an easily accessible repository for information about key client accounts.

The Intranet has also improved vertical communications between managers and the service workers out in the field. Alain Dehaze contrasts with the old vehicles: "We used to fax back and forth to the sites and people didn't get information in time." Today, the company has a site supervisor based with all major clients who will get the information on the Intranet and pass it on to the ISS workers at the site. The Intranet is also available to key clients through an "Extranet," password protected websites customized for clients, which futher bolsters integrated external communications. Explains Dehaze, "Our Extranet has three areas: documentation, communication, and quality." The document section contains ISS procedures, contracts, and other paperwork related to the particular client relationship. The communication section has monthly reports and news updates. In the third area of ISS's Extranet, the site manager enters quality data that have been agreed upon with the client. The Extranet plays a strategic role in building relationships with key clients. Dehaze points out that the Extranets have raised the bar for

ISS's client service. "It puts pressure on us to react rapidly to events." It requires the agility from ISS's administrative and field staff to respond to customers' needs within a moment's notice. Who would have thought that a cleaning company would lead the way into building client relationships in cyberspace?

The Internet is just as important for stakeholder communications. The virtual sphere is increasingly becoming the battleground where stakeholder relationships are melded and conflicts are fought out, giving the concept of "word of mouth" a completely new meaning. Instead of having each disgruntled customer bad-mouth a company to twelve people, they can all of a sudden vent their anger to twelve thousand people. For instance, Microsoft suffers from the online glare of over one hundred anti-Microsoft sites, or "rogue sites," which have names like Hate Microsoft and the Boycott Microsoft site. That's on top of the numerous rogue newsgroups, like Alt.destroy.microsoft. Bringing in lawyers to intimidate the creators of rogue sites only gives the sites more visibility. Companies must embrace negative as well as positive criticism and respond to it. Some companies even go to the extreme of exchanging links with their adversaries. A click on the company's official website takes the visitor to the rogue site, and vice versa. The lesson here is that companies need to keep their eyes and ears open to address online criticism with immediate and open communication. Doing that would have saved Intel the $475 million[7] it lost during the Pentium chip scandal when it neglected to respond to criticism raging in over twenty newsgroups, which finally exploded in the media. World-class companies need to have staffs dedicated to monitoring discussions on the Internet twenty-four hours a day. They need to respond to negative comments and alert people in their companies to problems raised in discussion groups and involve everyone in solving them. That applies even to companies like Saturn and FedEx, which actually have websites developed and maintained by enthusiastic customers and employees.

Turbocharged by the advances in digital technology, the unstoppable force of *vertical* online communications is shattering the big bureaucracies of the Production Century that were built for the sole purpose of controlling people and filtering information up and down the organizational hierarchies. The power of online *horizontal* communications is blowing up the God-given boundaries within companies—connecting people, information, and ideas. And finally, virtual *external* communications is enabling companies to attract, retain, and grow shrewd employees, patient investors, a supportive community, and profitable customers in real time. The Internet is integrated communications on Viagra.

Virtual Integration of the Supply Chain

The implications of the Internet are even more striking when companies get customers and the entire supply chain online, which is what Michael Dell, CEO of Dell Computer Corporation, has dubbed "virtual integration." His company has taken virtual integration further than anyone else. A custom-tailored computer that is ordered from its website at 9 A.M. Monday, can be on the delivery truck by 9 P.M. Tuesday. In that time span, the components of the computer are whisked in from the suppliers' warehouses to Dell's assembly plant. The computer monitors are sent directly to customers from Dell's supplier, Sony, without even passing Dell's Austin plant. A delivery company picks up monitors and computers separately and delivers them together to the customer. In addition, Dell has set up Extranets for several hundred of its largest client companies. For instance, employees of Eastman Chemical Company, which is one of Dell's clients, can design and order a customized computer on its "Premier Site." The computer is delivered from Dell's Austin plant, complete with Eastman's own proprietary software. By integrating electronic payment, Dell converts sales to cash in twenty-four hours, compared to rival Compaq's thirty-five days. Eastman's customized Premier Site also gives access to the same 45,000 pages of service information that Dell's own technicians use to diagnose problems. Figure 7.1 shows how Dell is shattering the entire supply chain by acting as manufacturer, retailer, information broker, and bank, linking online upstream with customers and downstream with suppliers. This newcomer is undermining the entire logic behind the Production Century division of labor between supplier, manufacturer, and distribution channel. Such virtual integration offers unprecedented opportunities for individual dialogue, mass customization, learning relationships, and, most importantly, big bucks, as evidenced by the fact that Michael Dell made himself the richest man in Texas at just over thirty years of age.

The Traditional Model

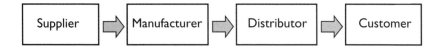

Dell's "Virtual Integration" Model

Figure 7.1. The traditional supply chain in the computer industry contrasted with Dell's "virtual integration," where Dell is manufacturer and retailer, linking customers and suppliers online.[8]

Clearly, service companies like ISS and FedEx have made greater strides into virtual integration than some of the manufacturing-based companies described in this book, which are prisoners of their offline distribution systems. Even a company as progressive as Saturn is not wavering its support behind its bricks-and-mortar stores. Its web-based "interactive pricing center" allows visitors to its website to design and price their own cars with colors and accessories, but stops short of selling the cars over the Internet. Customers still have to walk to the dealer to complete the purchase. "We will religiously protect our dealership relationships," contends Saturn public relations manager Greg Martin, whose company is spending $40 million upgrading its retail stores as this book is being written. Saturn might soon regret that it didn't put the same kind of money into building a virtual dealership. It won't take long for its competitors to take a page from Dell and offer customers the ability to configure their own car on the web, and have it assembled and delivered to the customer's doorstep in a couple of days. Competitor Chrysler estimates that one-third of all cars will be purchased over the Internet in just the next few years. That's the competitive environment Ericsson is already facing in the computer networking market, where competitor Cisco already earns two-thirds of its sales via the Internet. After only thirteen years of existence, Cisco is valued at three and a half times the value of

Ericsson. Hewlett-Packard is another latecomer to the Internet. It's toiling in the low-margin business of PCs and printers sold largely through independent and offline channels, while more agile rivals like Dell, Sun, and even IBM dominate the real growth markets of Internet servers and services. Dell and Cisco weren't on anyone's radar screen when I started researching this book in the early 1990s and are now ruling their respective cybermarkets. This new competition leaves companies like Saturn, HP, and Ericsson with no choice but to turn to virtual integration. They can take comfort in the fact that there is a precedent for offline companies successfully going online. Intel turned the switch in 1998 and was selling a whopping one billion dollars per month, half its sales and three times the online sales of Dell Computer, after only three months. The Swedish banks underwent a successful transition as well. Almost half a million people in this tiny country do their banking online, most of them with traditional banks that are offering online services.[9]

The barriers to virtual integration are typically not in the technology, nor in consumers' Internet savvy, but in industry structures. HP and Saturn are held back by the inevitable channel conflicts that come with virtual integration. Some companies are in a strong enough position that they can afford to alienate channel partners. The airlines, for instance, are not only competing with travel agents, but also slashing their commission rates. Companies that cannot afford to circumvent channel partners have to work with them. One strategy is to offer different brands or products on the Internet than the ones sold through retailers. Another option is to offer channel members better terms or commissions to cushion the negative impact on their sales. A third approach is to take orders on the website but have retailers deliver and collect payments. Whatever approach is used, producers are poised to find ways to shorten the selling chains and get closer to the end customer through virtual integration.

The Promise and Perils of High-Tech Communications

The digital communication of the Customer Century will be magnitudes more powerful than today's version. It will be as pervasive as electricity. In the early days of electricity, people thought it could only be used to bring light to the lightbulb. In much the same way, most marketers today think the Internet can only be used for e-mail and browsers. Soon enough, the Internet will proliferate to run everything in our home and at work, just like electricity. Computers are already being used to watch television, play video games, store and edit family photos and videos, turn off the air conditioner and turn on the oven, and stay in touch with friends. In the near future the wall screen or the projection on a car windshield will alert us of late-breaking news, an increase in a stock price, a score by our favorite hockey team, a message from our boss, or a traffic jam. If we want to know more, we can instantaneously interact and drill down for more information. We will move seamlessly between media that is "pushed" on us and information we seek to "pull" out. Information will be ubiquitous, transparent, and readily available. Yet it will be less intrusive than it is today. Intelligent electronic agents will carefully filter information for us and design our television schedule for the evening. We will be logged on at all times. The lockstep society where everyone gathered around the same television program will be a thing of the past. No longer will ink have to be squeezed onto dead trees that are shipped in trucks and airplanes in order for us to communicate.

Expect completely customized commercial breaks during television and radio programs, or even during telephone conversations if you choose free advertising-supported phone service. And then there are the "smart cards," which truly are the future of electronic commerce. Consumers everywhere will carry these multipurpose credit card look-alikes in their wallets and use them for everything from making payments to starting their cars. This is not science fiction. In fact, Americans are the late adopters. The cards are already in full swing in Europe, where almost a billion smart cards are in circulation! It stands to reason that within just a few short years, you'll be making your next travel reservation on your computer, popping your smart card into a reader, loading all the information on the card and using it as a ticket, boarding pass, baggage claim, charge card, and passport. Your frequent- flier points will of course be automatically credited to your account every time you use the card, as will your frequent brushing points every time you buy a tube of toothpaste in the grocery store. It will be a bonanza for integrated communicators, who will have complete up-to-the-minute information about your digital self. They will be able to use this information to target you with carefully crafted messages, service offerings, and custom-made products based on all your idiosyn-crasies—elevating integrated communications to new stratospheres.

Needless to say, the privacy issues that come along with this development are far-reaching and complex. Rather than belaboring them, I'll offer the following one-sentence summary: You give customers value and customers gladly volunteer their personal information. Most people are happy to share personal information with a company they have a relationship with, if they are sufficiently convinced that they will receive more personalized service. At least in the United States. But go to a pub in Dublin or a coffeehouse in Vienna and most people don't share this lax, pragmatic view. They are as suspicious about corporations infringing on their privacy as Americans are about the government intruding on theirs. In the European Union capital of Brussels, the suspicion has reached levels of paranoia. At the time that this book goes to press, the E.U. has just passed a law that essentially outlaws database marketing in all of its fifteen member countries.[10] The anachronous law makes it criminal for web hosts to place a cookie on visitors' hard drives without visitors' explicit permission. It also bans all forms of cross-marketing without permission from the customer, as in the case of airlines selling hotel accommodations to its travelers, for example. And more to the point, it bars any company doing business in Europe from transmitting personal data to any country, such as the United States, that does not have similar privacy protection.

Some European countries take their national privacy laws even further (which is just fine with the E.U.). For instance, in my native Sweden, a court ruled that American Airlines is not even allowed to keep information in its central database about what plane meal Swedish customers prefer. As a result, the Swedes have to repeat their request for vegetarian food every time they make an airline reservation. This is just a preview of the snags that might hit world-class companies as they develop worldwide customer databases. The seemingly rigid legislation expresses the deeply felt sentiment among many Europeans that individuals' private information should only be used with the utmost integrity. It would be a mistake for any manager to take these concerns lightly.

So far, sanctions against U.S. companies have been suspended while the U.S. and E.U. are negotiating. That gives a little breathing room for companies like Federal Express, which maintains a global database with every FedEx transaction of all its worldwide clients.[11] The database offers the delivery company tremendous leverage in the global marketplace, as long as E.U. legislation doesn't get in the way. Stay tuned for a trade war between the U.S. and Europe over privacy protection.

. . . And the Future of High-Touch Communications

In the Customer Century, everything that can be automated is becoming computerized, leaving only the true "people problems" to, well, the people. The counterintuitive implication of the Customer Century is that *high-touch* communication will be more and more important, along with the increasing prominence of *high-tech* communication. The gospel of good old-fashioned high-touch, face-to-face communication reverberates from the Xerox directors who take turns at the call centers, to the 50,000 Saturnites who make a pilgrimage to Spring Hill every year. It chimes resonantly from the team brief meetings that are cascaded every other week at D2D, to the Team Day festivities at Motorola. It echoes from the integrated marketing communications council meetings at Rockwell Automation, to the "buddy system" between employees of Ericsson and client BT. In the elusive Customer Century, high-touch and high-tech communication need to be leveraged off each other, each used for what it does best. The high-tech ways of online communications offer unprecedented efficiency in transactions, deliveries, information retrieval, and immediacy of communication. The high-touch vehicle of personal meetings, on the other hand, is unrivaled in its knack for bonding, building trust, developing ideas, and solving complex problems.

Even the darling of the digerati, Dell Computer Corporation, owes its success in large part to the high-touch channel of customer conferences held every six months around the world, "We send not only our top technologists and engineers, but also the real engineers, the people who usually don't get out to talk to customers because they're too busy developing products," comments CEO Michael Dell, adding, "The ratio is about one Dell person to one customer."[12] In the consumer retail market, Amazon.com is widely predicted to become the Wal-Mart of the Customer Century. Meanwhile, the Mall of America, the world's largest indoor shopping mall, just added an entertainment complex and a walkthrough aquarium. Its high-touch experiences attract more shoppers in one year than Walt Disney World, Disneyland, and the Grand Canyon combined.[13] Clearly, the real payoff in the Customer Century comes from using *high-tech* to free up people's time for more valuable *high-touch* human interaction.

A careful study of the matrix on the following pages makes it apparent that world-class companies are a combination of high-tech and high-touch communications processes. The matrix summarizes some of their more salient practices in each of the three dimensions of integrated communications. What's missing is the mass communication tools of the Production Century. We've come a long way from the time when communications was a process of packaging and delivering a persuasive message with a monologue of mass media to a mass audience. In the Customer Century, high-tech and high-touch communications processes will be carefully integrated to add value, facilitate dialogue, create meaning, and build relationships.

Company	External Communications	Vertical Communications	Horizontal Communications
ABB Sweden	• ABB Atom conducts personal one-on-one customer satisfaction interviews, and provides customers an action plan for improvements • Enlists managers as spokespeople • Developed strong relationships with the news media	• Strong focus on communications skills for managers • For the "T50" project, seven hundred managers went to a three-day conference. They held similar conferences at their companies	• Successful team projects featured in employee magazine and book • ABB Atom promotes job rotation by giving special bonuses • Focus on self-directed work teams

Company	External Communications	Vertical Communications	Horizontal Communications
ABB Sweden (cont.)	and used them to support the "T50" project, ran ads featuring success stories of the change process, and sold book describing a number of success stories • Customers and suppliers were provided educational seminars on the T50 project	• Chairman Percy Barnevik's "management by traveling around"	
Allen-Bradley and Rockwell Automation	• Integrated brand strategy with Rockwell Automation as endorsement brand. • Electronic literature management system and presentation templates for the sales force	• Managers communicate all relevant information to their immediate employees, supported with "briefing kits" complete with Q&A and feedback forms for questions they can't answer and for employee insights	• "Marketing Communicators Assistant Software" helps integrate communications planning • Integrated Marketing Communication Council has representatives from all businesses and a *Robert's Rules of Order* for decision-making
Danfoss	• Brings in groups of customers to meet assembly-line workers • Keeps stakeholders informed by sending out the employee newsletter to former employees, newspapers, politicians, union leaders, etc.	• Keeps assembly-line workers informed about the customer of each product	• Assigns horizontal process responsibilities at both senior and middle management levels for core competencies • "Room for Visions"—a building where teams converge to develop core competencies

Company	External Communications	Vertical Communications	Horizontal Communications
Danfoss (cont.)			• Policy of job rotation—managers encouraged to rotate jobs every five years
D2D	• Monthly customer satisfaction scorecards used as baseline for continuous improvement • Shares confidential profit and loss information for each client and project with its factory workers • All managers are company spokespeople to the media	• General manager holds "doughnut meetings" and "scotch on the rocks" meetings with small groups of employees. • Employee survey used as input for annual business planning, which is cascaded down the organization • Two-day cascade communications system every other week with "team talk" meetings held at all levels.	• Quality improvement teams • Awards for successful teams
Eastman Chemical Company	• 800 number that customers can access twenty-four hours a day to voice concerns; "customer advocates" follow up to resolve the complaints • Mobilizes grassroots organizations to help influence important policy issues • Community Advisory Panel act as a sounding board for various company initiatives and early warning for emerging issues	• Uses informal surveys with a panel of workers, for ongoing bottom-up communications • Communicates its strategic intent, mission, and drivers throughout the organization	• Corporate communications staff meets once a year with senior managers to discuss their communication needs and opportunities for improvements • Formal process for job rotation • Crisis plan is on the Intranet, where press releases are edited simultaneously from different sites

Company	External Communications	Vertical Communications	Horizontal Communications
Ericsson	• U.K. company has a "buddy system" with client BT to enable personal contacts and stronger ties • Global account managers • Trains part-time communicators to be company spokespeople	• Reversed burden of proof—constant information sharing among all employees • Places great importance on communication skills for managers to ensure effective cascade communications • Dual "management" and "technical specialist" career tracks to get managers with good communication skills	• Some units have "Stand Up" meetings every morning • Communications professionals have frequent council meetings • Intranet has chat groups on different subject matters
FedEx	• Provides customers their own computer terminals and software to print label, place orders, etc. • Package tracking on the web • "Service Quality Indicator" communicated daily to all employees • Full-service logistic provider to client companies, including warehousing • Constant tracking of customer satisfaction • "Strategic Communication Audits" • Every manager is required to spend one day	• "People-service-profit" mission of putting employees at the center is integrated in everything, including planning and bonuses • Internal TV show where employees can call in and speak to CEO directly • Managers are provided ongoing communications training, and their communications skills are assessed by employees every year in the "survey-feedback-action" process • "Guaranteed Fair Treatment Policy" and "Open-Door Policy"	• Twelve "Quality Action Teams" are responsible for working on key issues from the Quality Service Indicator • Cross-functional task force teams assigned for everything • Monthly international conference calls with communications directors globally • Job rotation • Single global PR firm

Company	External Communications	Vertical Communications	Horizontal Communications
FedEx (cont.)	each month out in the field with a salesperson • Strategic alliances with charitable groups like the Red Cross to provide aid and communicate the brand message • Speakers bureau, hub tours, and management conferences • Marketing department is organized on customer segments (rather than products) supported with extensive database • High-profile international lobbying		
HP	• Extending its brand focus beyond b-to-b to consumers • "Major Messages" binder used to integrate corporate messages • Central customer database with between 6.5 and 8 million names • Internal branding training program to educate all employees	• *Hoshin* planning process • PointCast Intranet system keeps employees informed about relevant news • Total job security encourages open communication • Employee publication citing opinions both negative and positive	• Intranet encourages open and critical discussion • Everyone works in cubicles to encourage open environment

Company	External Communications	Vertical Communications	Horizontal Communications
ISS	• Extranet to communicate with key customers • Global Account Managers • Aligns customer and employee satisfaction surveys and develops action plans for improvements	• Total Quality Management Institute—management training which is cascaded down to every organizational level • Intranet is available to site managers, who forward news to all employees	• Cockpit—internal Intranet site with performance matrix broken down for clients, countries, business units, etc. • Searchable database on the Intranet with competence of all employees
Motorola	• Led a high-profile integrated communications campaign with all key stakeholders to open trade with Japan	• CEO Bob Galvin engrained the issue of quality into his managers by putting it at the top of all meeting agendas • "Motorola University" provides training at all levels. Employees are trained to solve real problems together with their managers	• Focus on process improvements of communications services such as annual reports and press response • Team Day Awards Ceremony—Worldwide Total Customer Satisfaction team competition • "Communications Forum"—a joint meeting for all communications professionals
Philips	• Used news media during Operation Centurion to create a climate of crisis and willingness to change inside the organization • Formed "European	• Operation Centurion—communications cascade down multiple management levels • Town Hall meetings to support bottom-up communications	• Task forces assigned to strategic improvement areas staffed with people from different product divisions, countries, and ranks

Company	External Communications	Vertical Communications	Horizontal Communications
Philips (cont.)	Round Table" of business leaders	• Closes down all factories for a "Customer Day" for employee input and information sharing	
Saturn	• Homecoming events • Extended Family database on website for Saturn owners to connect with each other • Saturn Clubs—eighty chapters, 10,000-plus members • Integrating all "moments of truth" • Homey and inviting retail facilities with non-pressure sales approach • Enlists retailers as spokespeople with local media • Uses a lead agency for all marketing communications including all retail advertising	• The Saturn mission is reinforced in the induction training, on posters everywhere, in pocket cards, and in all communications • Managers of all ranks work side by side with employees for philanthropic projects such as building playgrounds • "Saturn Windows"—Satellite broadcasts to keep employees informed • Unique union-management partnership	• Everything is done by work teams, including the hiring of employees • Consensus decision-making—70/100 rule
Xerox	• Distributes 55,000 surveys every month—results are disseminated to everyone in the organization, who are encouraged to take	• Annual "communication blitz" with top 150 managers around the world • Deployed a three-year learning cascade to kick off its quality	• All employees are globally trained in the same structured teamwork process • Senior managers assigned responsibilities for core processes

Company	External Communications	Vertical Communications	Horizontal Communications
Xerox (cont.)	action, and 10,000 complaints followed up every month • Rank-Xerox Denmark assigns every employee to action teams responsible for areas of customer satisfaction improvement • Senior managers answer customer service calls once a month • Top managers assigned ongoing responsibility for a few clients	management transformation • All internal messages are related to one of the four core messages • Front-line workers are trained to act as "customer advocates"	• Sales reps can use the Intranet to get instant answers to customer questions, and share best practices and expertise • Teamwork Day held once a year to recognize outstanding teamwork

Bird Brains in the Customer Century

The changes taking place in business are both profound and irreversible. The Production-Century business model of building products and finding buyers for them, is being replaced with a Customer Century model of building customer relationships and finding ways to add value to them. The prevailing image of the Production-Century company is that of a machine. When it performs well it "runs smoothly" as a "well-oiled engine." In times of trouble, it needs to be "reengineered" and fixed up with "tools." That was fine and dandy in the stable times of the industrial age. But in the fast-changing times of the Customer Century, the metaphor of the company as a *living system* is much more appropriate. There needs to be a free flow of communication to enable people to adapt and reorganize around changing customer and stakeholder needs and demands. The stabilizing force is no longer maintained through command and structure but through ongoing and open communication.

What better example of an integrated, vibrant living system than the V-formation of geese? Guided by the magnetic pull from the North, they also rely on landmarks to help them navigate.

Sometimes when fog dissipates and the landmarks are clear, a V-formation can be seen turning around because they've gone off course. Like our feathered heroes, surveying the changing landscape in constant search of the common orientation point of the customer—is the first dimension of integrated communications. The navigational pull of the magnetic north is the vision—which provides vertical integration. And aligning the scattered parts of the organization in a V-formation is the horizontal integration. Together, the three dimensions that guide the geese, will also help guide your company into the Customer Century.

What to Do Monday through Friday Morning—A Summary:

- Integrate *external* communications by compiling customer and stakeholder information into a central customer database, identify the potentially most profitable customers and critical stakeholders, and analyze their needs. Use *high-tech* vehicles to customize communications, service offerings, and products. Integrate the *high-touch* communications channel of human interaction between people in the organization with key customers and stakeholders.

- Integrate *vertical* communications between the senior management and the front line, keeping the top brass in touch with the realities of the business, and employees in tune with the strategic context of their work. Use *high-tech* computer connectivity to reach all employees instantaneously and encourage open dialogue. Use *high-touch* interaction of the communications cascade to secure commitment and involvement from all management levels.

- Integrate *horizontal* communications by aligning the entire organizational structure, processes, and reward structure around customers instead of functions, business units, and geographic regions. Use *high-tech* communication for global access to information and people and for forming virtual teams and communities. Use *high-touch* face-to-face communications for teamwork, bonding, building trust, developing ideas, resolving conflicts, and solving complex problems.

Notes

1. Reichheld, Frederick (1996). *The Loyalty Effect,* Boston, Mass.: Harvard Business School Press.
2. According to a study by *USA Today,* CNN, and the Gallup Organization reported in *Inside PR,* April 28, 1997. p. 7.
3. Baca, Stephanie (1998–1999). "Hooray for Hollywood: How the Entertainment Industry Capitalizes on IMC." *Journal of Integrated Communications,* Volume IX, p. 15; and Wolf, Michael J. (1999). *The Entertainment Economy: How Mega-Media Forces Are Transforming Our Lives.* New York: Times Books/Random House.
4. According to study by Reserarch Systems Corporation, reported in Davidow, William H. and Malone, Michael S. (1992). *The Virtual Corporation.* New York: HarperCollins, p. 220.
5. David Stewart reports the following studies (1992, "Speculations on the Future of Advertising Research," *Journal of Advertising,* Vol. XXI, No. 3, September, pp. 1–18): Three-quarters of the cases studied by Robert Drane showed that advertising had little to no effect on sales (1988, "Boosting the Odds of Advertising Success," in *Evaluating the Effects of Consumer Advertising on Market Position Over Time: How to Tell Whether Advertising Ever Works,* Stephen Bell, ed. Cambridge, Mass.: Marketing Science Institute). A study by Anthony J. Adams and Margaret Henderson Blair showed that sales gains associated with advertising peaked after only a few weeks (1989, "Persuasive Advertising and Sales Accountability: Past Experience and Forward Evaluation," *Proceedings of the Thirty-fifth Annual Conference of the Advertising Research Foundation,* New York: ARF).
6. According to: Abraham, M. M. and Lodish, L. M. (1990). "Getting the Most Out of Advertising and Promotion." *Harvard Business Review,* May–June; and Jones, J. P. (1995). *When Ads Work,* New York: Lexington Books, as cited by Ambler, Tim (1996). *How Much of Brand Equity is Explained by Trust?* MCB University Press.
7. Estimate by eWatch, reported in "Are You in Control on the Internet." *PR Week,* November 16, 1998, p. 27.
8. Based on: Magretta, Joan (1998). "The Power of Virtual Integration: An Interview with Dell Computer's Michael Dell." *Harvard Business Review,* March–April, pp. 72–84.
9. *Svenska Dagbladet,* September 20, 1998, p. 40.
10. European Union's "Directory on Data Protection."
11. Hack, Becki, Heidi Schultz, Don Schultz, Linda Mullinix, Chris Cates, and Alexandria Womack (1998). *Integrated Marketing Communication, Consortium Benchmarking Study Best-Practice* Report. Houston, Tex.: American Productivity & Quality Center International Benchmarking Clearinghouse.
12. Magretta, Joan (1998). "The Power of Virtual Integration: An Interview with Dell Computer's Michael Dell." *Harvard Business Review,* March–April, pp. 79, 80.
13. Wolf, Michael J. (1999). *The Entertainment Economy: How Mega-Media Forces Are Transforming Our Lives.*

INDEX